Getting the Most from WordStar® and MailMerge®

Things MicroPro® Never Told You

M. David Stone

A SPECTRUM BOOK

PRENTICE-HALL, INC.   Englewood Cliffs, New Jersey 07632

Library of Congress Cataloging in Publication Data

Stone, M. David.
  Getting the most from WordStar and Mailmerge.

  "A Spectrum Book."
  Includes index.
  1. MailMerge (Computer program) 2. WordStar (Computer
program) 3. Business--Data processing. I. Title.
HF5548.4. M35S83 1983   652   83-22896
ISBN 0-13-3543820-X (pbk.)
ISBN 0-13-354390-0 (case)

This book is available at a special discount when ordered in
bulk quantities. Contact Prentice-Hall, Inc., General
Publishing Division, Special Sales, Englewood Cliffs, N.J. 07632

     4   5   6   7   8   9   10

To my father and, in memory, my mother

Manufacturing buyer: Joyce Levatino
Cover design by Hal Siegel

ISBN 0-13-354390-0

ISBN 0-13-354382-X {PBK.}

ReportStar is a trademark of MicroPro International Corporation. WordStar, MailMerge, SpellStar,
InfoStar, DataStar, StarIndex, and StarBurst are registered trademarks of MicroPro International
Corporation. CP/M is a registered trademark of Digital Research, Inc. Z-80 is a registered trademark of
Zilog, Inc. Punctuation + Style and The Word Plus are trademarks of Oasis Systems. Math* is a trademark
of Force Two, Ltd. Superfile is a trademark of FYI, Inc. VisiCalc is a registered trademark of VisiCorp.
ExecuPlan is a trademark of Vector Graphic Inc. Formula II is a trademark of Dynamic Microprocessor
Associates, Inc. DBPlus is a registered trademark of HumanSoft, Inc. dBASE II is a registered trademark
of Ashton-Tate, Inc. Magic Print, MagicBind and MagicIndex are trademarks of Computer EdiType
Systems. Sprint is a trademark of Qume Corporation. Diablo is a registered trademark of Xerox
Corporation Inc. Random House is a registered trademark of Random House, Inc. The Random House
Proof Reader, The Random House Electronic Thesaurus, Grammatik, and Strunk & White: The Program
are trademarks of Wang Electronic Publishing, Inc. Xerox is a registered trademark of Xerox Corporation.

Prentice-Hall International, Inc., London
Prentice-Hall of Australia Pty. Limited, Sydney
Prentice-Hall Canada Inc., Toronto
Prentice-Hall of India Private Limited, New Delhi
Prentice-Hall of Japan, Inc., Tokyo
Prentice-Hall of Southeast Asia Pte. Ltd., Singapore
Whitehall Books Limited, Wellington, New Zealand
Editora Prentice-Hall do Brasil Ltda., Rio de Janeiro

Contents

Preface

This book is about advanced WordStar, which makes it mostly about MailMerge.

WordStar, of course, is MicroPro International Corporation's powerful and very popular word processing program. MailMerge is an optional addition that MicroPro bills as suitable for producing form letters, printing mailing lists, and creating individual documents out of standard "boilerplate" paragraphs. MailMerge does all of this very well and can also do much more.

If you have MailMerge, but haven't figured out how to use it yet, or if you are using it, but only for the obvious applications, then this book is for you. If you don't have MailMerge because you thought it was just for form letters, mailing lists, or assembling boilerplate, then this book is for you too. This book not only shows you how to use MailMerge for the things MicroPro says it can do, it also shows you how to use it for other things as well—including things that MicroPro's documentation doesn't even begin to hint at.

Of course, any book that claims to be about advanced WordStar has to cover more than just MailMerge and this one does. It introduces you to WordStar's unsupported proportional space print feature, it shows you several known bugs in WordStar and how to avoid them, and it even takes a look at some ancillary programs you can use with WordStar—spelling checkers, footnote programs, thesaurus programs, and so on. It also includes a look at StarIndex, MicroPro's new indexing program. Mostly, this book shows you how to use WordStar to the fullest advantage—with special emphasis on MailMerge.

The fact is, MailMerge is a much more powerful program than MicroPro lets on. It is so powerful and so flexible that to really explain it properly would have nearly doubled the size of the WordStar reference manual. MicroPro chose instead to cram the information into about a third the space and then stay with the most basic uses of the program.

What else can you do with MailMerge besides the obvious? Quite a bit. The possibilities range from trivial to substantial.

To begin, you can use MailMerge effectively not just for mass mailings, but for the occasional single form letter as well. You can use it to print individual envelopes. It can also be used to assemble other things besides boilerplate, the chapters of a book for example. But all these things can be extrapolated easily enough from the MicroPro manual. There are some much more interesting possibilities.

For instance, you can use MailMerge to create a data entry screen for a free format "index card" data retrieval program. Or you can use it to turn WordStar into the report generator for a data base program, thereby adding all of WordStar's formatting capabilities to your finished reports. In fact, you can use WordStar and MailMerge as a data base program by themselves in many applications, thus saving you the cost of buying and learning a separate program.

Most interesting perhaps, you can use MailMerge as a limited programming language—much as VisiCalc and calc programs in general are limited languages—capable of solving only a certain kind of programming problem, but capable of doing it much more quickly and easily than if you started from scratch.

This book shows you how to do all this and more. Throughout the book are specific, fully tested, useable examples. The real value of this book, though, is not so much that it shows you specific ways to use WordStar, with and without Mail-Merge, but that it shows you possibilities. Once you see what sorts of things can be done—and *how* they can be done—you'll find your own applications.

One last note: Most of the ideas in this book can be used with other word processing programs as well, not just WordStar/MailMerge. Details will vary of course, depending on the program. Nevertheless, you'll find that most of the concepts will still apply to any program with substantially the same capabilities as WordStar. If you're using some other comparable program, then, you can treat this book as an advanced word processing guide that just happens to use WordStar/MailMerge as an example.

ACKNOWLEDGMENTS

More people than I can comfortably keep track of have had a hand in helping me put this book together. In particular, I must thank Bill O'Brien and Danny Wexler, both of whom provided generous amounts of help, information, and access to equipment. Thanks also go to John Schnell for adding his dBASE II expertise to the mix.

Each of the following individuals and business entitites has also given me generous amounts of time and information. FYI, Inc., HumanSoft, Inc., Wayne Holder at Oasis Systems, Bruce Wampler at Wang Electronic Publishing, Ben Jone at Computer Editype System, Chuck Woodford at Force Two, Ltd., Howard Radin at Dynamic Microprocessor Associates, Inc., and any number of people at MicroPro International Corporation.

Preliminaries:
A Quick Look
at WordStar
and MailMerge

Who This Book Is For
What Is Expected From the Reader
Differences Between Various Releases of WordStar/MailMerge
Multiple Printing—a Quick Warm-Up Exercise

WHO THIS BOOK IS FOR

This book is not an introduction to WordStar. Nor is it an introduction to using computers. There are other guides available that do both of these things quite well already. This, rather, is a "second" book. It is for WordStar users who are ready for advanced word processing techniques.

Introductory WordStar books are meant essentially as a rewrite of MicroPro's documentation. This book is meant to do much more. It is meant, quite simply, to explore the full capabilities of WordStar, with special emphasis on MailMerge. Although it includes an introduction to basic MailMerge, its real usefulness begins where MicroPro's explanations end.

You will find some overlap between the most basic material in this book and the most advanced material in MicroPro's documentation and in

---

various introductory WordStar books. The overlap, though, is minimal. It is there of necessity to establish definitions and concepts that the rest of the book can build on.

WHAT IS EXPECTED FROM THE READER

I start with the assumption that you are already reasonably familiar with basic WordStar and with the computer system you're using—at least to the extent of knowing how to boot up the system and knowing how to create, modify, and print a letter, memo, or whatever complete with print enhancements and dot commands when necessary.

Of course, even someone who is well versed in WordStar may be thrown by a reference to a command out of context. (Quick: What does ^QP do?) Whenever this book refers to a specific command, therefore, it will generally include at least a shorthand explanation along with it—even for the most elementary commands. (^QP means jump to the Previous Cursor position—"Quick Previous.") Similarly, whenever you see an instruction to do something—such as "read another file"—you will usually find the command along with it (in this case ^KR). All this explanation should serve to make the book understandable to all but the complete WordStar novice.

I make no assumption at all about how familiar you are with basic MailMerge. If you're like most people who bought MailMerge at the same time you bought WordStar, you probably took one look at the MailMerge documentation and proceeded to ignore the program—at least until you became thoroughly familiar with WordStar by itself. As of this moment, you may or may not have invested the time in getting MailMerge up and running. If not, this book will help. In particular, Chapters Four and Five will be useful as an introduction to MailMerge. These chapters cover the vast majority of MailMerge commands, introducing each and explaining each in context—meaning as part of an example and in terms of a problem that needs to be solved.

If you are already familiar with MailMerge, you might like to skip the introductory MailMerge chapters. If so, make sure you do not skip Chapters One through Three, which discuss some advanced WordStar capabilities that are independent of MailMerge.

DIFFERENCES BETWEEN RELEASES— FROM WORDSTAR 1.0 TO 3.3

Like most programs that have been around for any length of time, WordStar has undergone improvements since its original release. As of this writing, there are three basically different versions of the program floating around. These are 1.xx, 2.xx, and 3.xx. In addition, there have been minor improvements and revisions within each of these versions, so that if you are using release 3.xx, for instance, you might actually be using version 3.0, or

3.2, or 3.3, depending on when you bought the program and what machine you are using it on.

As far as this book is concerned, the only really important difference among these various versions of WordStar is between version 1.xx and all later releases of the program. The difference, quite simply, is that Mail-Merge will not work with version 1.xx. For purposes of this book, we will ignore 1.xx. Beyond that virtually everything in this book applies to any release 2.xx or later. The major exception to this is Chapter One, which deals with release 3.xx only.

For the most part, it doesn't much matter which version of WordStar you are using. Still, there are differences and it is important to know what they are. Here is a list of the key releases, followed by a quick rundown on the important differences between these releases.

The key revisions are:

1.xx, which we are ignoring completely,

2.xx, which can use MailMerge, but lacks column mode and horizontal scroll,

3.00 through 3.2x, which include minor changes from one revision to the next, and which work on different machines, but which are substantially the same from the user's point of view,

8-bit (CP/M) 3.3 and later, which include a new "Conditional Print" command in MailMerge.

16-bit (MS-DOS and CP/M-86) 3.3, which does not include the conditional print command, but does include all other minor improvements found in the CP/M 3.3 version.

WS 3.30
MM 3.31

THE DIFFERENCE BETWEEN 2.xx AND 3.xx

From your perspective—in terms of what you see on the screen and what features are available to you—there are three major differences between release 2.xx and 3.xx.

The first difference is that the menus were redesigned for release 3.00 to make them more readable and generally easier to understand. This is helpful while you are learning WordStar, but it doesn't affect using the program in any way, and doesn't much matter in terms of this book.

The second difference is that releases 3.00 and later include a column mode that lets you mark off a column of text, then move it, copy it, or delete it as a column. There are one or two examples in this book that make use of this feature in the form of column copy. (There is also a bug in the feature. You'll find the bug described toward the end of Chapter Fourteen.) If you are using an earlier version of WordStar, though, the lack of this capability presents only a minor problem. There is a little more work involved, but you can still get the same effect simply by copying an entire block of text margin to margin, then deleting what you don't want line by line.

The third major difference between release 2.xx and release 3.xx is in the way they handle lines that are longer than will fit on the screen. Release

2.xx wraps long lines. This means that each line is broken into two or more parts as necessary, but you can see it all at once. Releases 3.00 and later extend the line off the screen. This means you can't see the entire line at once, but in exchange for this, you get horizontal scrolling—meaning that your screen acts as a window that moves left and right. This lets you look at portions of the text as they will appear when printed out. While this can be a helpful feature for certain uses—like putting a final polish on a spreadsheet before printing it—it has little or no effect on most uses of the program. Here again, the difference between releases doesn't much matter in terms of this book.

The situation gets a little more complicated with the various versions of release 3.xx, but here again the differences don't matter very much—with one important exception. Release 3.00 is the original version of release 3.xx. All releases 3.00 and earlier were written to run on 8-bit machines using the CP/M-80 operating system.

Release 3.02 was the first version of WordStar written for the new generation of 16-bit computers. 3.02 had some serious limitations and serious bugs. It was quickly replaced by 3.20, then 3.21, and finally 3.24, each of which corrected various problems in the program. 3.2x was available for two operating systems—MS-DOS and CP/M-86.

Except for being able to run on different machines, the 16-bit version of WordStar 3.2 has exactly the same features and capabilities as WordStar 3.00. One complication is that the MS-DOS version of this release makes use of the IBM PC's function keys to perform certain commands. There has been no change, however, in the commands themselves or in the features available. The MS-DOS version, then, is basically standard WordStar that has been customized for the IBM PC. From our perspective as users, release 3.2x is, for all intents and purposes, identical to release 3.00. If you're using the MS-DOS version (or any other customized version for that matter) you can follow the examples in this book either by using the standard commands or by using the function keys—whichever you feel more comfortable with.

WordStar 3.3 is the most recent release as of this writing. This new version includes some minor changes in menus and some internal changes, many of which I'll mention as we go along. The biggest difference, though, is not in the program itself, but in the documentation. The manuals have been completely rewritten to make them much more readable and easier to use. As with the revised menus in version 3.∅, this is helpful if you're learning WordStar, but don't change the way the program works.

Version 3.3 is available in both 8-bit and 16-bit versions, both of which are essentially identical from the user's point of view, except for one feature. This one feature only exists in the 8-bit version. It is also the only additional feature in all WordStar releases since 2.0 that makes any real difference in terms of this book.

In the 8-bit version of WordStar 3.3, MailMerge includes a new Conditional Print command. This new command amounts to a powerful select feature, and gives MailMerge additional capabilities. Some examples in this book will take advantage of these capabilities. Obviously, if you have the 16-bit version of release 3.3, or any earlier version at all, you will not be able to use this feature. Where possible, then, I have also included an alternate example showing how to accomplish substantially the same thing without using the conditional print command. Where these alternatives are given, the examples are clearly labeled with the appropriate release numbers.

INCOMPATIBILITIES

There is, finally, one other thing you should be aware of about the various releases. Each release of WordStar is matched to its own set of MailMerge (and SpellStar) overlay files. This means that you cannot, for example, use MailMerge 3.3 with WordStar 3.00. This is something you have to be careful about if you decide to update your WordStar—particularly if you are planning to do something like keep WordStar version 2.xx for use with MailMerge version 2.xx, but buy WordStar 3.xx for its horizontal scrolling. It quickly can get confusing to have two or more versions of the same program floating around. If you wind up doing something like this, make sure your WordStar disks are clearly—and correctly—marked with the version number of the program.

Here again, though, this incompatibility of the various releases has no effect on most of the examples in this book. The only exceptions will be a few of the ancillary programs discussed in Chapter Sixteen. Even there, the only programs affected will be those that function as overlay files themselves.

MULTIPLE PRINTING

There's one last thing we need to do in this preliminary look at WordStar/MailMerge; namely, a quick, hands-on example of how to use it.

A good place to start is with the simplest thing you can do with MailMerge: print more than one copy of whatever you're working on. This will also serve as a convenient warm-up exercise to help establish some ground rules for the rest of the book.

If you recognize the importance of keeping a copy (a hard copy) of everything you send out, and particularly if you hate dealing with carbon copies and carbon paper, you've probably gotten in the habit of printing everything twice. Once for you and once for whomever you're sending it to. If you need a third copy—for a follow-up file, for instance—you print it yet again.

With the print function of WordStar, you can only print one copy at a time. For each additional copy, moreover, you have to wait until the previous one is finished before you can enter another print command. If you're printing four or five copies, you wind up spending most of your time twiddling your thumbs, waiting for each one to finish.

With MailMerge, though, you can enter the information once, then concentrate on something else while the computer prints all the copies you need.

A Quick Warm-up Exercise

All the examples in this book, beginning with this one, assume that you already know things like how to log onto the proper disk, how to open a file, and so forth. It's worth pointing out, though, that if you have a dual floppy machine, it's generally good procedure to put your program on one disk in drive A and your data on another disk in drive B. This puts the data files on a separate disk, thus giving you maximum disk space for files, and minimizing the chances of running into a disk full error.

If you do run out of disk space while working with a file, moreover, and if there is nothing you can afford to delete from your data disk, this gives you a simple way to save your work. Mark the beginning and end of your file (with ^**KB** and ^**KK**), then use the write a file command (^**KW**) to write the file onto the program disk. If that disk is also full, you can delete WSMSGS.OVR (with ^**KJ**) to make room. This will eliminate menus and many messages from your screen, but it won't keep WordStar from working. Later, you can copy the WSMSGS.OVR file back to your program disk from a back-up disk.

You should start by putting both WordStar and MailMerge on a single system disk—meaning a disk that will boot up. If you are ready for this book, you should know how to do that already. If not, you'll have to find someone to show you—try your dealer. Also, if you're ready for this book, you should already know enough not to use a distribution copy of anything, ever, once you've created your first back-up. But it won't hurt to remind you of that either.

Now, put the disk in drive A, put a formatted disk in drive B, boot up your system, go into WordStar, and log on to drive B. There are other ways to get to the same place, but if your disk is set up so that it automatically goes into WordStar when you boot up, then this is the natural route. If you haven't discovered this for yourself, you might like to know that when WordStar asks you for "NEW LOGGED DISK DRIVE," you do not have to add a colon after the drive letter—despite what the prompt says. This is one of those trivial savings of time and effort that adds up after a while.

Open a file—call it MTEST—and type in a few lines of text. Three or more lines from the previous paragraph will do nicely. Now close the file.

From the No-File menu, pick M for MailMerge. MailMerge will ask "Name of file to MailMerge?" or "Name of file to MergePrint?" depending on the release. Answer with ^**R** (Restore last entry). Since you haven't printed anything since you went into the program, WordStar will automatically enter MTEST, the first (and in this case last) file you edited. WordStar will then ask you a series of questions, just as it does in the standard print function.

If you've never used MailMerge before, the first thing you'll notice is how similar the questions are. In fact, with one exception, they are the same. They all have the same default settings as in the standard print function, and they are treated in the same way; you can answer each by hitting RETURN, you can bypass all remaining questions at any time by hitting ESCAPE, and you can abort the whole procedure whenever you like simply by entering a ^**U**.

The one exception—the only difference between Print and Merge-Print—is that in Merge-Print a new question has been added:

NUMBER OF COPIES (RETURN for 1)?

When combined with other MailMerge commands, this additional question gives MailMerge a number of capabilities, but the simplest and most straightforward use is fairly obvious. The default setting on this question is for one copy. If you bypass the question or enter a RETURN that's what you'll get. But if, for instance, you need three copies, all you have to do is enter **3** and MailMerge will print them for you.

Hit RETURN until you get to the "Number of Copies" question. Enter 3 at this point. Make sure your printer is on and ready (and loaded with fanfold paper). Now, hit RETURN in answer to the remaining questions, or hit ESCAPE to bypass them, and watch MailMerge print MTEST. You should wind up with three identical copies of MTEST, each one on a separate page.

The one other difference you will notice between printing and Mail-Merge–Printing is that MailMerge does not return you to the standard menu while printing. The only menu choice it gives you is "P for Stop Print." This means you cannot work on another file or do any file maintenance functions (renaming, copying, deleting, and so forth). You can, however, largely ignore your computer while MailMerge takes care of the printing.

This multiple printing capability is certainly useful, but it is hardly worth the cost of the program. Starting with Chapter Four, you are going to be introduced to some much more powerful uses of MailMerge. For the next three chapters, we are going to ignore MailMerge and discuss Word-Star by itself. After that we'll come back to MailMerge, first in a short introduction, and then—for the bulk of the book—in a careful exploration of possibilities.

1

WordStar's Unsupported Proportional Space Print Feature

Commands Introduced
^PP (Proportional Space Printing)

Uses Introduced
Proportional Space Printing

You won't find this mentioned anywhere in the MicroPro documentation, but if you have WordStar release 3.xx, you have a built-in (but unsupported) proportional space print feature. "Unsupported" means that if you try using it and you run into a problem, MicroPro doesn't want to hear about it. It's not that they don't know about the proportional spacing, it's just that they are already well aware that there are problems with it—which is precisely why they don't claim it as one of the features of the program in the first place.

The problems, however, are minor. They are so minor that you just might like to make use of this unsupported feature—assuming, of course, that you have a printer that is capable of proportional spacing. In general, daisy-wheel and thimble printers have this capability, while others do not. This is only a rule of thumb though. Check your printer's manual if you're not sure. Also, if you have a NEC 3550, be forewarned that some 3550's have a problem with the proportional spacing of lower-case l's. This apparently is dependent on which PROM is in the printer, but NEC has not been able to confirm this for me.

Proportional space printing is used almost universally in printed matter such as books, magazines, and newspapers. This book, for instance, is printed with proportional spacing and would probably look strange to you if it were not. In fact, whether you are consciously aware of it or not, proportional spacing is precisely what makes printed matter look "printed," or typeset, rather than typed.

Virtually all typewriters assign the same amount of space to each letter. This means that a narrow letter like an "i" or an "l" has a lot of empty space around it while a wide letter like a "w" or an "m" has very little space around it. Proportional space printing, in contrast, assigns different amounts of space to letters of different widths. For example, a "w" gets a larger chunk of space than an "a," which in turn gets a larger chunk of space than an "i." The result is that each letter has essentially the same amount of space around it regardless of the width of the letter.

For most purposes, it doesn't much matter whether you have proportional spacing. If you're writing a memo or a letter, for instance, it's certainly enough to have it typed well, and you might even prefer it to have a typed look. On the other hand, if you're dealing with an in-house report, or a proposal for a prospective client, or even a one-page circular for handing out on the street, you might want to give it a professional, typeset look. You can do this with proportional spacing.

Do not, by the way, confuse proportional space printing with WordStar's ability to vary the character width, or pitch, of printed copy. *Pitch* is a measure of the number of characters per inch, so that 12 pitch—the standard for elite typestyles—means printing at 12 characters per inch, while 10 pitch—the standard for pica—means printing at 10 characters per inch. This is another WordStar feature altogether that is fully supported by MicroPro.

Also do not confuse proportional space printing with microspace justification. This too is another WordStar feature altogether and is fully supported by MicroPro.

If you read your WordStar manual, you will find that microspace justification automatically uses less space for periods and commas, and more space for "m's" and "w's," which makes it sound very much like proportional spacing. In addition, both proportional space printing and microspace justification require a printer capable of incremental spacing—meaning that unlike a typewriter, which moves in fixed amounts, the printer must be able to vary how far it moves after each letter. The similarity between the two features ends here though.

The effects of microspace justification come into play mostly when you use WordStar's right justification feature—meaning that your right-hand margin is even rather than ragged. (This book is right justified. Typewritten material is ragged right.) If you use a printer that is not capable of incremental spacing, you will find that in order to keep the right edge of the text justified, WordStar has to insert space between the words. If your printer is capable of incremental spacing, though, and assuming your WordStar is installed correctly for the printer, microspace justification will spread that extra space more or less evenly throughout the line. This means that the words will still be separated a bit more than they otherwise would be, but it also means that the letters themselves will be separated more than they otherwise would be.

Proportional space printing, in contrast, leaves the amounts of space between words. In effect, it turns off the microspace justification so that the proportional spacing between letters can remain unchanged. But this is not precisely correct. In reality, there is still some adjustment within the words. The fact remains, though, that with proportional spacing most of the blank space does wind up between the words—not within them—which makes the statement close enough to the truth for our purposes. In a sense, proportional spacing still uses microspace justification but in a modified form. In fact, these two features are interrelated—a point we will come back to shortly.

Finally, when printing with proportional spacing, you need a proportional space printing element such as a printwheel or thimble, or whatever else is appropriate for your machine. A regular element won't look quite right because its type style was not designed for proportional spacing.

Be careful when getting a new printing element, by the way. There are several different "standard" sequences of symbols. Qume printwheels, for instance, come in word processing sequence and proportional space sequence, among others. Helping to confuse the issue is that some Qume printwheels that follow "word processing" sequence have "proportional space" typefaces. The point is, make sure you get an element with both the correct type sequence and the correct type style, or else your printer is going to print gibberish. If you have any doubts when buying the element, make sure you can return it.

WORDSTAR'S PROPORTIONAL SPACE FEATURE—THE BASICS

The proportional space command in WordStar is ^PP. You will not find this anywhere on your menu or in your documentation, but WordStar recognizes it nonetheless.

Like many of the print commands, including the ^PS, or underlining command, for example, ^PP functions as an on-off toggle at print time. This means that you have to be careful not to put the command in your file more than once. Otherwise, when WordStar runs across the command the second time, it will turn proportional spacing off.

Unfortunately, you cannot simply enter ^PP at the beginning of a file and get proportional spacing all the way through the way you can, for instance, enter ^PA at the beginning of a file and get 12-pitch printing all the way through. This is because the feature will only work on lines of text that have been microjustified. In fact, if you turn off microjustification at any point in a file (using the .UJ command), you will find that you have also turned off proportional spacing. This does not cause a problem when turning microjustification off for printing columns of numbers because numbers are all equally spaced to begin with. Also note that the presence or absence of microjustification has nothing to do with right justification being on or off, though the effect of microjustification when printing is more obvious when the text is right justified.

In WordStar, a line of text is microjustified whenever it is affected either by word wrap or by a paragraph reform. On entry, then, microjustification is automatic whenever word wrap takes you from one line to the next. The new line that you're typing on, however, won't be affected until word wrap takes you to yet another line and so forth. This means that the last line in a paragraph will not be microjustified until and unless you do a paragraph reform command (^B). This, in turn, means that to use WordStar's proportional space feature, you have to make sure you've gone through the whole file and reformatted each paragraph.

Very often you'll be able to do this simply by entering the command ^Q^Q^B. This will repeat the ^B command through the entire file, or until you abort it by hitting another key. There are some cases, however, where you cannot do this. If you are using indented margins, for instance, you will lose the indentations this way. The question, then, is whether the polished proportional space look is worth the extra work of going through the file paragraph by paragraph.

Once you've seen how good proportional spacing looks, you may well decide it is worth the work. Besides, the procedure becomes easy enough if you simply get in the habit of using the ^B command to advance the text during your final on-screen proofreading. This is a little less convenient than, for instance, scrolling the text with ^Z, but it will advance the text paragraph by paragraph, and will reformat each paragraph in the process.

I tend to use a combination of these two commands, scrolling the text and cursor to the top of the screen using ^Z, then using ^B to move the cursor through each paragraph as I read it. In fact, it's a good idea to use this technique whether you're planning on proportional space printing or not because it ensures that your paragraphs are formatted correctly in any case. It saves you the nasty surprise of watching part of a line print on your roller because you didn't realize it continued beyond the edge of the screen.

USING PROPORTIONAL SPACING

Using the proportional space feature in WordStar requires three steps. They are:

1. Enter the proportional space command ^PP along with the alternate pitch command ^PA. (The order doesn't matter, you can enter it as ^PP^PA or ^PA^PP.)
2. Enter the text as usual.
3. Reformat all paragraphs throughout the file.

Except for the reformatting of paragraphs, which you obviously can't do until after you've entered the text, there's no need to follow these three steps in any particular order. This means you can enter the proportional space command before or after you've reformatted the paragraphs. It also means that once you have a file that has been reformatted all the way through, you can convert it from typewriter-style printing to proportional space printing and back again, simply by entering or deleting the proportional space command. All this makes it relatively easy to convert a file to proportional space printing, even if you didn't originally have that in mind when you entered it.

Go into WordStar now and open a practice file. Call it PSPACE1. Enter the print command **^PP.** It will show up on your screen as **^P.**

Next enter the command **^PA** (alternate pitch). This command will show up on your screen as **^A** and give you proportional space printing at 12 pitch. This command is needed because the amount of adjustment that WordStar makes for each letter remains constant in absolute terms no matter what the pitch. With the wider overall spacing at the default setting of 10 pitch, the relative adjustment for each letter is much less obvious and the printout begins to lose its typeset look.

Now enter the next paragraph using the default tab at column 6 and the default margins at columns 1 and 65. You can start on the same line as the commands or go to the next line. Do not reformat the paragraph this first time through. If you find yourself having to reformat for any reason, delete the last line and retype it. You can end with a < RETURN > or not, the results will be the same:

As you will see once you print out this paragraph, WordStar's unsupported proportional space print feature works nicely most of the time. Unfortunately, it does not work perfectly—though we'll ignore that fact for the moment.

Close the file (**^KD**) and print it using the print command (**P**).

If you followed the instructions, it should print as four lines. Take a look at the first three. (It may help to cover up the fourth line for a moment.) You should immediately notice the difference between this and what you usually see with WordStar.

Part of the difference, of course, will be due to the new type style you're using, but the difference lies mostly in the proportional spacing. If you have any doubts about that, then take a look at the fourth line in comparison to the first three. Even a quick glance will tell you that it doesn't look right; a closer look will tell you why.

The exact effect will vary depending on the particular type style, but in general you should find that the "t" and the "h" in "though" will be separated a bit more than the rest of the letters in the word, the "mom" in moment will be bunched together to the point where the letters may be touching, and, finally, the "w" and "e" in "we'll" will also be bunched together, while the space on either side of the apostrophe will be exaggerated.

Now open the file again, reformat it with a **^B,** close it, and print it in the fully formatted version.

Once again, take a look at the printout. There will be no change at all in the first three lines. This time, though, the fourth line will also have a typeset look. In particular, the letters in "though," "we'll," and "moment" will be evenly spaced, and the gap on either side of the apostrophe will have disappeared.

Basically, that's all there is to it. If you do no more than follow the three steps we've just covered, you'll find that the proportional spacing works just fine the vast majority of the time. Errors will show up occasionally, though. There is a reason, after all, why this is an unsupported feature. If you can live with a little less than perfection, you might not even care about an occasional error.

On the other hand, you ought to at least be aware that there are two problems built into the proportional spacing. The two problems deal with one-line paragraphs and one-word lines, respectively. If you're a perfectionist, you'll be happy to hear that both problems can be solved to make the spacing come out right anyway.

Proportional Spacing and One-Line Paragraphs

The first problem shows up when printing any series of one-line paragraphs with a bidirectional printer. This problem can often be ignored, but it becomes obvious when the same words appear directly over each other in two or more lines.

Open a new file, PSPACE2, and enter the following:

This is a demonstration of proportional space printing.

This is a demonstration of proportional space printing.

This is a demonstration of proportional space printing.

This is a demonstration of proportional space printing.

This is a demonstration of proportional space printing.

You can type this in one line at a time, or you can type the line once, then mark it and use the block copy comand (^**KC**) to repeat it. The important points are that each line should end with a carriage return, and each word in each line should be directly over the same word in the line below it. Regardless of how you enter this in your file though, make sure to format each line when you're done using ^**B.**

Close your file and print it out. If you have a bidirectional printer, you will find that the proportional spacing works within each line, but that there is a problem going from one line to the next. Identical words in these identical lines do not print one directly over the other. Instead, some of the words in alternate lines will be offset, so that they look like this:

This is a demonstration of proportional space printing.
This is a demonstration of proportional space printing.
This is a demonstration of proportional space printing.
This is a demonstration of proportional space printing.
This is a demonstration of proportional space printing.

Strictly speaking, this is not a problem with the proportional space feature as such. The same offset problem will show up in any series of one-line paragraphs whenever they have been microspace justified (meaning whenever they have been reformatted with ^B). Try it and see. On the other hand, since there is generally no need to reformat a series of one-line paragraphs unless you're specifically setting them up for proportional space printing, you probably won't run into this problem except when doing proportional spacing.

In any case, the offset is not a serious problem. It is caused by the way that microspace justification interacts with bidirectional printing. Specifically, the line will print differently depending on whether it's being printed forwards or backwards.

The solution, then, is simple. Use the **.BP** (bidirectional printing) command to turn bidirectional printing off before these lines, and turn it back on after. The file, then should look like this:

```
.BP Off
            This is a demonstration of proportional space printing.
            This is a demonstration of proportional space printing.
            This is a demonstration of proportional space printing.
            This is a demonstration of proportional space printing.
            This is a demonstration of proportional space printing.
.BP On
```

If you don't use these commands too often, be forewarned that if you're using release 3.2 or earlier, a question flag will show up on the right hand column of your screen. You can ignore the flags; WordStar recognizes the commands anyway. If the flags bother you, you can use "0" and "1" instead of "Off" and "On." The two sets of commands are completely equivalent.

Go back to your file now, enter the bidirectional print commands, and print it out again. The problem will have disappeared.

This same problem can also show up in a much more subtle form. Open a new file, PSPACE3, and enter the following. Be sure to include a carriage return at the end of each line:

```
* This is a test of proportional space printing.
* But it doesn't quite work.
* Because of bidirectional printing.
```

As always with proportional space printing, be sure to put **^PP^PA** as the first entry in the file, and be sure to reformat all three lines with **^B.** Now close the file and print it out.

If you just take a quick glance at the printout, you probably won't see anything wrong with it. Take a closer look, though, and you'll see a slight problem. The asterisks are lined up one over the other well enough, but the first letter of the first word in each line shows the same offset we saw before. The offset is somewhat hidden here because the one line paragraphs are no longer identical. With the first two lines, for instance, you have to look closely to see the offset between the "T" in "This" and the

"B" in "But." Nevertheless, it is there and you can see it. It becomes more obvious if you compare "B" in "But" with the "B" in "Because," since in this case you are dealing with the same letter both times. As before, you can get rid of this problem by turning bidirectional printing off and on with the appropriate commands.

Finally, you'll find that more often than not, this offset problem isn't really a problem to begin with. Open the file PSPACE3 once again, delete the three asterisks, close the file, and print it out. You will find no problems this time. The first letter of each word will be lined up one over the other—just as the asterisks were lined up before. Since everything else in each line is different to begin with, the problem simply doesn't show up.

In general, if you are setting up a file for proportional space printing, you should keep an eye out for one line paragraphs. If any two lines in a row are identical to each other—even in just the first two or three words—then you should turn the bidirectional printing off. Similarly, if each line begins with an asterisk and a space, or a number and a space, or some equivalent format, you should turn it off. In all other cases, you can save yourself some work and speed up the actual printing by leaving everything as is.

Proportional Spacing and One-Word Lines

The second problem in WordStar's proportional spacing shows up in one-word lines. These can be one-word paragraphs (items on a list, for example, with each word followed by a carriage return) or they can be the last line in a longer paragraph. Either way, the problem and the cure remain the same.

Open another file, PSPACE4, and enter the following sets of words. The two indented sets of words should start at column six. The rest should start in column one. (It doesn't matter whether you indent by tabbing or by hitting the space bar.) Each line should end with a carriage return.

```
^PP ^PA
mom
moment
momentum

— mom
— moment
— momentum

     mom
     moment
     momentum

     — mom
     — moment
     — momentum
```

mom is
moment is
momentum is

a mom
a moment
a momentum

can
can't
canny

he can
he can't
be canny

Be sure to reform the entire file with ^B. Then close the file and print it out. Looking at this printout you'll see that as far as the first four sets of words are concerned, there is no sign of proportional spacing. In each case, the letters "mom" of "mom," "moment," and "momentum" are bunched together. It doesn't matter whether the word starts in column one or column six. It doesn't even matter whether you put the two dashes in front of the word. Quite simply, whenever there is only one word in the line, proportional spacing disappears.

This statement is always true, though it's not always obvious. Take a look at the next to last set of words (can, can't, canny). At first glance you may not see anything wrong with them, but take a careful look at the space around the apostrophe in "can't," and compare it with the same word in the last set of words (he can't). The space around the apostrophe in this last set is smaller. Here again, then, when dealing with one word on each line, the proportional spacing disappears; it's just hidden because there are no extra-wide or extra-narrow letters in the words.

Finally, take a look at the three remaining sets of words—each of which have lines with two words each. Notice that as soon as you have two words on each line instead of one word, the proportional spacing reappears.

The rule of thumb here, then, is to keep an eye out for one-word lines. Unless you are big on making lists, you should find that these are relatively rare to begin with. If you do happen to have one, you can ignore it unless it has one or more extra-wide or extra-narrow letters in it. Even then, you might decide to ignore it on the grounds that it won't be all that obvious. If you want to fix it, though, there is a way.

Go back into the file PSPACE4. You can ignore or delete everything after the first set of three words, because the rest of the file amounts to variations on a theme. What you have to do to get WordStar to print this correctly is enter a series of commands to change the pitch where necessary. You can do that, mostly, by using ^PN for 10 pitch and ^PA for 12 pitch.

For the "mom" in "mom," "moment," and "momentum," you need

to spread out the letters. You do that by using **^PN** to switch to 10 pitch, then **^PA** to switch back to 12 pitch.

After you enter the print commands, they will look like this on your screen:

```
^Nmom
mom^Aent
^Nmom^Aentum
```

In this case, there was no reason to tell WordStar to go back to 12 pitch after the first line. In general however, if you are dealing with the last line in a paragraph, you would need to include a **^PA** command after the word. You might even like to include it here, just for the sake of symmetry and making the file easier to read. In that case, you would have to add a **^PN** at the beginning of the next line as well, and your screen would look like this:

```
^Nmom^A
^Nmom^Aent
^Nmom^Aentum
```

There is another problem in this set of words. We skipped over it before, but it happens that the "u" and the "m" in "momentum" are also bunched together. This can be fixed with the same trick, so that your screen, finally, should look like this:

```
^Nmom^A
^Nmom^Aent
^Nmom^Aent^Num^A
```

The **^PN** command here has to be entered before the "u." Otherwise, the "u" will print at 12 pitch, and there will not be any extra space between the last two letters.

Close this file now and print it. You will find that all three words look at least acceptable. For most purposes, they would be more than adequate. If you really want to get picky, though, you might notice that "moment" and "momentum" are not quite proportionally spaced, for although the "m's" are widened slightly the way they should be, the "t's" are not narrowed the way they should be.

Of course, if you re-enter "can't" in its own line, much the same could be said about it. It looks at least acceptable, but there is still that extra space around the apostrophe.

Once again, there is a way to deal with this. We are now getting into the realm where—for this particular problem at least—the work may not be worth the return. On the other hand, the techniques involved have other uses as well, which makes it worth running through the example anyway.

Open the file PSPACE4 again. Insert a new line immediately after "mom" (using **^N** or RETURN). Enter the dot command **.SR 8**. This is the set roll command, which you probably don't use too often. It's there so you can control how far the printer will roll up or roll down in doing subscripts and superscripts. The default setting is **.SR 3,** or $3/48$ of an inch, but Word-Star will recognize and follow commands up to and including **.SR 255,** which is $255/48$ of an inch, or more than 5 inches. This gives the command some interesting possibilities beyond merely controlling the roll of subscripts and superscripts. What we've just done here is set the roll for $8/48$, or $1/6$ of an inch. At WordStar's standard line height setting of six lines per inch, this makes the subscript/superscript roll exactly equal to the distance from one line to the next. The reason for doing this will become clear in a moment.

Move the cursor to the "t" in "moment," and note the column number. (It should be column six.) Then hit RETURN. Assuming you are in insert mode, the cursor and the "t" will move to the next line.

Now enter the character width command **.CW 9** on the new line, and hit the RETURN again. **.CW 9** translates to roughly 13 pitch—$13\frac{1}{3}$ to be precise. Once again, the reason for doing this should become clear in a moment. The cursor and the "t" should now be on a new line again. Insert spaces in front of the "t" to move it over to column seven (not six).

Finally, insert a **^PT** before the "t," enter another **^PT** after the "t," and end the line with a **^PM.** This is another command you probably don't use too often. It will put a "–" flag in your right-hand screen column, and will send a carriage return to the printer without a line feed—meaning it will tell WordStar to overprint the next line.

At this point, your screen should look like this:

```
^A ^P                                        <
^Nmom ^A                                      <
.SR 8                                         <
^Nmom ^Aen                                    <
.CW 9                                         <
        ^Tt ^T                                —
^Nmom^Aent^Num^A                              <
can't                                         <
```

Close the file and print it out. The printed version should look like this:

```
mom
moment
momentum
can't
```

Compare the spacing between the "n" and the "t" in both "moment" and "momentum." In the first word, we finally have proportional spacing. In the second word, we still have that extra gap between the two letters.

This little exercise is complicated enough so that you may not understand what you just did. Take another look at the file and we'll go through it step by step.

Basically, this is just a roundabout way of doing what we did before when we changed the pitch with a ^**PA** or ^**PN.** The difference, of course, is that we don't have a simple print command that we can put into the middle of the word for the pitch that we want to change to. Instead, we're stuck with needing to use a dot command—which means that we have to go to the next line so that the dot can be in the first column. That, in turn, forces us to go to yet another line to type the rest of the word. Finally, we have to find some way to get the "t" on the same line as the first part of the word.

Probably the easiest way to see how we did all this is to follow it through from WordStar's point of view. WordStar reads ^**A**^**P** at the top of the file and sets itself for proportional spacing. It then starts printing the file, changing the pitch as necessary when it comes across the ^**PN** and ^**PA** commands in the next line.

The first interesting command that WordStar gets to is .**SR 8,** at which point it sets the subscript/superscript roll to $\frac{8}{48}$ of an inch. It then goes on to the next line and prints out "momen," once again changing pitch when it comes to the ^**PN** or ^**PA** commands.

At the end of that line, WordStar finds what it usually finds at the end of a line, namely a carriage return and a line feed. The line feed is there so the printer will move to the next line by rolling the paper $\frac{1}{6}$ of an inch.

The next thing WordStar sees is a dot command (.**CW 9**), which tells it to reset the character width. The line feed at the end of that line has no effect because lines containing dot commands do not print.

WordStar goes to the next line, and begins to print it using the new character width. The first thing it sees are the spaces. It then gets to the superscript command ^**PT,** which is now set to roll the paper backwards by $\frac{8}{48}$, or $\frac{1}{6}$, of an inch. This exactly cancels the one line feed since the first part of the word, and puts the "t" on the same line as the "momen." The second ^**PT** then tells WordStar to roll the paper back to where it was before the "t"—which, of course, advances the paper exactly one line.

The next command—the ^**PM**—sends a carriage return to the printer without a line feed command. This puts the printer back at column one, without skipping another line.

The next line, finally, begins with a new pitch command to cancel the .**CW 9** command just used. (In this case, the command is ^**PN** to spread out the first letters in "momentum." Usually the correct command would be ^**PA.**)

There is one other thing going on in this example. Notice that the "t" started in column six when it was on the same line as the rest of the word, but ended up in column seven. This is because in changing the pitch, the number of columns per inch, we have also changed the position of any given column on the page. If you decide to try for this kind of careful correction for proportional spacing, you'll find that knowing which column to use can be a problem because it depends on the character width you are using, the number of letters before the correction, and, finally, any adjustments in pitch that you already made in the first part of the word. If, for instance, you try the same trick with "can't," using .**CW 9,** you'll find that the " 't" should still start in column four.

If you use the following adjustment for "moment," you'll find that the "t" now winds up in column six on your screen instead of column seven, but is in the same spot as before on your paper. (There are two spaces in the last line after ^PN, and three after ^PA.)

```
^A ^P
.SR 8
momen
^N   ^A     ^Tt ^T
```

I started with the warning that this last fix probably wasn't worth the effort. If you apply it to this simple, four line example, for instance, you wind up with a file that looks like this:

```
^A^P                                                    <
^Nmom ^A                                                <
.SR 8                                                   <
^Nmom ^Aen                                              <
.CW 9                                                   <
          ^Tt ^T                                        —
^Nmom ^Aen                                              <
.CW 9                                                   <
      ^T ^Num ^A ^T                                     —
can                                                     <
.CW 9                                                   <
       ^T't ^T                                          <
```

Yet for all that work, the problem being solved is so minor that it's unlikely that anyone will notice the difference anyway. All of which means that you're probably safe in just ignoring it.

If you do decide to use this trick anyway, be sure to reset the .SR command to its default value of .SR 3 soon after. It's a good habit to get into, even if you know that you haven't used any subscripts or superscripts in the file.

Also, note that the .SR command cannot be inserted directly above the line where it is being used. (Between "momen" and "t" for example.) Otherwise the second half of the word will wind up on a line by itself. (It shouldn't, but it does. WordStar ignores the first ^PT command under those conditions.)

If you agree that this trick is too much work, but you still insist on perfect proportional spacing, then you should probably buy a program like MagicPrint, which is designed to work with WordStar. This will not only give you proportional spacing without problems, it will do several other things for you also. (See Chapter Sixteen for a discussion of MagicPrint.)

In the meantime, be assured that time spent learning how to fix this problem has not been wasted. You've just learned some tricks that you will be able to apply to other situations as well.

CONVERTING A FILE TO PROPORTIONAL SPACING

So far everything we've done has been piecemeal—a word, a sentence, or a paragraph. Granted, the polished look of proportional spacing is evident even when printing a single paragraph, but the difference between proportional space printing and normal printing becomes even more dramatic if you print out an entire page of text, particularly if you print it out both ways and compare the two. Also, going through a file and converting it to proportional spacing will give you a better idea of how much work is really involved in the process.

Take any file you have previously created—a letter, memo, or whatever. It should be long enough to fill at least one single-spaced page. Begin by making a copy of the file so the original can remain unchanged. At this point, you might like to print the file as is, using a 10 pitch or 12 pitch element, so you can have it to compare to the final output later.

Now enter **^PP^PA** (or **^PA^PP**) as the first characters in the file. Next, reformat the entire file, paragraph by paragraph, watching out for indented margins, columns, and other possible problems. While you're reformatting, watch for single line paragraphs. Turn bidirectional printing off and on (**.BP off** and **.BP on**) only as necessary.

Be sure to keep an eye out for single word lines as well. If you find any, use **^PN** and **^PA** to widen parts of the word where necessary. Don't bother with closing up the space around narrow letters.

Finally, close the file, and print it. Compare the result to what you're used to seeing with WordStar. The difference should be obvious.

GIVING YOUR PRINTED OUTPUT
THE FINAL "PRINTED" LOOK

Since the point of this exercise is to make your printed output look as much like typeset material as possible, there are two final considerations that you ought to keep in mind.

The first deals with right justification, which is used nearly as often as proportional spacing in books, magazines, newspapers, and the like. In general then, if you're using proportional spacing, you should make sure that right justification is on, whether you normally use it or not. WordStar as distributed, of course, comes up with right justification on, so unless you usually turn the feature off with the toggle **^OJ,** or you've reinstalled your WordStar to come up with it off, you'll automatically be using this anyway.

The second consideration deals with the spacing between lines. The "best" spacing will vary depending on the type style, paper size, and your own taste. In general, though, standard typewriter double-spacing won't look right, while standard typewriter single-spacing will be a bit difficult to read. To give your printout that final polish, then, you should play around with the line height (**.LH**) command until you find the spacing that looks right.

With the printwheel I usually use, 5.3 lines per inch (**.LH 9**) looks about right on 8½ by 11 inch paper. You might like to use 5.3 lines per inch as a starting point, then adjust to your taste.

In this chapter, I've gone into great detail on the proportional space feature because this is the only place you're likely to find any information about it. That leads me to a disclaimer.

This entire discussion of WordStar's proportional space feature is based on my own experimentation with it, using two computers (a Vector 3 and an IBM PC), four printers (a Diablo 630, a Qume Sprint 3, and two NEC 3550's), and three different versions of WordStar (3.00, 3.24, and 3.30). I have tried to put the feature through its paces, but as with any attempt to document any computer program, there may well be problems that I've missed. If you find any, I'd be interested to hear about them. In the meantime, the information in this chapter should serve as a good starting point if you want to try using this feature.

2

A Hidden Twist on Two-Column Printing

Concepts Introduced
Snaking

Uses Introduced
Two-Column/Multicolumn Printing

Proportional space printing isn't the only unsung printing capability hidden in WordStar. As the title of this chapter indicates, WordStar is also capable of two-column printing, or multicolumn printing in general, for that matter.

Of course it's no secret that WordStar will let you create as many columns as you like on the screen and then print them that way. There are problems with doing that though, not the least of which is that if you add or delete material, and then try to reformat using ^B, the columns become hopelessly intermixed.

If the only time you use columns is when you're dealing with numbers, this is not really a problem. In the first place, you are unlikely to do extensive editing and reformatting on numbers, and in the second place, you will normally enter each line as a separate "paragraph" with its own hard carriage return.

If you are dealing with columns of text, though, the intermixing definitely becomes a problem; it puts real limits on your ability to edit the text at will. As it happens, though, there's a way to avoid the intermixing and keep the ability to edit easily.

MULTICOLUMN FORMATS

There are three ways to get a multicolumn format with WordStar.

The first and most obvious way is to set tabs for your columns, then enter the text or numbers by tabbing from one column to the next. You can do this either by entering the lines across—meaning one entry in each column, one line at a time:

```
1       2       3
4       5       6
7       8       9
```

Or, you can get the same effect by entering one column at a time, top to bottom, moving over to the next column to enter it, and so forth:

```
1       4       7
2       5       8
3       6       9
```

Either one of these variations works well enough with numbers or with lists of words. Either one, moreover, can be set to give you a hard carriage return at the end of each line automatically. All you have to do in the first method is enter the columns with INSERT ON. In the second method, you enter the first column with INSERT ON, then enter the remaining columns with INSERT OFF.

Neither of these variations, though, works very well when entering continuous, readable text. MicroPro suggests that in entering text, you first enter one column with appropriate margins, then, with INSERT OFF, use the margin release command (^OX) to go outside the margins and proceed to enter the second column. If you set a tab at the first letter of the second column, and clear all other tabs, then each time you reach the end of a line, you can use TAB as if it were a return.

The major problem in this approach, of course, is one we've already touched on. If you have to make changes anywhere in the text, except the last line, there is no easy way to reformat without getting the two columns hopelessly mixed together.

There is a second fairly obvious method for entering text that at least partially solves this problem. If you enter all of the text in a single continuous column, you can edit and reformat to your heart's content. Then, once you are satisfied that you are finished, you can count the number of lines, mark the beginning and end of the second half of the column, and finally, use the column move feature to transfer the second half of the column to the right half of the screen.

This approach works well enough as long as you really are finished with your edits before you do the column move. If you have to make further changes, though, you're right back where you started, with the problem of intermixing the columns.

One way out of the problem, of course, is to move the right-hand column back where it started. That means you have to mark the beginning and end of the column, then add enough blank lines below the columns so the block can be moved without interfering with other text.

In adding those blank lines, though, you've also added a hard carriage return in each line, so that WordStar will see each line as a separate paragraph. This means that reformatting the text will become something of a chore. Once you're finished with reformatting, you still have to move the right-hand column back to right side of the screen, then delete all those extra lines you put in. This all adds up to a lot of extra work—enough to discourage me, at least, from making a change I might otherwise want.

If this isn't discouraging enough, there's another possible problem. In printing, WordStar sees the text as one wide column rather than two narrow ones. Microspace justification, therefore, will adjust the spacing within the entire line, not within each column. That means that if you want the right-hand column to be left justified, you have to turn off the microspace justification with the **.UJ 0** command. (And turn it back on after the columnar section of the file.)

This is not the problem, since turning off microspace justification is easy enough to do. The problem shows up if you happen to want to print with proportional spacing, because turning off the microspace justification also turns off the proportional spacing.

The third approach to creating columns solves both of these problems at once. It does so by borrowing a trick from word processors that lack WordStar's on-screen formatting.

Both of the approaches we've discussed so far make full use of the on-screen format feature—meaning that for a two-column format, for example, you see both columns on the screen at once. WordStar will print both columns at once, beginning with the first line of each column, then the second line of each column, and so forth.

Most word processors do not do that. To begin with, most word processors do not have on-screen formatting, meaning that you generally see the text on the screen in one continuous block, usually filling the screen from edge to edge regardless of the width of the columns. To use a columnar format with this kind of word processor, you have to tell the program to create the columns at print time. These word processors will print the left-hand column first, top to bottom, roll the printer back to the first line of the column, then print the right-hand column. This is sometimes called snaking.

The advantage of snaking, as far as WordStar is concerned, is that it frees you to enter the text in one continuous column, then edit it and reformat it as many times as you like. A secondary advantage is that it also lets you use proportional space printing because you no longer need to turn off the microspace justification.

SNAKING

The idea of creating columns with snaking instead of on-screen formatting is all very nice, but it is not at all obvious how to make WordStar jump through this particular hoop. After all, MicroPro clearly intended on-screen formatting not only to replace the need for snaking, but to be an improvement on it. (For most purposes it is.) Snaking, at any rate, is not a feature that is intentionally built into the program.

The key word here is "intentionally," because whether MicroPro intended it or not, the capability is there if your printer can handle it. All you have to do is trick WordStar into doing it.

You do that by taking advantage of the **.SR** command for setting the subscript/superscript roll. Add in the subscript and superscript commands themselves (**^PV** and **^PT**), plus the page offset command (**.PO**), and suddenly you have snaking.

PRELIMINARY DECISIONS

As with anything you plan to print, the first thing you need to know is what you want the printout to look like. This decision covers all the usual choices about pitch, lines per inch, ragged right versus right justified, and so forth. In addition, with the two-column format, you also have to decide how wide you want the columns to be and where you want them on the page.

Assume, for example, that you want each column to be three inches wide, with half an inch between them, and with one-inch margins on either side of the page. The next decision you have to make is choice of pitch. This will affect both the number of characters per column and the page offset commands you use to position the columns on the paper.

In general, you will probably want to use 12 pitch for two-column format. For any given width of line (in inches), the extra two characters per inch make ragged right look less ragged, and leave fewer gaps in a line that has been right justified. This difference is minor in a line that is 60 or 70 characters wide. It is glaringly obvious, though, in a line that is only 30 or so characters wide.

Assuming 12 pitch, and a three-inch wide column, you should set your margins at 1 and 36 (3 inches x 12 characters per inch). Add any other formatting commands that you want, then go ahead and type in the text as usual.

The Basics of Snaking

The basic trick of snaking is simple. You start out with the file in the form of one long column entered, edited, and formatted to the proper margins. Then all you need to do is break each section in half, and tell WordStar to roll back the paper and put the second half on the right side of the page.

Here's an example that shows the basic techniques for a single, short section of text. The commands that relate to snaking are in boldface.

One warning before you try this example though. All the sample files in this chapter assume you are using a friction feed, or roller, to advance the paper. If you usually use a tractor, you should take it off the printer. A unidirectional tractor feed will not work for snaking at all. A bidirectional tractor feed can be made to work, but the mechanics of moving the paper back and forth may require that you adjust the commands a bit. In general, with a bidirectional tractor feed, you will have to roll the paper back further than you really want to go, and then roll forward again before printing the second column.

Before Entering the Commands for Snaking:	After Entering Commands for Snaking:
^A ^SSectionA ^S	.PO 10
AAAAAAAAAAAAAAA	^A ^SSection A ^S
AAAAAAAAAAAAAAA	AAAAAAAAAAAAAAA
AAAAAAAAAAAAAAA	AAAAAAAAAAAAAAA
AAAAAAAAAAAAAAA	AAAAAAAAAAAAAAA
AAAAAAAAAAAAAAA	AAAAAAAAAAAAAAA
AAAAAAAAAAAAAAA	AAAAAAAAAAAAAAA
AAAAAAAAAAAAAAA	**.SR 48**
AAAAAAAAAAAAAAA	AAAAAAAAAAAAAAA
AAAAAAAAAAAAAAA	**.PO 54**
AAAAAAAAAAAAAAA	^TAAAAAAAAAAAAA
AAAAAAAAAAAAAAA	AAAAAAAAAAAAAAA
	AAAAAAAAAAAAAAA
	.SR 0
	AAAAAAAAAAAAAAA
	^TAAAAAAAAAAAAAAA
	.PO 12

Converting the text on the left into example on the right takes only a few simple steps. First, you have to enter a page offset (**.PO**) command to give you the one-inch left margin. Notice that in this example, a one-inch margin requires a setting of **.PO 10** because the page offset command comes before the **^PA** command for 12 pitch. Notice also that all later page offset commands come after the **^PA** command, and are, therefore, measured in terms of 12 pitch.

Next, you need to find the halfway point. Count the number of lines, and divide by 2. Mark that point by adding a blank line between the first half and second half. If there is an odd number of lines (as in this example), the first "half" winds up one line longer than the second half. In this example, then, with 11 lines of text in the original file, the dividing point is after the sixth line. (Eleven lines of text does not include the section heading.)

Third, you have to tell WordStar to move this second half of the section over to the right side of the paper. You do that with another page offset command that you enter in the line you just created. This takes just a bit of arithmetic: Given a 1-inch margin (12 characters), a 3-inch column on the left side (36 characters), plus a half inch between columns (6 characters), the proper setting is **.PO 54** (12 plus 36 plus 6, or alternately, 4.5 inches times 12 characters per inch).

You also have to tell WordStar that this is the place where it is going to roll the paper back. You do that by entering the **^PT** command (superscript roll) before the first character in the second half of the section.

Having done that, your next step is to tell WordStar how far to roll the paper back by resetting the **.SR,** or set roll command. Determining the value for this also takes a bit of arithmetic. If you are printing with WordStar's default of 6 lines per inch, each increment of 8 on this value will tell WordStar to roll back one additional line. The value for this setting, then, would be 8 times however many lines there are in the first half of the section. In this example, you want to roll the paper back 6 lines, so the correct setting is **.SR 48** (for 8 times 6).

Watch out here. The obvious place to put the **.SR** command is on a line directly before the second half of the section. This will not work. As I mentioned in the last chapter, if the **.SR** command is placed immediately before the **^PT** command, WordStar will often get confused and ignore the **^PT** altogether. The safest place to put the **.SR** command is either at the top of the file, or one line before the end of the first section. Either of these spots is obvious enough to make the command hard to overlook if you have to go back to the file to re-edit and reformat.

There is one last thing to do. Up to this point you have used the **^PT** command only once—to roll the paper up. As far as WordStar is concerned, your whole right-hand column is a superscript. The next time it sees a **^PT,** it is going to roll the paper down. You have to reset WordStar by tricking it into thinking it's done that already.

You do that by using **.SR 0** to set the roll to zero, then adding another **^PT**. Notice here again that you should not put the **^PT** immediately after the **.SR** command. Other than that, you can insert these commands pretty much anywhere in the text. Probably the best place is toward the end of the column, where it will be easy to find and adjust if you make changes later.

Finally, unless the end of this section is the end of the file, you have to reset the left margin to one inch with a page offset command (**.PO 12**).

Snaking with a Two-Column Format

The basic trick for making WordStar snake may be simple, but the actual application can get a little sticky. To begin with, there are two different formats for two-column printing. Each one requires a slightly different approach.

One format divides each page into sections and snakes each section so that it takes the form:

Section A
AAAAAAAAAAAAAAA   AAAAAAAAAAAAAAA
AAAAAAAAAAAAAAA   AAAAAAAAAAAAAAA
AAAAAAAAAAAAAAA   AAAAAAAAAAAAAAA
AAAAAAAAAAAAAAA   AAAAAAAAAAAAAAA
AAAAAAAAAAAAAAA   AAAAAAAAAAAAAAA

Section B
BBBBBBBBBBBBBBB   BBBBBBBBBBBBBBB
BBBBBBBBBBBBBBB   BBBBBBBBBBBBBBB
BBBBBBBBBBBBBBB   BBBBBBBBBBBBBBB
BBBBBBBBBBBBBBB   BBBBBBBBBBBBBBB

Section C
CCCCCCCCCCCCCCC   CCCCCCCCCCCCCCC
CCCCCCCCCCCCCCC   CCCCCCCCCCCCCCC
CCCCCCCCCCCCCCC   CCCCCCCCCCCCCCC

The other format does not divide the page into sections, though it may divide the text into sections so that it takes a different form:

Section A   BBB Continued
AAAAAAAAAAAAA   BBBBBBBBBBBBB
AAAAAAAAAAAAA   BBBBBBBBBBBBB
                 BBBBBBBBBBBBB

Section B
BBBBBBBBBBBBB
BBBBBBBBBBBBB   Section C
BBBBBBBBBBBBB   CCCCCCCCCCCCC
                 CCCCCCCCCCCCC

We'll tackle this continuous format first because it's a little easier to create than the section format. The complication with the continuous format is that WordStar only recognizes settings for the **.SR** command up to and including **.SR 255.** This works out to a maximum superscript roll of 255/48 inch, or roughly $5\frac{1}{3}$ inches. On an 11 inch sheet of paper, with top and bottom margins of perhaps one inch each, this still leaves you nearly 4 inches short of rolling to the top of the page. You can get these extra 4 inches, though, by combining a superscript command with a subscript command.

The following example shows only 30 lines of "text," but the settings on the various commands assume a full page. The example is based on using WordStar's normal default of 66 lines per page—with 55 lines of text, a top margin of 3 lines, and a bottom margin of 8 lines. If you change any of these defaults, the settings for many of the commands will also have to change.

As far as the commands for page offset and for 12 pitch are concerned, the same comments apply here as before, so we will ignore them this time through. Some of the lines have been numbered, as WordStar will number them, to make the example easier to follow.

```
.PL 121
.PO 10
.SR 0
 ^a^SSection a^S           < Line 1
 ^VAAAAAAAAAAAAAAA          < Line 2
.SR 220
AAAAAAAAAAAAAAA            < Line 3
AAAAAAAAAAAAAAA
AAAAAA . . .
AAAAAAAAAAAAAAA
AAAAAAAAAAAAAAA
AAAAAAAAAAAAAAA
AAAAAAAAAAAAAAA
AAAAAAAAAAAAAAA
AAAAAAAAAAAAAAA
       *   *   *
 ^SSection b^S
BBBBBBBBBBBBBBB
BBBBBBBBBBBBBBB
BBBBBBBBBBBBBBB ^V         < Line 55
.PO 43
 ^T                        < Line 56

BBBBBBBBBBBBBBB            < Line 57
.SR 0
BBBBBBBBBBBBBBB
 ^TBBBBBBBBBBBBBBB
BBBBBBBBBBBBBBB
BBBBBBBBBBBBBB
       *   *   *
 ^SSection c^S
CCCCCCCCCCCCCCC
CCCCC . . .
CCCCCCCCCCCCCCC
CCCCCCCCCCCCCCC
CCCCCCCCCCCCCCC
CCCCCCCCCCCCCCC
CCCCCCCCCCCCCCC
CCCCCCCCCCCCCCC
CCCCCCCCCCCCCCC            < Line 110
.PO 12
```

Notice that the first thing in the file is a page length command (**.PL 121**). This is critical because WordStar's line counting function doesn't know anything about rolling the paper back. If you don't adjust the paper length, WordStar will count 55 lines of text, then send a form feed to the printer, no matter where you happen to be on the paper. The setting of 121 comes from adding 3 (for the top margin) plus 8 (for the bottom margin) plus 55 (for the left-hand column) plus 55 (for the right-hand column)—all of which gives us a page length of 121 lines, with 110 lines of text.

The next thing we want to do is convince WordStar that it has rolled the paper down for a subscript, so that later we can roll up with a second subscript command. This is really the same trick we did before with the superscript, but in reverse. We do it here by setting the subscript roll to zero with a **.SR 0** command, followed by a **^PV** two lines later. (As with the superscript command, there should be at least 1 line of text between the **.SR** setting and the **^PV** or else WordStar may get confused.)

The next step is to reset the subscript/superscript roll for use when we want to roll the paper up. The setting of **.SR 220** comes, once again, from simple arithmetic. We know we want to roll the paper back a total of 55 lines. Each increment of eight on the **.SR** command still equals 1 line, of course, for a total of 440 as the desired **.SR** setting (8 times 55). But we also know that we are going to add two "roll-ups" together, so the value for the **.SR** command becomes 440 divided by 2, or 220.

We end line 55, then, with the second subscript command, **^PV.** This rolls the paper half way up. Line 56 then starts with a superscript command, **^PT,** which rolls the paper the rest of the way up. (In between we add a page offset command so the second column will print on the right half of the page.) Notice that in this example, the superscript command is followed immediately by a carriage return (meaning the **^PT** is on a line by itself), so that the second column will have a blank line directly across from the section heading in the first column. All that remains now is to set the **.SR** value to zero again, and follow that with a second **^PT** to reset the superscript command.

When WordStar reaches line 110 on the screen, it will send a form feed to the printer and start the next page. As far as the format commands are concerned, each following page is a repeat of this first one, except that new pages do not need a command for page length or pitch, and they do not need to start with a new **.SR** command because this is already set at zero. Each new page does need a new command for page offset, but starting with the second page, the 1-inch margin is figured in terms of 12 pitch for a setting of **.PO 12.** The settings for the last page in your file, finally, are adjusted as necessary so that both columns will be the same length.

Snaking with a Two-Column Section Format

In one way, at least, snaking with a section format is a little easier than snaking with a continuous format. Unless you have very long sections, you will generally be able to use the superscript command by itself, rather than having to use superscript plus subscript. Even so, setting up a section format is a little trickier than setting up a continuous format because of a not-so-obvious problem that shows up in separating the sections.

If, for instance, you add blank lines between the sections, the simplest thing to do is add the lines once, in moving from one section to the next, then roll the paper back only to the top of the new section. If you do that, though, you will have blank space on the paper that WordStar's line counting function doesn't know about. This means that the end of the page on the paper will not match the end of the page according to WordStar.

If you add blank lines (or asterisks or whatever) to separate the sections, then, you also have to make sure that you add the same number of lines to each of the two columns. Then, of course, you have to adjust the **.SR** command to take the extra lines into account.

Here's a short example of how to set up a section format. The only thing new in this example is the use of blank lines. These are indicated with a number sign (#). The reason for each is explained within the file. The values for the set roll command are based on the number of blank lines plus lines of text. Other than that, the example should be self-explanatory.

If you want your printed page to look like this:

```
Section A
AAAAAAAAAAAAAAA     AAAAAAAAAAAAAAA
AAAAAAAAAAAAAAA     AAAAAAAAAAAAAAA
AAAAAAAAAAAAAAA     AAAAAAAAAAAAAAA
AAAAAAAAAAAAAAA     AAAAAAAAAAAAAAA
AAAAAAAAAAAAAAA     AAAAAAAAAAAAAAA
AAAAAAAAAAAAAA
        *           *           *
Section B
BBBBBBBBBBBBBBB     BBBBBBBBBBBBBBB
BBBBBBBBBBBBBBB     BBBBBBBBBBBBBBB
BBBBBBBBBBBBBBB     BBBBBBBBBBBBBBB
BBBBBBBBBBBBBBB     BBBBBBBBBBBBBBB
```

Your file should look like this:

```
.PL 121
.PO 12
^A ^SSection A ^S
# (for blank line between section heading and first line)
AAAAAAAAAAAAAAA
AAAAAAAAAAAAAAA
AAAAAAAAAAAAAAA
AAAAAAAAAAAAAAA
AAAAAAAAAAAAAAA
.SR 64
AAAAAAAAAAAAAA
.PO 54
# (For blank line opposite section heading)
# (For blank line between section heading and first line)
```

```
^TAAAAAAAAAAAAAA
AAAAAAAAAAAAAAAA
AAAAAAAAAAAAAAAA
.SR 0
AAAAAAAAAAAAAAAA
^TAAAAAAAAAAAAAAAA
# (For blank line to balance the last line on the left column)
.PO 12
# (For blank line between end of section A and asterisks)
        *              *              *
# (For blank line between asterisks and beginning of section B)
^SSection B ^S
# (For blank line between section heading and text)
BBBBBBBBBBBBBBBB
BBBBBBBBBBBBBBBB
BBBBBBBBBBBBBBBB
.SR 72
BBBBBBBBBBBBBBBB
.PO 54.
^T (To balance blank line before asterisks)
# (To balance line of asterisks)
# (To balance blank line after asterisks)
# (To balance line with Section Heading)
# (To balance blank line after Section Heading)
BBBBBBBBBBBBBBBB
BBBBBBBBBBBBBBBB
.SR 0
BBBBBBBBBBBBBBBB
^TBBBBBBBBBBBBBBBB
.PO 12
```

Nothing, not even snaking, will make editing as easy in two columns as it is with WordStar's normal one-column format. If you have to go back to the file and make major changes in the text, you will find that you have to reformat the entire file once again for two columns. Though with snaking, at least, you won't have to put it back into a one-column format first. The real advantage to snaking shows up when you only need to make minor edits in the text, along with minimal changes in the dot commands that control the columnar format.

In general, then, you will want to do as much editing as possible before setting up your file for columns. It is also a good idea to keep an unformatted copy of the file on disk in case major changes are necessary. By going back to the unformatted version, you can at least avoid having to delete the format commands you've already put in the file.

Format Files, Forms, and Form Letters
WORDSTAR WITHOUT MAILMERGE

Uses Introduced
Creating Standard Format Files
Forms and Form Letters Without MailMerge
Address Files

Odds are that just about every time you open a new file, the first thing you do is a series of standard entries. This may include things like entering commands for pitch and line height, or entering a format line for tabs and margins. It also may include some additional largely mechanical entries—things like entering your name and address in a letter file, or finding the right line for entering the date.

One of the nice things about WordStar (or any other good word processor for that matter) is that you can use it to do all the mechanical work for you. All you need is a format file.

FORMAT FILES

Format files are one of those simple ideas that seem incredibly obvious once you've thought of them or been introduced to them. By the same token, they are one of those simple ideas that, if left to your own devices, you may never think of.

Quite simply, the idea is that for any given format, you create a standard file. From then on, having done the work once, you use the Read a file command (^**KR**) to read that format into a new file whenever you need it. The purely mechanical work is then reduced to two keystrokes, and you can get on to doing the real work.

If you're like most people, there are several standard formats that you use consistently. In my case, the basic choices include a letter format, a manuscript format, a billing format, and a memo format. Within each of these categories there are variations, so that for the letter format, for instance, I not only have a version for my preprinted letterhead, I also have a version for printing on fanfold paper. Similarly, I not only have a HEADELIT, for writing book and article manuscripts at 12 pitch (which I happen to prefer), I also have a HEADPICA, for the benefit of those editors I know who prefer seeing manuscripts printed at 10 pitch.

The idea is to keep all these format files on the same disk as your master working copy of WordStar. That way, any time you open a new file, an appropriate format file is available to read from the working disk no matter what data disk you happen to be using.

Here is an example of a simple format file, HEADLTR. As the name implies, this is designed as the heading for letters. Specifically, this is the format file I use for letters on my preprinted stationery. With a little modification such as adding or subtracting blank lines as necessary, you should have no trouble adapting it for your own use. As an added convenience, this file also includes a section for the envelope that goes with the letter.

The "#" signs on the left side indicate a blank line. The first "#" represents the first line in the file.

FILE: HEADLTR

A Standard Format for Use with Preprinted Stationery

```
#
#
..To print out put top of letter just under bail, left side at 7.
..
-----! --------------------------------------------------------------------------------
#
#
#
#
#
#
```

```
#
#
#
#
#
#
NAME
#
Dear Whoever:
#
..lh16
START
#
#
#
Sincerely,
#
#
#
#
M. David Stone
.PA
..ENVELOPE
..The following is for the envelope to go with the letter.
..The top of the envelope should be at bail.
..The left edge at the arrow.
^A
.PL 25
.PO 48
^C
.LH 8
#
#
#
#
#
#
^A
```

This example really consists of two different formats—a letter format
and an envelope format. One reason it makes sense to join them together,
of course, is that you'll usually want an envelope whenever you write a letter. But even if you don't plan to print both at the same time, or if you want
several copies of the letter and only one copy of the envelope, it's still easier to create them together, then use the Write a file, **^KW,** command to
write the envelope to another file.

The way you use the HEADLTR file is to:

1. Open a new file,
2. Read this into the new file using the read a file command (^KR),
3. Type the date, using the "D" of DATE as a guide for the first letter (after which you delete DATE, of course),
4. Enter the name and address, the salutation, and the body of the letter, using NAME, WHOEVER, and START respectively as your guides,
5. Enter the address in the ENVELOPE section of the file. (The easiest way to address the envelope is to use the block copy command (^KC) immediately after you've entered the address at the top of the letter. Mark the beginning and end of the address, jump to the end of the file (using ^QC), then use ^KC to copy the address.)

In addition to saving a few keystrokes here and there, the most important thing that this file will do for you is eliminate the need to remember how many blank lines go where, and what column to use for starting the date. The point is, you figure out the correct lines and column one time, and never have to do it again.

There are a few other things worth noting in this file. To begin with, one of the first things in the file is a nonprinting reminder of how to line up the paper in the printer. (This was entered with the ".." command, which tells WordStar not to print the line and saves you the chore of deleting it before printing.) Ideally, you should be consistent in all your files, so the paper will always go in the printer the same way. In the real world, that's not so easy. If you put notes like this in your files, you'll waste less paper and less time whenever you've strayed from your usual format.

The format line is also entered as a nonprinting line. If you're not familiar with format lines, take a look at your WordStar manual. The basic point is that you can set margins and tabs with a single command, ^OF. MicroPro, incidentally, calls this "Ruler from Line." A better mnemonic is on-screen Format line. This format line is there to use or not, depending on the length of the letter and your own taste. For short letters, you will probably want to stay with the default margins of 1 and 65. For longer letters, though, you might prefer using this wider line and fewer pages.

Take a careful look at the "DATE" line. This is set up so that the spaces are at 10 pitch, but there is a ^PA command before the date itself so the text will print out at 12 pitch. This gives the file a little more flexibility. You may, for instance, usually use 12 pitch, but occasionally want to use 10 pitch—on a short letter perhaps. Since the date is already positioned in terms of 10 pitch, you won't have to do anything but delete the ^PA command. Either way, with the command there or not, the date will still print at the same position on the page.

The line height command (.LH 16) is in the file for the same reason—flexibility. It is entered with two dots rather than the usual one, so that

WordStar will normally ignore it, and print with the default line height of (**.LH 8**), or six lines per inch. For a short letter, though, you will probably want double spacing, in which case you only have to delete one dot to transform this into an active command.

Because the envelope portion of this file has to go on a new "page" (meaning on an envelope), it begins with a **.PA**, the new page command. It is also clearly marked as a separate section with nonprinting notes and reminders about how to place the envelope in the printer.

There should be little or nothing in this part of the file that isn't obvious if you are familiar with basic WordStar. Even so, there are a few interesting wrinkles that make it worth going over quickly.

The page length command, **.PL 25,** sets the page length at twenty-five lines. This is more of an esthetic refinement than anything else, though it does save some wear and tear on the printer by telling it to roll just far enough for the envelope to come out.

The page offset command, **.PO 48,** tells WordStar to count 48 columns on the printer before it starts printing the first column that shows on the screen. This setting is designed to print the address 4 inches in from the left edge of the envelope (4 inches at 12 columns per inch equals 48 columns). The correct setting for this value will vary somewhat depending on how you have the envelope positioned in the printer and what pitch you are using, but the point is that by using the page offset command to indent the address, you are free to enter the address starting in column one on the screen, without having to move the cursor to the correct column for each line of the address.

Notice, though, that in order for this to work, WordStar has to be set at 12 pitch before it gets to the page offset command. Otherwise it will count spaces in whatever pitch it was set to at the time. That's the reason for the **^PA** command one line above the page offset command.

Of course if you are printing the envelope at the same time as the letter, and you are already using 12 pitch, then you don't need another **^PA** command here. Still, it will do no harm, and by including it, you will avoid a problem that might otherwise show up at times.

The next command, **^PC,** tells WordStar to stop printing at that point. This gives you a chance to put the envelope in the printer instead of watching WordStar print the address on your roller.

The **.LH 8** line height command, setting WordStar for six lines per inch, is there once again for assurance. If you are already printing at six lines per inch, it has no effect. But if you are double spacing the letter, using **.LH 16,** this command will reset the line height for printing the envelope.

The final **^PA** is the last character in the file. Since we have already set the file at 12 pitch, this command will have no effect whatsoever. It is there as a marker, to let you know that this is the right line to start the address on. Any other marker, a letter or word, would have to be deleted. This one can be left where it is.

One other thing. WordStar as distributed will automatically print page numbers on the bottom of each page. If your working copy of Word-

Star is set to do that, you should add the additional dot command .OP (omit page numbers) at the beginning of the file; otherwise your envelopes will be numbered as pages. A second alternative is to reinstall your Word-Star so that it will not print page numbers unless you tell it to. Most of the examples in this book (including this one) assume that you have done that. For directions on how to reinstall WordStar, see Appendix D.

SOME THOUGHTS ABOUT FORMAT FILES

There are a few things you should keep in mind when you start creating a set of files for your own use.

To begin with, the easiest way to create a format file is to take advantage of the ^KW (write a file) command. The next time you write a letter, for instance, you could simply mark the beginning and end of the part you want to keep and write it to a file. Be sure to go back to the new format file later, though, and delete the parts you don't want (the specific name and address, the specific date, and so forth). Otherwise you'll have to delete these things every time you read the format into a new file.

While you're at it, take the time to design some flexibility into the format to make it easier to vary the pitch, the margins, or whatever. You don't have to do this all at once, but when you find yourself having to make changes on the basic format, take a look, and see if there's a way to design those changes into the standard file.

Another important point is to be consistent in naming the files. If you use HEADLTR for your letter format, then use HEADBILL and HEAD-MEMO, not BILLFORM and MEMOFORM. The more consistent the names are, the less often you'll find yourself trying to read in a file that doesn't exist. By the time you finish looking at the disk directory for the right name, then giving the command to read the file again, you will have wasted most of the time you're supposed to be saving by using format files in the first place. This is particularly true if you're logged in on your data disk on drive B, and the format file is sitting on drive A, so that you have to take the time to log onto another disk before you can look at the directory.

There's another benefit of having the names of each format file begin with the same letters. All your address files will show up together and alphabetically on your WordStar disk directory (HEADBILL, HEADELIT, HEADLTR, and so forth). If you forget the name you've given a format, this will make it much easier to spot it, particularly if you have many files on your disk.

Finally, to give you a better sense of the real value of format files, here is another, somewhat more complex, example.

CREATING YOUR OWN LETTERHEAD

There are times when you must use preprinted stationery to create the "right" impression in your letters. There are also times, however, when you don't really need to bother. In those cases, you can just as easily use fanfold paper and a format file with your address already in it. If you take the time to design your file carefully and have a letter-quality printer, you can still make the letterhead look nearly as good as preprinted stationery—particularly if you are using a heavy weight paper and carbon ribbon. This kind of file can also be useful if you happen to run out of preprinted stationery, or if you've moved and don't have any stationery with the new address yet.

At any rate, here is an example of what you can do. I've left out the envelope section this time. You should be able to add it back in easily enough. Just remember that in order to add your name and address on the envelope, you'll have to set both the top margin and page offset to zero, using **.MT 0** and **.PO 0**, respectively. Otherwise you won't be able to print the return address in its usual position at the top left-hand corner.

FILE: HEADLTR.FUL

For Use Without Preprinted Stationery

```
.PO 4
.MT 0
^D ^B ^SYour__Name__Here ^A_____ ^S ^B
^N                ^A                          111 Whatever Street
^N                ^A                        City, State   Zip Code
^N                ^A                                    Phone ^D
#
#
.PO 8
.MT 3
#
#
#
#
                                                                    DATE
#
#
#
#
#
NAME
#
Dear WHOEVER:
#
..LH 16
START
#
#
Sincerely,
```

```
    #
    #
    #
    #
Your Name Here
```

This example demonstrates the real value of format files. It is long enough and complicated enough so that under most conditions it simply wouldn't be worth the work involved if you had to enter the information from scratch each time. By reading it in from a standard file, though, you can put an attractive heading on your letter with just a few keystrokes.

For the most part, this file is concerned with design considerations. For the design to look right, for instance, the heading should be wider than the body of the text. The first command in the file then, (**.PO 4**), sets the page offset to four columns. Notice that this is reset to the usual default of eight columns immediately after the heading.

The second command in the file (**.MT 0**) sets the top margin to zero so that the paper won't advance at all before printing. This makes it much easier to position the paper in the printer in terms of judging where the heading should go, particularly if you're using single sheets rather than fanfold paper. This value is also reset to the normal default (**.MT 3**) immediately after the heading.

The heading itself gets its preprinted look through a judicious use of boldfacing, underlining, double striking, and careful counting of spaces so that the address lines are flush right—meaning that, as with right justification, they all end at the same place. In this case, notice that instead of letting WordStar adjust the positioning for you, you have to add the spaces manually, exactly where you want them.

Also adding to the preprinted look is that the name is set for 10 pitch, while the address is set for 12 pitch. The line across the heading, moreover, is printed at 12 pitch, boldface, and double strike, to give it as solid a look as possible. In addition, be sure to put an underline between first, middle, and last names, or else you'll wind up with blank spaces there instead. The address and phone number, finally, are printed with double strike to give them a darker, crisper look than the body of the letter will have.

Each of the three lines with the address and phone number is set to "print" some spaces in 10 pitch and the rest of the line in 12 pitch. The number of spaces printed at 10 pitch in each line is exactly equal to the length of your name, which makes them exactly equal to the number of spaces printed at 10 pitch in the first line. This makes it much easier to keep the address lines flush right with the underlining of the first line.

Finally, notice that I did not include the final flourish of proportional space printing in this file. You can do this of course, but unless you either have a dual element printer or want to print out the body of the letter with proportional spacing also, you'll have to stop the printer (by including a **^PC** command in the file) and change print elements. This is more work than I, for one, am usually willing to do.

FORMS AND FORM LETTERS—WITHOUT MAILMERGE

If you're even vaguely familiar with MailMerge, or any other mailmerging program (with a small "m"), you have probably noticed that format files do some of the same things for you that mailmerging does, except that they do it under conditions where it would be silly to even consider using Mail-Merge.

Specifically, format files provide you with a basic form. All you have to do is fill in the blanks—just like filling in the blanks in a form or form letter with MailMerge. The blanks in this case happen to be the entire letter, report, manuscript, or whatever, but the concept is the same. In fact, the basic idea of format files can be extended much further, so that you can use this same approach for forms and form letters.

For letters, for instance, you could write a standard letter, leaving blanks for the date, name, address, and so forth. Then, whenever you need to send the letter, you would open a new file, read the standard letter in, and fill in the blanks.

You could do exactly the same thing with forms—personnel forms, invoices, or whatever—create a standard form, read it into a file when needed, and fill in the blanks.

In either case, you can automate the process somewhat by marking the blanks with a symbol you know you will never use in the body of the text—something like "@@@." Then, once you've read the form or letter into your new file, you begin by telling WordStar to find the first "@@@" and delete it. You do this with the **^QA,** or find and replace command. When WordStar asks you what to find, you enter "@@@" followed by a RETURN. When WordStar asks you what to replace it with, you simply enter a RETURN, which tells WordStar to replace it with nothing, or, in effect, to delete it. Also, when WordStar asks for options, enter "N"—replace without asking. That way, WordStar will delete the marker without first stopping to ask you for permission.

After you fill in the first blank, you then enter **^L** (repeat last find command). WordStar finds the next marker and deletes it, you fill in the blank, enter another **^L,** and so forth.

This all adds up to more than simply a cheap and easy way to avoid buying MailMerge to produce forms or form letters. Granted, you could use this trick to replace that particular capability of MailMerge, but that misses the point. In certain cases, there are some real advantages to using this approach instead of MailMerge, and in other cases there are real disadvantages.

Basically, there are two disadvantages. To begin with, using format files is going to take more time than using MailMerge. With format files, you have to wait as you open each file, you have to wait while WordStar reads the format into the new file, you have to wait during each find operation while WordStar looks for your markers, and finally, you have to wait for WordStar to write the file to disk when you're finished.

Taken individually, none of these waits is unreasonably long—unless you have an extremely long file. Taken together, though, they begin to add up. If you're doing more than one form or letter at a time, each additional one adds that much more waiting time. With MailMerge, on the other hand, most of the waiting time disappears. As for what remains, you only have to go through it once for each session, rather than once for each form or letter.

In general, then, if you do only one or two forms or letters at any given session, and if your format file is short enough to fit in your computer memory all at once, the extra time involved in using format files will be minor. If you do many forms or letters at a time or if your file is extremely long to begin with, you will probably find that the extra waiting time is costing you more—in dollars and cents—than it would cost to buy Mail-Merge.

The second disadvantage of using format files is relatively minor. Every time you read a form or letter into a file and write it to disk, you are taking up space. This can be easily corrected, of course, by deleting the file from the disk when you've finished printing it. But here again this is an extra step, which adds that much more time to creating the forms or letters.

As it happens, this "disadvantage" can become an advantage—if you happen to want a copy of the form or letter on disk for future reference.

If you're an employer, for instance, you might like to keep your personnel records on disk so you can call them up and enter changes easily. Usually you would think in terms of a data base management system for this sort of thing, but if you only have a handful of employees, and you have no other use for a data base program, there's no point in buying one. You can use MailMerge for this application by telling it to "print" to disk, but it happens that using MailMerge to create disk files is a little clumsy. Worse, it is risky if you are using any release earlier than 3.3. If you tell MailMerge to use a file name that's already on the disk, release 3.3 will tell you about it and ask whether to overwrite the file. Earlier releases, though, will overwrite the file without warning you about it.

In this kind of application, WordStar by itself will not only do everything you need, it is actually preferable to MailMerge.

A second advantage that format files have over MailMerge is that with format files you use WordStar as usual, with all of WordStar's editing capabilities. This means that after you've filled in a blank space and gone on to the next, you can still go back and make changes if you notice you made a mistake.

With MailMerge you can't do that. If you enter information at print time in response to prompts on the screen, then once you've moved past any given prompt you don't have the ability to back up and change your answer. (There are ways to get out of this corner once you've painted yourself into it, but for this kind of application, they are too clumsy to be useful. We'll get to them later.) For this reason alone, if you're only printing one or two forms or letters at a time, and if they're not terribly long, you may be better off using format files over MailMerge.

A related advantage that format files have is that they allow for more mucking around with the finished product. For instance, if you are a free lance picture researcher working for several clients on any number of different projects, you may have a semistandard request letter for pictures. You need a different letter for each project, because you have to describe the project in the body of the letter. In addition, you may also want to customize the letter each time you use it, so that it doesn't read too much like a form letter.

You may, for instance, occasionally want to use phrases like "As I told you over the phone," or, "Thank you for your time over the phone," or even "I haven't been able to reach you by phone," depending, of course, on the circumstance. On top of all this customization, you may need to describe the particular picture you want in some detail.

In this situation, there will still be parts of the letter that are identical from one to the next except for blanks to be filled in. For the most part, though, this level of customization goes beyond what you can do easily with MailMerge by filling in blank spaces. In particular, MailMerge will only provide you with prompts. A format file, in contrast, will let you see your customizations in context, and will leave you free to use full WordStar editing capabilities for the parts that need to be rewritten. In this kind of application, all this customization also has the effect of turning this semistandard form letter into the kind of individual letter that you will probably want to keep on a correspondence disk anyway.

ADDRESS FILES: SEMIAUTOMATIC ADDRESSING OF LETTERS AND ENVELOPES

There is at least one other MailMerge-like capability that you can use WordStar for by itself. This is the semiautomatic addressing of letters and envelopes.

This is another one of those simple, obvious tricks that is easy to overlook. The magic is done courtesy of the ^KR command once again, and a set of short address files, each one containing a different name and address. All you need to do is create an address file for each person you normally write to. Then, whenever you're writing a letter to that person, you read the address into the letter file.

Obviously, this trick is most useful for people that you write to fairly frequently. More often than not, though, if you send any letters at all to some person or business, you will eventually wind up sending more.

You don't have to put in much effort to create address files. All you have to do whenever you write a letter is mark the beginning and end of the address block, and write it to another file. (You can even include the salutation.)

As simple as this sounds, it can get messy if you're not careful, especially if you write letters to many different people. Here are a couple of hints to help keep things straight.

First, as with format files, the name of all address files should begin with the same letters—and for the same reason: so they will all show up together, listed alphabetically, on your WordStar disk directory. NA, for name and address, is a good choice in this case—NABILL, NAJIM, NACONED, and so forth. This, once again, will make it much easier to find the file you want, if you forget the name. It will also tell you immediately that some given file is an address when you are looking at the directory at some later point and trying to figure out what's on the disk.

If you're dealing with a company, and particularly if you deal with more than one person in that company, it can often be helpful to use a file name with both the company name and the initials of the particular person (NAMICPRO.JL and NAMICPRO.MHG, for instance).

Finally, since the number of address files will tend to grow with time, it can be helpful to keep your disks organized either by project, or in terms of the businesses or people that you deal with. That way, instead of having an overwhelming number of address files on your master working disk, you can keep specific address files on the same disks as the projects—and correspondence—they are needed for. This not only cuts down the number of address files on any given disk, it automatically eliminates addresses you no longer need once you finish a project or stop dealing with the particular company.

When you've filled up a disk, you can carry all the address files you still need over to a new disk with a simple copy command. This assumes that you're at least vaguely familiar with your operating system, in which case the command should look something like:

PIP A:=B:NA*.*

This is the correct format for CP/M. Other operating systems vary. If you are not familiar with your operating system, you can still copy the files individually with WordStar's copy a file command.

Everything that we've done in this chapter—format files, forms, form letters, and address files—has been with WordStar alone. In each case, we've squeezed a little more usefulness out of this program by using techniques and concepts that are similar to what we can do with MailMerge. Up to now, though, we've used those concepts in a limited way. It's time to take a look at MailMerge itself, and see how those same techniques can be used with software designed to provide full-fledged mailmerging capabilities.

Envelopes I

AN INTRODUCTION TO MAILMERGE

Commands Introduced
.AV (Ask for variable)
/O (Omit if value not given)
.DM (Display message)
.RP (Repeat file)

Concepts Introduced
Variables
Entry Time Instructions
Prompts vs. Variable Names
Maximum Length for Variables

Uses Introduced
Printing Individual Envelopes

This chapter and the next are meant primarily as an introduction to using MailMerge. This chapter introduces a few basic commands and shows, step by step, how to develop a file suitable for producing individual envelopes. In Chapter Five, you'll see how those same commands (plus a few more) can be used to create files for other common applications, including the printing of labels, forms, and form letters.

If you are already familiar with MailMerge commands, you can safely skip both chapters, though you might like to look through them quickly anyway. Chapter Five, in particular, contains some tricks you may not have discovered on your own as yet.

We're going to start with envelopes for three reasons.

First, envelopes are short—short enough to warrant using examples throughout the chapter, and short enough to warrant your taking the time to try these examples for yourself.

Second, envelopes are bare bones simple. As far as MailMerge itself is concerned, there is almost no difference between designing a file for envelopes, forms, or form letters. With envelopes, though, there is little excess baggage to complicate the issue.

Third, it's a safe bet that you mail things occasionally and can make good use of a file that prints envelopes. The file we are going to wind up with at the end of this chapter will do just that. It's meant for those times when you have a check to mail, or a form, or some other odd item, and all you need from WordStar is an envelope by itself.

Individual envelopes are something that many people don't bother using their word processor for, on the grounds that it's easier to put an envelope in a typewriter than it is to create a file and print the file out.

The argument has merit. Creating a file for an envelope is clumsy. You have to open the file, you have to find the right line and the right column to start typing, you have to type in the address, you have to close the file, and so forth and so on.

Of course you can simplify things by creating an envelope format file. In fact, we've already created one in Chapter Three—as part of the format file for letters. Even so, if all you need is an envelope by itself, without a letter or somesuch to go with it, it's still easier to put the envelope in a typewriter and type the address.

With MailMerge, though, you can arrange things so it's just as easy to do it on the computer—meaning that all you have to do is put the envelope in the printer and type the address. You do this magic by taking advantage of a single MailMerge command, namely **.AV,** or the ask for variable dot command.

.AV—Ask for Variable

This first MailMerge command immediately brings us to the one concept you must understand in order to use MailMerge: Variables. Quite simply, a variable is anything that changes, or varies, from one printing to the next. With envelopes, for example, you need a different name and address on each one, so the name and address are the variables in that file.

When you print with MailMerge, the dot command **.AV** tells WordStar to ask you for the variable it should use. WordStar will not begin printing, moreover, until you give it an answer by typing it in from the keyboard.

Creating a file using the ask for variable command is really a two-step procedure. First, you have to create a format for MailMerge to follow. Then you have to tell MailMerge to ask you for each of the variables in the first place.

A file designed to print an envelope, then, might look something like this:

FILE: ENV1 (Partial File)

For Printing Individual Envelopes

(Notice that the page offset is set to 40 in this file rather than 48. This is because the file is designed to print at 10 pitch rather than 12 pitch. The file starts on the next line of text.)

```
.AV NAME
.AV NUMBER-STREET
.AV CITY-STATE-ZIP
.PL 26
.PO 40
#
#
#
#
    &NAME&
    &NUMBER-STREET&
    &CITY-STATE-ZIP&
```

This file has been left with some serious shortcomings in the interest of keeping it simple. Before we examine and correct those shortcomings, let's take a look at the file the way it stands and see how it works.

To begin with, if you eliminate the **.AV** commands in the first three lines, you are left with something that looks very much like the format file we created in Chapter Three, but with one major difference. Instead of indicating the proper line to start the address as a whole, this file indicates the proper starting point for each line within the address.

Notice that each address line is indicated with *exactly* the same words that follow the **.AV** commands in the beginning of the file. Notice also that each address line starts and ends with an ampersand (**&**).

Each of the items following the **.AV** command is a variable. And each of the specific items—NAME, NUMBER-STREET, CITY–STATE–ZIP—is a variable name.

When you put two ampersands close together in a file (&NUMBER–STREET&), it serves as a signal to MailMerge that the text inside the ampersands is a variable. MailMerge looks for a variable name that matches this text, then substitutes the specific variable for the variable name.

This is not as confusing as it may seem at first glance. Basically, when you Merge-Print this file, what happens is this: Where WordStar sees ".AV

NAME" it will ask you to enter the name to use in printing the envelope. Where it sees ".AV NUMBER–STREET," it will ask for the number and street, and so forth. Where it sees "&NAME&," it will print the name you entered. Where it sees "&NUMBER–STREET&," it will print the number and street, and so forth. Try it and see.

Open a file, ENV1, and enter the partial file as it is given here. Remember, the number signs (#) are there just to help you count lines. Don't put them in the file. Also, don't forget to add the dot command **.OP** (omit page numbers) if you need it.

After you finish entering the example, close the file (^KD). Put an envelope in your printer, then hit "M" for MailMerge from the Opening Menu (or No-File Menu, depending on the release). WordStar will ask you, "Name of File to MailMerge?" or "NAME OF FILE TO MERGE-PRINT?" depending on the release. Enter ENV1.

The default settings on the Merge-Print questions are fine here. Simply hit ESCAPE to bypass them, or hit RETURN in answer to each. Make sure your printer is on and ready, with an envelope properly positioned.

MailMerge will come up with its single menu choice:

"P = Stop Print"

It will then prompt you, item by item, with the names of the variables. The program automatically adds a question mark to the variable names, so that where the file reads ".AV NAME," the prompt reads "NAME?".

Notice that you can only answer the prompts line by line. Once you have entered a variable by hitting RETURN, MailMerge moves on to the next prompt, without giving you another chance to correct mistakes. That means you have to double-check each line before you hit RETURN.

If you've already hit RETURN and then realize you've made a mistake, there is a way out, but it's a little tricky. If you hit the "P" to stop print, MailMerge will interpret it as an entry, not as a command. What you have to do is hit RETURN, then quickly hit the "P"—about as quickly as if you were drumming your fingers on the keyboard. This will give you the Word-Star Print Paused menu, with its choices:

"Y" TO ABANDON PRINT, "N" TO RESUME, ^U TO HOLD

At this point, you can enter a "Y" and start over again. You might like to try this trick a couple of times now, just to get a feel for it.

When you're satisfied that you can abort the printing when necessary, go ahead and try out the ENV1 file.

Once again, from the No-File Menu, enter "M" for MailMerge.

Enter "ENV1" for "Name of File," followed by ESCAPE.

MailMerge will prompt with "NAME?"

Enter you own name, then hit RETURN.

MailMerge will prompt with "NUMBER–STREET?"

Enter your own number and street, then hit RETURN.

MailMerge will prompt with "CITY-STATE-ZIP?"

Enter your own city, state, and zip code, then hit RETURN.

MailMerge will respond by printing your name and address.

You now have a self-addressed envelope for future use. You created it by putting the envelope in the printer, and typing your name and address.

You will, by the way, find that files with **.AV** command lines will generally run much more quickly if you turn off the file directory before you call up MailMerge. (Use "F" from the Opening Menu.) Try it both ways and see.

Envelopes with More Than Three Address Lines

USING THE "/O" (OMIT) COMMAND

ENV1 works, but it has one major drawback: it only has room for three lines in the address. You'll often find that you need four lines or more. You might, for instance, need the name of the addressee, his or her title, the department or office he or she works in, and so forth and so on—up to seven lines long. If you put all this in one file, the address block itself would look like this:

```
&NAME&
&TITLE&
&DEPT-OR-OFFICE&
&COMPANY–NAME&
&NUMBER–STREET&
&CITY–STATE–ZIP&
&COUNTRY&
```

If you were to create a file around this address block, you would find that it would work, but only if you remember exactly what you're doing. The problem here is that this file is going to print seven lines no matter what.

If you need fewer lines, for a three-line address for instance, you could still use the file by ignoring the prompts and blindly typing in the address as the first three lines. If you then enter RETURN for the remaining lines, MailMerge will obediently print out blank lines, and you will have a three-line address.

The problem comes when people use the file without knowing that they're supposed to ignore the prompts. If they enter the address as asked for, they will wind up with several blank lines in the middle of the address block. If this is a file that you don't use too often, one of those people might well be you.

One way out of the problem would be to change the prompts to something noncommittal like ADDRESS-LINE-1, ADDRESS-LINE-2, and so forth, but specific prompts are not only nice to have, they can be essential in many applications. Another way around the problem would be to create a different file for each possibility, but you would soon find yourself with a ridiculously large number of files for creating envelopes.

Fortunately, there's a better solution. You can tell MailMerge to omit a variable in printing if that variable hasn't been given a value. This means you can create a file that has room for seven address lines, but will only print the lines you give it. Take a look at ENV2.

FILE: ENV2

For Printing Individual Envelopes

```
.AV NAME
.AV TITLE
.AV DEPT-OR-OFFICE
.AV COMPANY–NAME
.AV NUMBER–STREET
.AV CITY–STATE–ZIP
.AV COUNTRY
.PL 26
.PO 40
#
#
#
&NAME/O&
&TITLE/O&
&DEPT-OR-OFFICE/O&
&COMPANY–NAME/O&
&NUMBER–STREET/O&
&CITY–STATE–ZIP/O&
&COUNTRY/O&
```

The only thing new in this file is that each variable name in the address ends with a "/O." (That's the letter "O" not the number "zero.") Yet this one change transforms this into a much more useful file. Each "/O" command tells MailMerge either to print the appropriate variable in that spot, or to omit the line entirely if no variable was given. Create an ENV2 file and try it.

When MailMerge prompts with "NAME?", "NUMBER–STREET?", and "CITY–STATE–ZIP?", enter your own name and address. On all other prompts, enter nothing. Simply hit RETURN.

MailMerge will respond by printing a three-line address, just the way you want it: No blank lines, no cryptic prompts, and no need for you to remember anything except to answer the questions as asked.

.DM—DISPLAY MESSAGE

At this point, we have a useful file for producing individual envelopes, but there are a few more refinements that are worth putting in.

First, if you're like me, you will at least occasionally find that you've entered an address without putting an envelope in the printer. Unless you're planning on mailing the roller, that doesn't help much.

It would be nice, then, if you could get WordStar to stop, and remind you to check for the envelope. You can, by using two commands: one to stop printing, and one to put the reminder on the screen.

WordStar's print pause command, ^**PC,** will stop the printing easily enough. Put this in the file, and when WordStar runs across it, it will stop, and prompt you with "Enter 'P' to resume printing."

The reminder to check for the envelope is entered courtesy of a Mail-Merge command, **.DM** (display message). To use this, you start a line with **.DM,** then type whatever you want to see on the screen at print time.

In this case, you want to enter the following lines in the file:

```
.DM Place Envelope in Printer and hit Space Bar
.DM Then P to Resume Printing
^C
```

There are several points to keep in mind here.

First, the ^**PC** command must come after the reminder itself. If it comes before, WordStar will read the pause command, then stop before it gets to the **.DM** commands.

Second, you do not have to put the print pause command on a line by itself. It is a good idea, though, because it makes the command harder to overlook. This makes the file more readable in the sense of being easier to understand if you go back later to redesign it for any reason.

Third, if you put the reminder and pause before the prompts for the address, there will be a strong tendency to ignore it. These lines should be entered after the **.AV** commands, but before the blank lines (or carriage returns, if you prefer) for advancing the envelope.

Finally, notice that the reminder has been broken into two lines here. MailMerge will display a line up to the width of the screen, but if you make the line wider than the margins you are using in the file, you run the risk of accidentally reforming the **.DM** line and breaking it in two.

While we are putting messages in the file, there are other reminders you might like to include. For instance, if you don't use this file too often, are you going to remember exactly how to use it? Are you going to remember how to line up the envelope in the printer, or are you going to have to figure it out all over again? What if someone else uses the file who's never seen it before? The solution, of course, is to use the **.DM** command to add whatever reminders you're likely to need.

You might, for instance, start with a "sign-on" statement telling you exactly what the file does—something like:

This File Prints Envelopes from Screen Input.

Also, after the reminder to place the envelope in the printer, you might like to include an instruction on how the envelope should be positioned—something like:

Top of Envelope Should Be at Bail,
Left Edge of Envelope Should Be Flush with Guide.

VARIABLES: PROMPTS AND VARIABLE NAMES

When we clarify things in the file, it would also be nice if we could make the prompts a bit more readable. Up to this point, we've been using variable names for prompts, but variable names have limitations. They cannot, for instance, contain spaces or commas. This is why we've been using "CITY–STATE–ZIP" rather than "CITY, STATE, AND ZIP."

LEGITIMATE VARIABLE NAMES

A variable name can consist of anywhere from 1 to 40 characters. Those characters are generally letters. Numbers and dashes (-) may also be used, but not as the first character in the name. This means MailMerge will recognize "A1" or "A-1" as an acceptable variable name, but it will ignore "1A" or "-A1." Other symbols such as @, !, #, and so on cannot be used at all. Here again, if you try using them, MailMerge will ignore the variable name entirely.

One other thing: MailMerge does not differentiate between upper-case and lower-case letters in reading variable names. It will, in fact, turn all lower-case letters into upper-case letters. This means it doesn't help to enter a variable name as "NUMBERandSTREET" in the hope of improving readability. MailMerge will change this to "NUMBERANDSTREET?" when it puts the prompt on your screen.

Some acceptable variable names are:

A1
NAME
HOW-MUCH-DO-YOU-OWE
WHOSYWHATSITS

Some unacceptable variable names are:

1A (starts with a number)
NUMBER AND STREET (a space is an unacceptable "symbol")
!()*&%&* (all unacceptable symbols)
WHAT-ARE-YOU-GOING-TO-PUT-HERE-IF-I-LET-YOU (too long)

SEPARATE PROMPTS

The limitations on variable names are not all that severe. Still, if you want to go beyond those limitations, MailMerge gives you another choice: separate prompts. Basically, in the absence of a separate prompt, the variable name becomes the prompt. Adding a separate prompt takes very little extra work. The key points about prompts are:

They are enclosed in quotes (single or double).

They are followed by a comma.

They go between the **.AV** command and the variable name.

MailMerge accepts them and puts them on the screen exactly as they are written—upper-case and lower-case letters, commas, spaces, and all.

All of which means, for instance, that in order to transform the prompt "CITY–STATE–ZIP?" into the prompt "City, State, and Zip Code," we only have to change the **.AV** command line from

.AV CITY–STATE–ZIP

to

.AV "City, State, and Zip Code: ", CITY–STATE–ZIP

Notice here that the variable name is still "CITY–STATE–ZIP," and that it is the variable name that needs to show up in the format section of the file, surrounded by ampersands.

Also notice that the use of separate prompts frees us to use shorter, more easily entered variable names. This means that the **.AV** command line here could become:

.AV "City, State, and Zip Code: ", Z

In which case, "Z" (for Zip Code) would be the variable name, and all we would have to put in the format section of the file would be

&Z&

or

&Z/O&

While this trick can get confusing on a long or complicated file, it can also be helpful—particularly if you use it with care. On a short, unambiguous file it can help simplify things. If you use separate prompts, you can then use the variable names "A1" through "A7" for the seven address lines, and the format section of the file would become:

&A1/O&
&A2/O&
&A3/O&
&A4/O&
&A5/O&
&A6/O&
&A7/O&

The Maximum Length Command

There is one other problem in the ENV2 file that can get us in trouble. It is possible to enter a variable that will print past the edge of the envelope. MailMerge allows you to enter a maximum length command to prevent this possibility.

In general, when you respond to a prompt on the screen with Mail-Merge, the maximum length of your answer is limited by how much room is left on the same line as the prompt. If your screen is 80 characters wide, you will generally, for technical reasons, have 78 characters available to use on a prompt line. If your prompt is "NAME?", which takes up 6 characters, MailMerge will allow you to enter a response of up to 72 characters (78 minus 6). This works out to $7\frac{2}{10}$ inches if printing at 10 pitch.

Because an envelope is $9\frac{1}{2}$ inches long, and the address is set to start printing 4 inches in from the edge of the envelope, you only have $5\frac{1}{2}$ inches of envelope left to print on. Anything longer than that will print on the roller.

Even a line that's short enough to fit on the envelope, moreover, may still be long enough to make the envelope look out of balance. One way to avoid both of these possibilities is to tell MailMerge not to accept more than an arbitrary number of characters for any given variable.

If, for instance, you want each address line to end at least $1\frac{1}{2}$ inches from the right edge of the envelope, then you're left with a maximum length for each address line of 4 inches. ($9\frac{1}{2}$ inches for the width of the envelope, minus 4 inches for the left margin, minus $1\frac{1}{2}$ inches for the right margin.) This works out to 40 characters at 10 pitch. You tell MailMerge by adding a comma after the variable name, followed by the maximum acceptable length of the variable.

For an envelope designed to be used at 10 pitch, the **.AV** command line for the name would become

.AV "Name: ", A1, 40

and WordStar would simply refuse to accept more than 40 characters in response to the prompt.

You can also use the maximum length command as an error-checking feature. You could, for instance, use a separate prompt for the zip code, and add a maximum length command of five. This won't keep you from entering an incorrect zip code, but it will keep you from accidentally entering an extra digit.

There are one or two more refinements worth making in this file. You may have noticed that after last prompt the roller advances slightly before you are reminded to put an envelope in the printer. This means that addresses will print at a different position depending on whether you put the envelope in the printer before or after you answered the prompts.

This is not an important problem, but it is so easy to eliminate that it would be silly not to. What WordStar is doing is putting a top margin on the envelope. To get rid of it, you only have to add a line at the top of the file, and enter the dot command **.MT 0** (margin top—set to zero). You should also add three blank lines to the file because the original format was based on WordStar's default setting of three lines for the top margin.

Finally, you are free to enter any other WordStar print commands or dot commands that suit your taste. You can, for instance, change the number of lines per inch using the **.LH** (line height) command or the number of characters per inch using the **.CW** (character width) command. Don't forget, though, that if you make this sort of change you may also have to adjust the file. If you change the pitch before the page offset command, for example, you are also changing the positioning of the address on the envelope.

Following is the finished ENV file. Before you look at it, try recreating it yourself by starting with ENV2 and adding each of the refinements we've discussed, step by step.

This file also includes a return address in case you don't have preprinted envelopes. (Notice that the return address is preceded with a page offset command **.PO 0**, so it will print ½ inch from the edge of the envelope.) You can eliminate the return address, of course, if you don't need it.

FILE: ENV

Finished File for Printing Individual Envelopes

```
.PL 26
.MT 0
.DM This file prints envelopes from screen input.
.DM It will Automatically Print the Return Address.
.AV "Name of Addressee: ", A1, 40
.AV "Title: ", A2, 40
.AV "Dept or Office: ", A3, 40
.AV "Full Name of Company: ", A4, 40
.AV "Number and Street: ", A5
.AV "City and State: ", A6
.AV "Zip Code: ", A7, 5
.AV "Country: ", A8
.DM Place Envelope in Printer.
.DM Top of envelope should be just above printer head.
.DM Hit Space Bar, then P to Continue Print.
^PC
.PO 5
^AYour Name
Your Number and Street
Your City, State, and Zip^N
#
#
#
#
```

```
#
#
.PO 40
&A1/O&
&A2/O&
&A3/O&
&A4/O&
&A5/O&
&A6/O& &A7/O&
&A8/O&
```

PRINTING MORE THAN ONE ENVELOPE AT A TIME

USING MULTIPLE PRINTING

You will sometimes find that you need to print a few envelopes at once. (Not a whole bunch of envelopes—we'll save that for later.) When this happens, you will not want to spend time calling up MailMerge for each individual envelope. It is much better to call up MailMerge once, tell it to use the ENV file once, then just enter names and addresses. There are two ways to do this.

The first, and simplest way, is to make use of the multiple printing feature. When calling up MailMerge, simply enter the number of envelopes you need when prompted for the number of copies. If you're not sure how many that is, then pick any number larger than you'll need. After that, use the file as usual. There are one or two points you should be aware of, though.

First, when MailMerge prints your envelopes using the multiple print function, the 16-bit version of WordStar will print all the way through, but the 8-bit version will stop when it still has one character to go. This is not a problem. After you finish answering the next set of prompts, the last character will print and WordStar will roll the envelope out of the printer. Printing will then stop again and the reminder to put the new envelope in the printer will appear on the screen. After you position the new envelope, you enter a SPACE and a "P" to start printing again. At this point, WordStar will print the next envelope up to (but not including) the last character. This procedure repeats until the last envelope. What happens then depends on whether WordStar realizes it is at the last envelope or not.

If the number of envelopes you are printing matches the number of envelopes you told MailMerge that you needed, then the last envelope will print all the way through—last character, last form feed, and all. If WordStar thinks there are more envelopes to print, it's going to stop with one character to go and wait for you to answer the next set of prompts.

All you have to do is answer the prompts with a RETURN all the way through. After the last RETURN, WordStar will print the last character and spit the envelope out of the printer. Next, you hit the space bar, and WordStar will tell you to enter "P" to continue printing. Instead of entering one

"P," though, enter two of them, very quickly, one right after the other. This will give you the prompt:

"Y" TO ABANDON PRINT, "N" TO RESUME, ^U TO HOLD

At that point you enter a "Y," printing will end, and you will be returned to WordStar's main menu.

MULTIPLE PRINTING WITH .RP (REPEAT) COMMAND

The second way to use the ENV file for more than one envelope at a time is to include a **.RP** command (repeat) within the file itself. Then you can bypass the questions when calling up MailMerge. Using the repeat command is reasonably similar to using the multiple print feature, but setting the command up to work is a little tricky.

First, when MailMerge is getting all its variables from the keyboard by way of the ask for variable command, it will ignore the repeat command unless you include a number specifying how many times to repeat the file. The safest thing to do is pick a number much higher than you will ever need—**.RP 50** should do.

Second, you have to make sure that the **.RP** command is not the last entry in the file, or else WordStar may ignore it. If you put it toward the end, it must be followed by a carriage return, so that your screen will look like this:

```
.RP                                        M (MailMerge Flag)
                                           < (Hard Carriage return flag)
```

In general, though, it is safer to put the commands toward the top of the file. That way you won't have to worry about forgetting the final carriage return.

Another important point in writing the file for use with the repeat command is that you must end the file with **.PA,** the command for a new page. If you leave this out, MailMerge will not roll each envelope out of the printer as the envelopes are done. Instead, it will keep counting lines until it reaches the end of the "page," at which point it will finally send a form feed to the printer. This will affect printing differently depending on the page length you are using, but whatever the effect, it will not be the one you want.

Assuming you remember to add the new page command, multiple printing with the repeat command follows pretty much the same pattern as with the multiple print feature. If you're using release 3.3 in particular, the only differences are minor. The entire address is printed on the envelope at once, for example, instead of being printed up to the last character.

With earlier releases, there are other minor complications. In particular, MailMerge is somewhat unpredictable about exactly when it will start printing. Generally, it won't print any of your first envelope until you're finished answering the prompts for the second. But if you enter enough data, printing will sometimes start while you're still entering the second address.

With earlier releases, the actual printing procedure when using the repeat command works something like the following.

1. Turn off the file directory with F.
2. Tell WordStar to Merge-Print ENV.
3. Answer the prompts for the first envelope.
4. Position an envelope in the printer.
5. Enter a SPACE and a "P."
6. Answer the prompts for the next envelope.
7. At this point WordStar will print the first envelope, roll it out of the printer (courtesy of the **.PA** command), then give you the prompt to position another envelope. You go back to step three and continue this way until you have answered the prompts for the last envelope.

Aborting printing short of 50 envelopes (or whatever number you've set the **.RP** command to) also works pretty much the same way with the repeat command as with the multiple print feature. You answer the last set of prompts with RETURN, enter a space to get the "ENTER P TO RESUME PRINTING" prompt, then hit "P" twice quickly to abort printing.

Don't forget that if you're using an older release of MailMerge, your printer is one address behind your entries. Make sure you print that last envelope before you abort printing.

THE MULTIPLE PRINT FEATURE VERSUS THE REPEAT COMMAND

Choosing between using the multiple print feature and the repeat command has mostly to do with your own needs in the way you use a particular file.

The major advantage of using the multiple print feature is that you only call it up when you need it. In terms of the envelope file, this means that when you're doing only one envelope, you don't have to do any extra work at the end to abort the printing.

The major advantage of using the repeat command is exactly the opposite: The multiple printing is always there. With the envelope file, once again, this means that when you're doing more than one envelope, you don't have to do any extra work at the beginning. If you rarely do more than one envelope at a time, then, it doesn't make much sense to put the repeat command in the file. On the other hand, if you rarely do only one at a time, it doesn't make much sense to leave it out. Of course, if both situations are reasonably frequent, you can write two files, one with the command and one without it.

So much for envelopes. If all these design considerations dealt strictly with envelopes, they wouldn't be worth discussing. The point, of course, is that they don't. If you think of MailMerge as a musical instrument (a piano with its keyboard seems appropriate), then up to now we've been learning scales. It's time to get on to a few simple tunes.

Some Basic Applications

LABELS, FORMS, AND FORM LETTERS

LABELS

There is not a lot of difference between printing addresses on envelopes and printing addresses on mailing labels. In fact, if you take an "envelope" file, and compare it to a "mailing label" file, you'll find that the only important differences lie in the format commands. These are basic WordStar considerations and have nothing to do with MailMerge as such. All of which means that if you start with the envelope file that we developed in the last chapter, it takes very little work to convert it into a file for printing mailing labels.

The Occasional Single Mailing Label

Open a new file, MAILING.LAB, and use the **^KR** (read a file) command to read in the file ENV. All you have to do now is go through the file line by line, and make the appropriate format changes, along with a few changes in the text.

This example is based on labels that are 4 inches wide by $1\frac{7}{16}$ inches long. (These are designed so that there is an additional $\frac{1}{16}$ of an inch between labels, and therefore, exactly $1\frac{1}{2}$ inches from the top of one label to the top of the next.) The example also assumes that each time you print a mailing label, you need a separate label with your return address on it.

Given these assumptions, the file should look like this:

FILE: MAILING.LAB

For Printing Individual Mailing Labels

```
.PL 9   1 1/2 inches at 6 lines per inch
.MT 0 Note: There is no room for top or bottom margins
.MB 0
.DM This File Prints Mailing Labels from Screen Input
.DM It is designed for labels that are 4" by 1 7/16"
.DM It will Automatically Print the Return Address
.DM on a Second Label
..NOTE: Maximum length commands are 35 characters, or 3 1/2
..inches to allow for 1/4 inch margins on each side of label
.AV "Name of Addressee: ", A1, 35
.AV "Title: ", A2, 35
.AV "Dept or Office: ", A3, 35
.AV "Full Name of Company: ", A4, 35
.AV "Number and Street: ", A5
.AV "City and State: ", A6
.AV "Zip Code: ", A7, 5
.AV "Country: ", A8
.DM Place Labels in Printer and Hit Space Bar,
.DM then P to Continue Print.
```

```
.DM Top of Labels should be just above printer head.
^C
.PO 3 For roughly 1/4 inch margin on each side
Your Name
Your Number and Street
Your City, State, and Zip^N
.PA  TO ROLL TO TOP OF NEXT LABEL FOR MAILING ADDRESS
&A1/O&
&A2/O&
&A3/O&
&A4/O&
&A5/O&
&A6/O& &A7/O&
&A8/O&
```

Notice that something new has been added in this example. In addition to reminders that will show on the screen at print time telling you what size labels to use and so forth, the file also contains reminders that will not display on the screen. The page length command, for instance, is followed by a note that explains it. (You can do this because WordStar will interpret the dot command correctly, then ignore the rest of the line.) This second set of reminders is there to help make the file easier to change if you need to, by drawing your attention to the reasons for each of the format commands.

If you think of this file as a short program (and it is really), then taken together, the two sets of reminders turn it into something that programmers like to call a self-documenting file. (If the idea of MailMerge as a programming language bothers you, then feel free to ignore it for now. We'll come back to this idea in a later chapter.)

Finally, one minor point: The correct value for the page offset command will vary somewhat depending on how the labels are positioned in your printer. The setting **.PO 3** assumes that column one on the printer is column one on the paper.

OTHER LABELS—FILE FOLDERS

With all the modifications we've been doing, you may have lost sight of how to create a MailMerge file from scratch. Just to fix the process in your mind, let's go through it once, this time with file folder labels. It works out to a simple three-step procedure.

The first step is to decide on the format you want and create what amounts to a format file. Start by measuring your file folder labels. Mine are 3½ inches by $^{15}/_{16}$ of an inch. (Once again, with $^1/_{16}$ of an inch between labels.) This measurement will tell you most of what you need to know about the various format commands.

You also have to decide what you want the labels to say. I usually use two lines. One for the category (correspondence, catalog, project, client information, or whatever), and one for the name of the particular folder.

Once you've designed and entered the format section of the file, the next step is to tell MailMerge to ask you for the variables. In this case, that's simple enough because there are only two variables to deal with.

The third step, finally, is to decide what notes you want to put in the file to remind yourself how to use it.

If you take the time to go through these three steps carefully, you should wind up with something like this:

FILE: FOLDER.LAB

For Individual Labels for File Folders

```
.PL 6 For one-inch labels at six lines per inch
.MT 0
.MB 0
.DM This File Prints File Folder Labels from Screen Input
.DM It is designed for labels that are 3 inches by 1.5 inches
.DM And is meant to be used when printing ONE LABEL ONLY
.DM
.DM
.DM
.DM
.DM CATEGORY (Permissible categories are Correspondence,
.AV "Catalog, Project and Client Information): ", A1, 30
..NOTE: Maximum length of 30 for three and one-half inch labels
.AV "Folder Name: ", A2, 30
.DM Place Labels in Printer and Hit Space Bar,
.DM then P to Continue Print.
.DM Top of Labels should be just above printer head.
^C
.PO 0
&A1&
&A2&
```

The difference between this file and the file MAILING.LAB is mostly that this file is shorter. Still, there are one or two new tricks here in the way this file uses the display message command.

The four blank **.DM** lines improve the readability of the screen at print time by visually separating the "sign-on" message from the first prompt. Also notice, after the four blank lines, how the **.DM** command has been combined with the **.AV** command to give a longer, more informative prompt. This kind of information can be particularly helpful if you are setting up the file for someone else to use. But it is also a convenient way to provide information on the screen that you usually find yourself having to look up.

The last thing to notice in this file is the instruction that it is "meant to be used when printing one label only." This comment means just what it says. The file is not designed to print more than one label at a time, at least not conveniently.

To begin with, there is the Pause Print command. It may be a good idea when printing one label, but once you've put the sheet of labels in the printer, you don't need to stop after each one. Granted, it's a good idea to glance over at the printer and double-check, but most of the time you shouldn't have to do anything. Using the print pause command, which requires two separate entries plus disk access time to get started again, seems like overkill.

Another problem is that labels are commonly set up on sheets with two or three across, but this file prints only one column. This means that after you finish the first column on a sheet, you then have to load the same page into your printer again to do the next column.

Of course, if you're only printing a few labels, you might be willing to put up with these minor inconveniences. But if you're reorganizing all your files, for instance, or if you've saved up a double handful of folders before doing any, these "minor" inconveniences may not seem so minor after a while. In that case, you are better off designing a separate file to print more than one label at a time.

Printing Multiple Labels—File Folders

Most of the format considerations for printing multiple labels are the same as they are for individual labels. The one difference is that with multiple labels, you not only have to consider the individual labels, you also have to consider the layout of the pages of labels.

The particular labels I've used for this example come on tractor feed paper, which is designed so that the distance between labels is constant—meaning there is no top or bottom margin to the "pages" of labels, and, therefore, no extra space between the bottom label on one "page" and the top label on the next.

The whole point of this design (and the reason for the quotes around "page" in the last paragraph) is that it lets you ignore the question of "pages of labels" altogether. As far as designing your file is concerned, the only page length you need worry about is the distance between the top of one label and the top of the next—in this case, a constant one inch. There is a second difference in layout that cannot be ignored: These labels are set up three across on the page.

Your first impulse might be to design the file so that in bare bones form (before the reminders are added) it looks something like this:

```
.PL 6
.MT 0
.MB 0
.RP 100
.AV "Category: ", A1, 30
.AV "Folder Name: ", A2, 30
```

```
.DM
.AV "Category: ", A3, 30
.AV "Folder Name: ", A4, 30
.DM
.AV "Category: ", A5, 30
.AV "Folder Name: ", A6, 30
.PO 3
&A1&            &A3&            &A5&
&A2&            &A4&            &A6&
.PA
```

The idea here is to have MailMerge ask you for all the variables for one label at a time, then after three labels, print the three across, and finally, start the cycle over again.

This won't quite work because of what happens in the format section of the file. Specifically, when MailMerge inserts the variables, it will also move the rest of the line over, so that the placement of the variable in the second column of each line (&A3& or &A4&) will depend on the length of the first variable (&A1& or &A2&). And, of course, the placement of the third variable will depend on the length of the first and second variables combined.

What you are dealing with here is a multicolumn format. Basically, you have two choices for how to produce it. First, you can use the snaking trick covered in Chapter Two. If you're using a tractor feed, this approach can cause a problem. As pointed out in Chapter Two, many bidirectional tractor feeds need some running room to adjust for the mechanics of moving the paper back and forth. This means that to get the file working with a bidirectional feed may take some fooling around with the setting of the **.SR** command. Of course, if you are using a unidirectional tractor, you won't be able to use the trick at all.

The second approach to the problem is to enter each of the variables on its own line, then use the overprint command (^**PM**) so that WordStar will print three variables across on each line. If you take this approach, the format section will look something like this on your screen:

```
.PO 0
&A1&                            — (Flag for Overprint next line)
        &A3&                    —
                &A5&    < (Hard Carriage Return)
&A2&                            —
        &A4&                    —
                &A6&    <
.PA
```

The advantage of this second approach is that it doesn't matter what kind of paper feed you are using—friction feed or tractor feed, bidirectional or unidirectional—the file doesn't care. It will print the labels correctly regardless.

THE CLEAR SCREEN COMMAND

There is one new command you'll want to add to the multiple label file, the **.CS,** or clear screen command. This command does just what it says, it clears the screen of all messages up to that point.

In a file like this, designed as it is for printing multiple labels, the screen can get confusing after a while. By clearing the screen after each set of three labels, though, it becomes easier to read. It becomes even easier if you remember to turn off the screen directory before you go into Mail-Merge, another good reason to turn the directory off.

Here then is a complete file suitable for printing file labels on fanfold paper. The format section includes the flags that should show on your screen. (The columns themselves are much narrower than they should be in your file. They were set up this way to make room for the flags.)

FILE: FOLDERS.LAB

For Printing File Folder Labels on Continuous Tractor Feed Paper

```
.PL 6  (for one-inch labels)
.MT 0
.MB 0
.RP 100  (Any random number higher than you're likely to need)
.DM This File Prints File Folder Labels from Screen Input.
.DM It is designed for labels that are 3 inches by 1.5 inches
.DM And are mounted 3 across on FANFOLD sheets.
.DM It is meant to be used when printing MULTIPLE LABELS.
.DM
.DM
.DM
.DM Category (Permissible categories are Correspondence,
.AV "Catalog, Project and Client Information): ", A1, 30
..[NOTE: Max length of 30 is for three and one-half inch labels]
.AV "Folder Name: ", A2, 30
.DM
.AV "Category: ", A3, 30
.AV "Folder Name: ", A4, 30
.DM
.AV "Category: ", A5, 30
.AV "Folder Name: ", A6, 30
.DM Check Labels in Printer. Then hit RETURN to print.
.AV "Top of Labels should be just above printer head.", A7
.CS
.PO 0
```

```
&A1&                              — (Overprint next line)
        &A3&                      —
                &A5&      < (Hard Carriage Return)
&A2&                              —
        &A4&                      —
                &A6&      <
.PA
```

Notice that this file demonstrates a different way to hold up the printing and remind you to check the labels. The last **.AV** command isn't being used to ask for a variable. In fact, it contains a variable name that doesn't exist in the format section of the file. The command is there only to remind you to glance at the labels. Because it is an **.AV** command, though, rather than a **.DM** command, MailMerge will hold up printing until you give it an answer—a RETURN will do.

The advantage of using this trick instead of using a print pause command is that getting the printing started is easier and faster this way; you only have to hit RETURN once. The disadvantage (and the reason we didn't use this trick before) is that if you are rushing though several "non-answers," as you may be with an address, you are likely to accidentally overshoot and enter this last return before you mean to. On this file, the overshooting is unlikely to begin with. And because the labels are continuous, it is unlikely to make much difference if you do happen to overshoot occasionally.

PRINTING MULTIPLE LABELS ON SINGLE SHEETS OF LABELS

One last comment on labels. If you are using single sheets instead of fanfold sheets, you'll have to make some changes to this last file, but the changes are less than you might expect.

First, you have to think in terms of the length of the sheet rather than the length of the label, which means you have to change the page length command. If the labels and layout are the same as in the example, for instance, with eight rows to a page, the page length becomes **.PL 48** (eight inches times six lines per inch).

Second, since you don't want WordStar to spit the page out of the printer after the first row is printed, you have to delete the new page command, **.PA,** at the end of the file.

Third, you need to make WordStar advance to the next row of labels after it prints each set of three. You do this by adding four blank lines to the format section of the file. This gives you a total of six lines per label.

Finally, you have to remember to tell MailMerge to stop after each page when you call it up in the first place. And that's it. The reason this will work is that the **.RP** or repeat command does not automatically force a new page at the end of the file. Instead, it continues counting lines through however many repetitions until it reaches the full page length. This saves you from having to type the format for an entire page of labels just to make the file work with individual sheets.

FORMS

The only important difference between using MailMerge for envelopes or blank labels and using MailMerge for forms is that forms contain some text mixed in with the variables.

If you're using preprinted forms, moreover, there isn't even any text. This generally complicates the formatting of the file, though, because you have to match the placement of the variables with the blank spaces on the form. The point is, in a very real sense, an envelope or a blank label is already a simple form, and a preprinted envelope is, in effect, a preprinted form.

Similarly, the labels printed by FOLDERS.LAB can be turned into "forms built from scratch" simply by changing the format section of the file to this:

```
Category: &A1&                          — (Overprint next line)
        Category: &A3&                  —
                Category: &A5&          < (Hard Carriage Return)
File Name: &A2&                         —
        File Name: &A4&                 —
                File Name: &A5&         <
```

This new format will produce a simple form that looks like this:

```
Category:
File Name:
```

(along with whatever variables you use to fill in the blanks.)

The only additional thing you have to worry about with forms, then, is the formatting itself. With a preprinted form, that means taking a ruler, measuring the distance between lines and the distance between blanks on the same line, then doing a little simple arithmetic to calculate the proper line heights and the proper number of blank spaces to use. (Note the use of the plural in "line heights." Forms that were not designed for use on computers generally have strange variations in vertical distance between lines. These appear to have been selected at random, and often require you to adjust the line height at several places within the file.)

In most cases also, on a preprinted form, you will have to use the Overprint Line command when there is more than one variable on a line. The exceptions will be for variables like social security number, where the number of characters will always be the same.

BUILDING A FORM FROM SCRATCH

The major advantage of building a form from scratch is that you can design it any way you like. Even though you may use someone else's general layout, for a standard invoice form for example, you are still freed from the tortuous route of having to carefully measure the form and then force your printout to fit those measurements.

The procedure, as always, is to design the form, build the format section of your file around that design, then add MailMerge commands and reminders as necessary. You can design the form directly on the screen, or put it on paper first, then enter it in WordStar. Either way, this is the stage also to include any printing commands that you need. You might, for instance, want to print the background text of the form with double strike, to give it a darker preprinted look in comparison to the variables that will be filling in the blanks.

When you think you're done with the form itself, and before you do anything else, print it and see what it looks like. Make sure you're happy with it. This will be the easiest time to make any changes.

The next step is to adjust the file so the text will print in the proper format, no matter how much the length of any given variable changes. This means putting text on separate lines on the screen when necessary, then using the overprint command to make them show up on the same line on the paper.

When you think you're finished with this stage, print the form again and make sure it still comes out the way you want it. Here again, this will be the easiest time to make any changes.

Next, add the variable names where you want them to show up within the form, then go to the top of the file and add the appropriate .AV commands to go along with them. Maximum length commands become particularly important in building forms because the number of spaces available for each variable is sharply defined by the design of the form. If you use short variable names in a complicated form, be careful to use abbreviations that are easy to follow for future reference. In an invoice form, for example, you might use "BA" for lines in the billing address, "SA" for lines in the shipping address, and so forth.

Finally, go through the file and add whatever reminders you might need—both to use the file and to help you remember how you designed it should you ever need to change it.

FORM LETTERS

If there is "not much of a difference" between creating files for forms on the one hand, and files for labels or envelopes on the other, then there is just a smidgen more difference in creating files for form letters.

Form letters come in two basic varieties—those in which the text remains identical from letter to letter, and those in which the text varies from one letter to the next.

Form Letters with Unchanging Text

You've just moved to a new house and are about to have the housewarming party to end all housewarming parties. You've already invited all your friends by phone, but the directions are complicated, so you've drawn a map, and made umpteen copies of it at your local copy shop. Now all you have to do is mail a copy to everyone who's coming to the party.

You need a letter to go with the map. It only has to be a few lines, something like:

> Dear WHOEVER,
>
> I'm glad you can make it to my housewarming party on May 3. Here are the directions. If you have any problems with them, give me a call. Either way I'll expect to see you at the party. Until then, take care.

A form letter like this, which keeps exactly the same text for each letter, is really no more than a very simple form. Designing it takes exactly the same considerations as designing any other form. In fact, we can back up a step and create a form letter "form"—meaning a standard MailMerge file that can serve as a starting point for any form letter.

FORMLTR: A FORMAT FILE FOR CREATING FORM LETTERS

Begin by opening a file, FORMLTR. This format file for designing form letters is going to have a great deal in common with a format file for envelopes. In fact, considering that the name and address are going to be among the variables in most form letters, the file ENV is a good place to start. Use the ^KR command to read ENV into FORMLTR.

The major thing that's lacking now is the letter format itself. This should be entered between the .AV commands from the ENV file, and the envelope format from the ENV file.

There are a couple of shortcuts you can take in entering the letter format. You can, for instance, use the block copy command (^KC) to copy the address block from the envelope section. Notice in passing that since these variables are the same in both cases, you will only have to answer the prompts once for the address to print on both the letter and the envelope. When you're done, you should have two new variable names in the file—one for the date, and one for the salutation. Your next step is to add two .AV commands to ask for these variables.

Finally, add any additional format commands that you need, and enter any reminders that you would like in the file. The final file should look something like the following.

FILE: FORMLTR.FMT

Format File for Creating Form Letters

```
.PL 66 (Resets page length to 11 inches after envelope)
.PO 8 (Resets page offset for letter)
.MT 0
.RP  This will have no effect unless a number is added
```

.. after the command
.. NOTE: This is a standard file for creating form letters
.. Once it has been modified for some particular letter, delete
.. this reminder, and complete the next line.
.DM This file prints WHICH FORM LETTER from screen input.
.DM It will Automatically Print the Return Address.
.DM On both the letter and the envelope
.AV "Name of Addressee: ", A1, 40
.AV "Title: ", A2, 40
.AV "Dept or Office: ", A3, 40
.AV "Full Name of Company: ", A4, 40
.AV "Number and Street: ", A5
.AV "City and State: ", A6
.AV "Zip Code: ", A7, 5
.AV "Country: ", A8
.AV "Date: ", DATE
.AV "Salutation: ", SALUT
#
.DM Place Stationery in Printer and Hit Space Bar,
.DM then P to Continue Print.
.DM Top of page should be just under bail.
^C

                                        Your Name
                                        Your Number and Street
                                        Your City, State, and Zip

#
#
#

                                    &DATE&

#
#
#
#
#
#
&A1/O&
&A2/O&
&A3/O&
&A4/O&
&A5/O&
&A6/O& &A7/O&
&A8/O&
#
Dear &SALUT&:
#
        TEXT OF LETTER GOES HERE
#

Sincerely, Yours Truly, Best Wishes, Best (DELETE ALL BUT ONE)
#
#
#
Your Name (ENTER FIRST NAME ONLY or FULL NAME, AS APPROPRIATE)
.PA (Rolls the letter out of the printer)
.PL 26 (Resets Page Length for Envelope)
.DM Place Envelope in Printer and Hit Space Bar, then P to Continue Print.
.DM Top of envelope should be just above printer head.
^C
.PO 5
^AYour Name
Your Number and Street
Your City, State, and Zip ^N
#
#
#
#
#
.PO 40
&A1/O&
&A2/O&
&A3/O&
&A4/O&
&A5/O&
&A6/O& &A7/O&
&A8/O&
.PA (Rolls the envelope out of the printer)

What you have just created, once again, is a format file for form letters. You can now use this to create the form letter to go with your map, or to create any other form letter.

Close this file, and open a new one, PARTY. Read in FORMLTR, make the appropriate changes in the reminders throughout the file, then enter the text of the letter in the format section. ("I'm glad you can make it to my housewarming party on May 3. Here are the directions . . . .")

Next, close the file and try printing one copy. You may have to add or delete blank lines to make the letter sit right on the page. (This positioning depends on the length of the letter and will vary from one form letter to the next.)

Once you're satisfied with the way the letter looks, add a number to the **.RP** (repeat) command. Printing the letter PARTY now becomes a simple matter calling up the file with MailMerge, answering the prompts, then following the directions for alternately placing stationery or envelopes in the printer. With FORMLTR, meanwhile, you now have a standard file to serve as a starting point for creating any future form letters.

All of which brings us, finally, to form letters that include variables within the text of the letter.

FORM LETTERS WITH VARIABLE TEXT

Not too long ago, I bought a car that meets all the technical specifications to qualify as a lemon. Fortunately I had the foresight to get towing insurance as well, which means that I periodically find myself sending towing bills to my insurance company, along with a standard letter that covers the various nuggets of information they want before they'll send me any money.

This form letter, LEMON, differs from the form letter PARTY in one important respect. In LEMON, it is the text that varies from one letter to the next, while the address block remains the same. In bare bones form, the letter looks like the following example.

FILE: LEMON

A Form Letter with Variables Inserted in the Body of the Text

```
.AV "Today's Date: ", LTRDATE
.AV "Amount of Towing Bill: ", HOWMUCH
.AV "Towed From: ", FROMWHERE
.AV "Towed To: ", TOWHERE
.AV "Cause of Towing: ", PROBLEM
.AV "Date of Towing: ", DATE

&LTRDATE&

The Lemon Tree Insurance Co.
34 Park St.
Orange, N.J.

Attn: Towing Unit

re: policy 123-333-456

Dear Sirs:

     Please find enclosed the original copy of a bill for
&HOWMUCH& for towing my 1982 Lemon from &FROMWHERE& to &TOWHERE&
on &DATE&.

     The reason for the towing was a problem with &PROBLEM&.

     Thank you in advance for your speedy attention to this
matter.

Sincerely,

M. David Stone
```

There's nothing particularly new in what we've done here except that for the first time, we've put variables within continuous text. We can do that and still wind up with well-formed paragraphs with the correct margins and so forth because MailMerge has a capability, called print-time line-forming, that will reformat the text as necessary. In essence, Mail-Merge will insert the variables, then do what amounts to a paragraph reform before printing each paragraph.

PRINT-TIME LINE-FORMING

The whole subject of print-time line-forming can seem a bit overwhelming; there are half a dozen different commands related to this one function. It's much simpler than it seems though.

In fact, you only have three basic choices. They are **.PF off**, **.PF on**, and **.PF Dis** (for "discretionary").

.PF off turns the feature off entirely.

.PF on puts the feature under your control. This has the effect of bypassing WordStar's on-screen formatting feature, and letting you use additional dot commands in the file to control margins, line spacing, and justification.

.PF Dis is the default setting. It functions, in effect, as an "automatic pilot" that takes care of most situations without your help, and lets you ignore this feature the vast majority of the time.

The best way to get a handle on what this feature does is to look at what would happen if it were not there—or equivalently, what happens if you turn it off with the **.PF off** command.

Without print-time line-forming, MailMerge inserts the variables, then prints out the file line for line, as it was entered without reformatting the paragraphs. Under most conditions, this will not give you a well-formatted letter. In fact, if your variables are either much longer or much shorter than the variable names within the text, it will effectively destroy your right margin.

In the LEMON letter, for instance, if you had the car towed from "New York, New York" to "San Francisco, California" for "several thousand dollars," and you include a **.PF off** command in the file, MailMerge will obediently insert the variable in the second line of this paragraph:

Please find enclosed the original copy of a bill for

&HOWMUCH& for towing my 1982 Lemon from &FROMWHERE& to &TOWHERE& on &DATE&.

And will then print:

". . . several thousand dollars for towing my 1982 Lemon from New York, New York to San Francisco, California . . ."

except that it will print all this on one line, which would put the end of that line well beyond the edge of the paper.

If you leave the feature at its default setting, in contrast (or set it to **.PF on,** for that matter), MailMerge will reformat the text as it goes, and produce a perfectly acceptable, well-formatted paragraph:

Please find enclosed the original copy of a bill for several
thousand dollars for towing my 1982 Lemon from New York, New
York to San Francisco, California over a period of three weeks
in March.

There are two things to notice here. First, the right margin has been maintained throughout. Second, in reformatting the text, MailMerge has changed this paragraph from three lines to four. This means that in a longer letter the positioning of page breaks may change. You can still ensure well-formatted copy, though, by making liberal use of the conditional page command **(.CP n).**

Everything we've covered so far about print-time line-forming applies whenever the feature is working, whether it is set at **.PF on** or at the default setting of **.PF Dis.** The difference between these two settings shows up when you try adding additional print-time line-forming commands to a file. You might, for example, decide you want to print the LEMON letter with double-spacing to see what it looks like. You could always reformat the file, of course. It's much easier, though, to take advantage of the print-time **.LS** (line spacing) command, and enter **.LS 2** before the body of the letter. If you do that, the first and second paragraphs will print with double-spacing as expected, but the third will not.

What happens is that MailMerge will only obey the line spacing command when the line-forming feature is actively working. The print-time line-forming does not become active within any given paragraph unless MailMerge finds a variable in that paragraph. Since there are no variables in the third paragraph, then, the line-forming feature will not become active, and MailMerge will ignore the line-spacing command. The point is, if you want MailMerge to follow your instruction throughout the file, then you have to make sure the line-forming feature is on throughout the file. And that, finally, is what **.PF on** is for.

If you add **.PF on** to the file, the feature will remain active from that point on (or until MailMerge runs across another command, turning it off). In this case, adding **.PF on** after the salutation ensures that the whole letter will print with double spacing.

The first point to remember about print-time line-forming, then, is that you can usually ignore it. The second point to remember is that if you want to print with a different format than the one you used in editing, you must enter a **.PF on** command in the file to give you "manual" control.

ADDITIONAL PRINT-TIME LINE-FORMING COMMANDS

The line spacing command is just one of several commands that are meant to be used along with the **.PF on** command. Each of these commands deals with a single aspect of formatting. As with the **.PF** command itself, each has three possible settings—On, Off, and Dis (for "discretionary" once again). As with the **.PF** command also, the default setting for each is "Dis." This means that if you set the **.PF** command to "on," it will have no effect unless you add one or more of these additional line-forming instructions to the file as well.

The specific commands are listed as follows.

.OJ—*sets output justification for printing.* The command is followed by "On" for right justified printing, "Off" for ragged right, or "Dis" to return to the default setting.

.IJ—*input justification.* This functions largely as excess baggage because there is little or nothing you can do with it that you can't also do with the **.OJ** command. Set this "on," and MailMerge will interpret text as right justified, then print it that way. In other words, the effect will be the same as if you set the output justification "on." Similarly, set this "off," and the effect will be the same as if you set the **.OJ** command to off.

MicroPro says that this command exists so you can force MailMerge to read text correctly where it might otherwise get confused. If, for instance, you've written a paragraph where each line happens to be the same length, MailMerge will interpret it as right justified even if you meant it to be ragged right. When MailMerge adds the variables and reformats the paragraph, then, it will right justify it as it goes.

You can force MailMerge to read the input as ragged right, though, by adding the command **.IJ off,** in which case MailMerge will reformat the text using ragged right. On the other hand, you can also force ragged right printing in this situation by using the **.OJ** command.

The MailMerge 3.3 manual and reference card list only these two commands and the **.PF** command itself, for a total of three print-time line-forming commands. In fact, however, there are either one or three additional commands, depending on the release that you're using. We've already touched on the line spacing command. The other two are **.RM** (for setting the right margin) and **.LM** (for setting the left margin). These were removed from MailMerge "because they never functioned correctly," according to MicroPro. What that translates to is that there are some bugs in these features, but my own experience is that they work more often than not. Here is a description of these three commands.

.LS—*sets line spacing for printing.* The command is followed either by the desired line spacing (**.LS 2**) or by "Dis" to return to the default setting. Line spacing can be any number of lines from 1 to 9. This is not listed as a MailMerge feature on release 3.3, but the program recognizes and obeys the command anyway.

.RM—*sets right margin for printing.* The command is followed by either the column number of the right margin, (**.RM 55**) or by "Dis" to return to the default setting. Right margin can be any number from 1 to 240. This command is not recognized or obeyed by release 3.3.

.LM—*sets left margin for printing.* The command is followed, once again, either by the column number of the left margin (**.LM 25**) or by "Dis" to return to the default setting. Left margin can also be any number from 1 to 240. This command is not recognized or obeyed by release 3.3.

Using the Print-Time Line-Forming Commands

Even if you mostly ignore the print-time line-forming feature, leaving it on automatic, you should be at least vaguely aware that there are times when there is good reason to print with a different format than the one you used in editing.

You might, for instance, want to print with right justification, but edit with ragged right, to make it easier to spot extra spaces between words during editing. Or you might want to experiment with different formats, without having to reformat the entire file each time. Or, if you need to print text that's wider than the screen, but you still want to see it all at once while editing, you can use the right margin command, if you have it available.

Possible Problems with Automatic Print-Time Line-Forming

You should also be aware that there are times when the default setting for this feature can be fooled into making a mistake, so that you don't have any choice but to enter commands manually. Specifically, you need to watch out for one-line paragraphs.

The basic cause of the mistakes is simple. The automatic feature makes its "judgments" on one paragraph at a time. A multiline paragraph contains unambiguous information about its own margins, line spacing, and so forth. A one-line paragraph does not. When the automatic print-time line-forming feature comes across a one-line paragraph, then, it has to make what amount to guesses. Sometimes those guesses are wrong.

There are two situations in particular that you should keep an eye out for. The first long line in any file, if it contains a variable, will be formatted for the default right margin of 65. Try entering and printing this file, and see what happens:

```
.AV VARIABLE
Watch what happens to one line with &VARIABLE&.
```

If you enter a sufficiently long answer for the variable prompt, it will "word wrap," in printing, to a right margin of 65. This will happen even if the rest of your file is formatted for a right margin of, for instance, 78 (for 12 pitch). This, obviously, will make the first paragraph too narrow to fit the format for the rest of the page. The solution is to use the **.RM** command, if available in your release, so that the file reads:

```
.AV VARIABLE
.RM78
Watch what happens to one line with &VARIABLE&.

.RM Dis
```

Notice the **.RM Dis** command after the single line. This returns the right margin control to the default setting, and ensures that any indented paragraphs will retain their indentation. Also notice that in this case there was no need to include a **.PF on** command because there was only one line to deal with, and because that line contained a variable.

If you're using version 3.3, you could probably get away with turning print-time line-forming off before this line and turning it back on after. If the variable is unusually long, though, you may find yourself with the opposite problem of winding up with the first paragraph being to wide to fit in with the rest of the page.

The other choice is to reinstall your copy of WordStar so it comes up with the default right margin that you want to print with. This is a reasonable alternative if you typically use some particular margin setting. In fact, if you typically use two or more different margin settings—65 for 10-pitch printwheels and 78 for 12-pitch printwheels for example—you might want to keep more than one WS.COM file on the disk. You can install each for a different default setting, and keep track of which is which by giving them appropriate names (WS65.COM and WS78.COM for example). You can use as many COM files as you need with a single set of overlay files.

The word wrap problem can show up in different guises. Try creating an envelope file, for instance, by using spaces in each line to position the address instead of using a page offset command.

Now, in response to the "NAME OF COMPANY:" prompt, enter "American Telephone and Telegraph Information Systems." (Ignore the fact that you would normally abbreviate it to AT&T.) You'll find that Mail-Merge will print this out as:

American Telephone and

Telegraph Information Systems.

Here again, one solution is to enter an appropriate right margin command—though in this case, you could just as easily enter a **.PF Off** command without creating a problem.

The automatic print-time line-forming feature can also be confused by format changes within a file. If, for instance, you have just included a series of indented paragraphs, and follow them with a one-line paragraph, there is no way for the automatic feature to "know" whether the new paragraph should be indented or not. (It will assume it should be unless told otherwise.) Here again, the solution is to include one or more format commands as necessary, to provide unambiguous instructions to MailMerge.

USING AMPERSANDS WITHIN A FORM LETTER

It is perfectly all right to use ampersands (&) in the middle of a letter, or any other MailMerge file for that matter. When MailMerge comes across an ampersand in the middle of a file, it looks for another ampersand. If it doesn't find one within 40 characters (the maximum length for a variable name), it simply prints the first ampersand literally, the way it shows in the file. Even if it does come across another ampersand in the next 40 characters, it will still print both ampersands (and the text between them) just as they show in the file, unless the text exactly matches one of the variable names being used in that file. The odds against this happening accidentally are long indeed. If you would like to change the variable name marker from ampersands to something else, though, there is a way. See Appendix D for details.

Assembling Boilerplate
AND OTHER STUFF

Commands Introduced
.FI (File insert)
CHANGE
.SV (Set variable)

Concepts Introduced
Command Files
Master Files
Slave Files

Uses Introduced
Inserting Paragraphs into Letters
Chaining Chapters into Books
Master Files—for Date Entries
            —for Repeating a Letter

Do not skip this chapter.

One of the most powerful MailMerge commands is the **.FI** (file insert) command. The easiest way to describe this command is to say that it does exactly the same thing as the read a file command, except it does it at print time only, reading the file onto the paper, instead of reading it into another file on the disk.

This is the command that lets you assemble letters (or whatever) from "boilerplate"—meaning commonly used portions of text that you don't want to type each time you use them.

But the command does much more, so much more, in fact, that it is fair to say that most of the truly interesting applications of MailMerge grow directly out of this capability. In this chapter, we will stay primarily with the simplest, most straightforward uses of the **.FI** command—beginning with boilerplate assembly. Toward the end of the chapter, though, we're also going to stray into some of the more interesting uses.

Once again, do not skip this chapter, even if you think you don't need to know how to assemble boilerplate, and even if you already understand how to use this command.

The .FI (File Insert) Command

Very often, when you are writing a large number of letters (or legal contracts or whatever), you will find that although they are all substantially the same, they are also different enough to keep you from using a single, standard form letter. Even so, you are likely to have portions of text—be they sentences, paragraphs, pages, or book length—that are exactly the same from letter to letter. These portions are the boilerplate.

We've already looked at one variation on this basic theme in discussing format files in Chapter Three. The example, remember, put you in the position of a free lance picture researcher working for several different clients on any number of different projects. The assumption was that you needed to write a large number of similar, but highly individualized letters, so that there was no point in creating a form letter with MailMerge. The solution was to create a format file and customize it for each letter you wrote.

The format file for that situation might look something like the following. (Items that could be treated as simple variables are in upper-case letters. All words and phrases that are subject to change are surrounded by parentheses.)

(DATE)

(NAME)
(ADDRESS)

Dear (WHOEVER):

(Thank you for your time on the phone today. As we discussed,) I am doing picture research for a (VIDEO? SLIDE?) program on the subject of (WHATEVER). This show is being produced by (CLIENT) for (CLIENT'S CLIENT). Its (working?) title is (TITLE). It is meant for the (WHICH) market, and will be distributed by (WHO).

I am looking for pictures of (WHATEVER). In particular I am hoping that you can provide me with (full description, or list as appropriate). (Please find enclosed Xeroxes of pictures that I found (where) and that were credited to you. These would be extremely useful for this project.)

If there are any forms you need filled out before you can grant permission to use your pictures, please let me know. Also, if there are any fees or special procedures involved, please let me know about those as well.

Thank you for your help.

Sincerely yours,

Ima Researcher

The first thing to notice about this format file is that it is going to produce precisely the sort of highly individualized, essentially unique letter that you are going to want to keep a copy of on a correspondence disk.

The second thing to notice is that different paragraphs in this letter need different degrees of individualization. To begin with, the second paragraph is almost entirely individualized; there is hardly anything in it that won't be based on the particular situation and the particular letter.

At the other extreme, the third and fourth paragraphs are strictly boilerplate, and there's no reason you shouldn't treat them that way. All you have to do is create a file, call it CHNKFILE, with these two paragraphs in it. Then you enter,

.FI CHNKFILE

in the format file instead of the two paragraphs. When MailMerge reaches this command in printing, it will look for CHNKFILE on the disk, then print it before printing the rest of the letter. (The rest of the letter, in this case, is the signature block. I've left this in the format file because you may want to vary this depending on previous contacts or phone conversations.)

What you are doing here, essentially, is using the file insert command to keep from having to save a few extra lines of text on disk every time you write a letter. In this case, the savings in disk space is trivial (or perhaps nonexistent, considering the length of the letter, and considering that there is a minimum size for any file no matter how little information is in it). Still, consider what would happen if CHNKFILE were a three-page permissions letter instead of just six lines.

If, under those conditions, you include CHNKFILE in each letter, you will wind up using an awfully lot of disk space just to store 40 or 50 copies of CHNKFILE. Of course, there's the time you spend twiddling your thumbs while WordStar reads all that text into your file each time, or is saving it to disk.

All of which brings us, finally, to the first paragraph. I've saved this for last, because in terms of customization, it lies somewhere between the two extremes of fully customized on the one hand, and straightforward boilerplate on the other. The first line of this paragraph is going to change from one letter to the next. The rest of the paragraph is going to change from project to project, but is going to be identical for all letters dealing with any one project.

Of course the original idea was that you were working on a large number of projects, sending only one or two letters for each one. In that case, treating this as boilerplate is hardly worthwhile. But if we change the situation so you are working on only a few projects, and are sending 20 or 30 letters for each, it suddenly makes a great deal of sense to treat this paragraph as boilerplate.

The trick, very simply, is to create a separate paragraph for each project, and put each one in a separate file. That way, you only have to type each paragraph once. After that, whenever you write a letter, you simply choose the paragraph you need for that letter.

Here's an example. You're working on three projects: One on modern banking, one on the history of film, and one on the Heisenberg uncertainty principle. Here's what one of the paragraphs might look like:

I am doing picture research for a video program on
the Heisenberg uncertainty principle. This show is being
produced by Random Media for Wave Productions. Its working
title is "Heisenberg May Have Been Here." It is meant for
the home market, and will probably be distributed by Wave
Productions.

This would be in the file HUPPROJ. Equivalent paragraphs for the other projects would be in the files BANKPROJ and FILMPROJ. The first paragraph in the format file, meanwhile, would become:

(Thank you for your time on the phone today. As we
discussed,) .FI HUPPROJ or BANKPROJ or FILMPROJ

There are several things to notice here. First, the boilerplate, meaning any one of the "PROJ" files, starts in the middle of the paragraph. The first line of this paragraph stays in the master format file because it needs to be individualized for each letter.

In order for this to work, you *must not put* a hard carriage return after the partial paragraph in the format file. If MailMerge sees a hard carriage return, it will start printing HUPPROJ, the inserted file, on the next line. If you use a soft return, though, the inserted file will be treated as a continuation of the current paragraph, MailMerge will continue printing without skipping any lines or spaces, and the two parts of the paragraph will be joined without any seams showing.

The only way to get a soft carriage return is to let WordStar put it there for you with word wrap. This means you have to enter spaces or random characters to get the cursor beyond the margin, then let word wrap take you to the next line. At that point, you must go back and delete the random characters, even if they are spaces or tabs. Otherwise MailMerge will insert the spaces in printing the letter.

In order for this trick to work, you also must have print-time line-forming on and active while printing, or MailMerge will not wrap the first line properly. The feature will turn on automatically if the paragraph has a variable in it, but in this case there is none, which means that you have to add **.PF On** at the beginning of the paragraph.

The final format file for the text of your letter is displayed in the following.

FILE: LETTER.FMT

A Sample Format File for a "Customized" Boilerplate Letter

DATE

NAME
ADDRESS

Dear WHOEVER:

(Thank you for your time on the phone today. As we discussed,) .FI HUPPROJ or BANKPROJ or FILMPROJ
I am looking for pictures of (WHATEVER). In particular I am hoping that you can provide me with (full description, or list as appropriate). (Please find enclosed Xeroxes of pictures that I found (where) and that were credited to you. These would be extremely useful for this project.)

.FI CHNKFILE

Sincerely,

Ima Researcher

One more thing before you try duplicating this file. When using file insert commands, you have to be careful with hard carriage returns. Double-check to make sure you haven't put them where they don't belong (as in this example), and double-check to make sure you have put them where they do belong. The inserted file must end with a carriage return, unless you want MailMerge to come back to the master file and keep printing without skipping any lines or spaces.

In this particular case, it wouldn't make much difference if you ended CHNKFILE without a carriage return. MailMerge would come back to the master file, read the next carriage return, and go to the next line anyway. The only effect would be that you would lose one blank line between the end of CHNKFILE and the signature block.

If you left the last carriage return off a "PROJ" file, in contrast, you would lose the blank line between the first and second paragraphs. If there were no blank line between the paragraphs, moreover, MailMerge would join the two paragraphs. If the next line were another **.FI** command, Mail-

Merge would tack the command itself on to the end of the PROJ file instead of reading it as a dot command. The last line of HUPPROJ, then, might be printed as:

distributed by Wave Productions. .FI FILE2

This is not a trivial difference.

LETTERS COMPLETELY FROM BOILERPLATE

There are times when you might want to assemble letters completely from boilerplate. Suppose you've been running a typing service that you're about to expand into a word processing service. Odds are you want to tell your clients about it. Odds also are that you'll want to send a letter to prospective clients as well. While you're at it, you might as well tailor each letter to the individual client or prospect. You can do all this very easily with one semistandard letter with three paragraphs.

The first paragraph introduces your new service. It comes in one version for old clients ("As one of our valued customers, we want you to know that we have recently upgraded our service"), and another version for new prospects ("We think you'll be interested in a new service we are introducing").

The second paragraph is customized for the particular kind of business, and comes in however many versions you can think of. ("To better serve the legal profession, we have a 50,000 word legal dictionary online to catch and correct spelling errors.")

The third paragraph again comes in two versions, one for old clients ("We hope you have found our work valuable in the past") and another for new prospects ("We believe we can be of value to your company, helping you cut costs and increase productivity").

Once you have these various paragraphs created and saved in different files, you can design the body of the letter in just three lines, so that the text of the letter becomes as simple as:

```
.FI NEWCLINT.1
.FI LAWYER
.FI NEWCLINT.3
#
```

This example does not end with a **.FI** command, but rather with an additional blank line after the last command. This is extremely important. *The File Insert command should never be the last line of a file.* If it is, MailMerge often gets confused and does something unexpected.

.SV—THE SET VARIABLE COMMAND

You can go one step further with a boilerplate letter and put variable names into the inserted paragraphs. This means you can customize sentences, so you can take something like: "We believe we can be of value to your company, helping you cut costs and increase productivity." and turn it into:

"We believe we can be of value to &COMPANY-NAME&, helping you cut costs and increase productivity."

The easiest way to do this is to enter the correct variable into the letter file, along with the name, address, and file insert commands. The command that lets you do this is the **.SV,** or set variable command. Simply enter it in the file, followed by the variable name, a comma, and the variable itself:

.SV COMPANY-NAME, Strunk, Strunk, and White

What the **.SV** does is take the variable name on the left side of the comma, and set the value to whatever you put on the right side of the comma. Be careful not to enter extra spaces in the line. If you enter "Strunk, Strunk, and White" followed by four spaces, the variable will read as "Strunk, Strunk, and White   "—and that is what will be entered in the body of the letter.

Your format file for this letter, then, might look something like this:

```
.SV COMPANY-NAME, > > > >ENTER
DATE

&COMPANY-NAME&
NAME
ADDRESS

Dear WHOEVER:

.FI NEWCLINT.1 or OLDCLINT.1
.FI LAWYER or ARCHTECT or BIZEXEC or WRITER or ADAGENCY
.FI NEWCLINT.3 or OLDCLINT.3

Sincerely,
```

And an individual letter would look like this:

```
.SV COMPANY-NAME, Strunk, Strunk, and White
June 4, 1992

Mr. Strunk
&COMPANY-NAME&
P.O. Box 999
Berlin, N.Y.

Dear Mr. Strunk:

.FI NEWCLINT.1
.FI LAWYER
.FI NEWCLINT.3

Sincerely,
```

COMMAND FILES

The **.FI** command will also let you create command files, meaning files that contain nothing but commands. This book, for instance, is being written with WordStar. Each chapter is a separate file. I could print it one chapter at a time, but I won't. What I will do (or will have done) is create a file called PRINT, make sure there's paper and ribbon in the printer, and go have dinner.

The file will look something like this:

FILE: PRINT

For Chaining Chapters of a Book

```
.HE MailMerge Book/ Stone / Page #
.FI PREFACE
.FI PRELIMS
.FI CHAPTER1
.FI CHAPTER2
ETC
```

Note that you can put a single header in the command file, as I've done here, but make sure that you don't have alternate headers in your individual files. If MailMerge finds any, it will start printing with the new header.

Also note that if you want each chapter to start on a new page (as I do), you can either end each file with a new page command (**.PA**), or put the new page commands in the command file, between the **.FI** commands. But be sure to do only one or the other, not both. Unless, of course, you want an additional blank page between sections.

THE CHANGE COMMAND

You can also tell MailMerge to change disks. Using the book example again, you may have room for only two chapters on each disk. In that case, your file might look like the following.

FILE: PRINT2

For Chaining Chapters of a Book Using Different Disks

```
.HE MailMerge Book/ Stone / Page #
.FI PREFACE
.FI PRELIMS
.FI CHAPTER1 CHANGE
.FI CHAPTER2
.FI CHAPTER3 CHANGE
ETC
```

When MailMerge runs across ".FI CHAPTER1 CHANGE," it will stop printing and put a message on the screen telling you to change disks. If you put in the wrong disk, moreover, so that MailMerge can't find the proper file (CHAPTER1 in this case), MailMerge will tell you that also, and give you another chance to put in the right disk.

In order for the CHANGE command to work, the WordStar files, the MailMerge overlay file, and the command file (PRINT2) must all remain in the machine. In other words, these files must be on a different disk than the one being changed. You can include as many CHANGE commands in a file as you need.

MASTER FILES

There are other uses for command files. Suppose, for instance, you have a form letter that you use frequently, usually printing one letter at a time but occasionally printing several at once. On those days when you're sending several letters, you might like to avoid having to enter the same date over and over. You can do that with a simple command file.

FILE: FORMLTR.MAS

For Automatic Entry of Date when Printing Multiple Letters

```
.AV DATE
.FI FORMLTR.SLA
#
```

The "MAS" and "SLA" endings here stand for master file and slave file, the point being you call up the master file and let it call up the slave file. FORMLTR.SLA is set to repeat. It functions just like any other form letter. You can add variables, file insert commands, and anything else you like. When it repeats, it starts at the beginning of FORMLTR.SLA, not FORMLTR.MAS, which means that MailMerge will not ask you for the date again. Instead, it remembers the answer you gave the first time and keeps using it.

There are one or two more variations worth going into at this point both for the sake of clarity and for the sake of demonstrating the flexibility of the **.FI** command. This file, for instance, can be used to enter the date for any form letter. It will first ask you to enter the date, and then ask for the form letter to use. Your answer to the second question becomes part of the **.FI** command to call up that file.

FILE: DATE.GEN

For Automatic Entry of Date with Multiple Printing of Any Form Letter

```
.AV DATE
.AV "NAME OF FILE TO USE:", FILE
```

```
.FI &FILE&
#
```

If you often use several different form letters at a single session, you should find the next file useful.

FILE: DATE.MAS

For Use with DATE.SLA—Will Enter Dates Automatically When Printing a Series of Different Letters

```
.AV DATE
.FI DATE.SLA
#
```

DATE.SLA

```
.AV "Name of Letter to Print: ", FILENAME
.FI &FILENAME&
.FI DATE.SLA
#
```

The first file here, DATE.MAS, will ask you the date, then pass you over to DATE.SLA. This second file will ask you the name of the form letter to print. When you finish the letter, you are then returned to the beginning of DATE.SLA (because of the command ".FI DATE.SLA") and asked for the name of next letter file. You can answer with " **^R**" to repeat the same letter, or you can enter a new file name.

Another way to get multiple copies from any of these examples, finally, is to add the command

.AV "How Many Copies: ", HOWMANY
to DATE.SLA, then add the command

.RP &HOWMANY&

to each of your form letters. Then, whenever you call up a letter through DATE.SLA, it will repeat &HOWMANY& times. If you answer with a RE-TURN only, or call up the letter directly, the **.RP** command will be read as incorrect and otherwise ignored.

We have barely scratched the surface of what you can do with master and slave files, but we've gone far enough to give you some idea of the possibilities. That's enough for right now. We'll be using master and slave files from now on, though, in some of the more interesting applications in this book.

Conditional Printing

HOW TO USE THE FEATURE
IF YOU HAVE IT, AND SOMETIMES
EVEN IF YOU DON'T

Commands Introduced
.IF (IF)
.EX (Except when, or unless)
.EF (End command—End if)
.AND. (AND)
.OR. (OR)
GOTO (Go to the designated EF command line)

Concepts Introduced
Conditional Statements
Conditional Commands

Other Material Covered
Using the File Insert Command to Create Conditional Commands

If you liked the file insert command, you'll love the conditional print commands. This sentence is a conditional statement. *If you don't know what that means, or even if you do, then read on.* This sentence is also a conditional statement. In fact, it is a conditional command; it tells you to do something—if certain conditions are met.

Conditional statements, and particularly conditional commands, are what the MailMerge conditional print commands are all about. They are a way to tell MailMerge to do something *"IF* this is true," or *"EXcept when* this is true."

If you're putting a letter together from boilerplate, for example, you might want to tell MailMerge, in effect, "If the client is a lawyer, print this paragraph, otherwise skip it." Or you might want to say "Unless the client is a lawyer, print this paragraph." Either way, the conditional print commands give you an easy way to do that.

This is all good and well if you are using the CP/M version of release 3.3 or later. If you are using an earlier release of the CP/M version, though, or even release 3.3 of the 16-bit version, it doesn't help very much. These releases do not have the conditional print feature. If you're using one of these other releases, though, you will probably be interested to learn that you can do many of the same things without the conditional print commands. Specifically, you can often use the file insert command to trick MailMerge into obeying a conditional command anyway.

CONDITIONAL PRINT COMMANDS

The basic format for a conditional command in MailMerge is simple and well defined. It must take one of two forms, either:

"**IF** this is so, do that," or "**EX**cept when this is so, do that." The dot commands for these two formats are certainly easy to remember. They are **.IF** for "IF" and **.EX** for "EXcept when."

Both formats are otherwise identical. Each consists of two parts, one on each side of the comma. On the left side is a conditional statement, and on the right side is the command to be followed if that condition is met.

THE CONDITIONAL SIDE OF A CONDITIONAL COMMAND

The "conditional" part of a conditional command is always defined by giving a variable name, along with the conditions it has to meet. If this part of the conditional command reads

    .IF &CLIENT& = "Lawyer"

for example, it tells MailMerge to read and follow the command only *if* the variable "CLIENT" is in fact "L-a-w-y-e-r." If the condition reads

    .EX &CLIENT& = "Lawyer"

it tells MailMerge to read and follow the command *except when* the variable CLIENT is "L-a-w-y-e-r." In either case, the match must be exact. If, for example, CLIENT is in upper-case letters as "L-A-W-Y-E-R", it will not match.

There is a way to write the command so that variations in capitalization will match. We'll come back to it later. There are also other choices besides "equals" for comparing the variable name to your chosen condition. We'll come back to these later as well.

The Command Side of a Conditional Command

The command side of a conditional command is limited. In fact, there is only one command you can use: **GOTO.** This can be in upper- or lower-case letters. It can also be abbreviated to **G** or **g,** but it always means the same thing.

The command **GOTO** does pretty much what it sounds like. It tells MailMerge to jump to a different spot in the file. The "where" is indicated by another dot command, **.EF.**

MicroPro calls **.EF** the end command. A better mnemonic might be the End If command. (The mnemonic doesn't work if you're using the **.EX** format, but it still makes the commands easier to remember. At any rate, that's what I'll use in this book.) The end if dot command must be located after the conditional command in the file. You may identify it with a *label* or not. Labels may be from 1 to 20 characters long. Aside from this limit on length, they follow pretty much the same rules as variable names. As with variable names, labels are limited to using letters, numbers, and hyphens, meaning that they cannot include other characters or spaces. As with variable names also, the first character in a label must be a letter. **A, A1,** and **A-1,** then, are all acceptable labels, while **1, A 1,** and **-6A1** are not.

Using the Conditional Print Command

Assume you're a management consultant writing a letter to all your clients. There's a section in the letter that you only want to include in those cases where your client is a lawyer. You could create a different file for each version of the letter, of course, but then you have to remember which file to use for which client. By using the conditional print commands, you can create one file and let MailMerge figure out which version of the letter to use.

The body of your letter might look something like this:

FILE: CONDITIONAL
BOILERPLATE EXAMPLE

For Creating Two Versions of a Letter

Dear &SALUT&:

This is the first paragraph, which is included on all letters.

.EX &CLIENT& = "Lawyer" GOTO SHORTFORM

This section goes to lawyers only.

.EF SHORTFORM

This is the last paragraph, which is also included on all letters.

The conditional command here tells MailMerge that except when the client is a lawyer, it should jump to the **.EF** command line, eliminating everything between the conditional command line and the end if command line. "Everything" in this case is a single line, but it really doesn't matter how long or short the section is. Considering that this is boilerplate, moreover, you could easily put the text in another file and replace it here with a file insert command.

This file uses a label: SHORTFORM. This tells MailMerge to look for an **.EF** command line that includes the same label. In this case, the label is excess baggage. You could enter the GOTO command simply as "**GOTO**," or "**G**," and enter the end if command similarly, as **.EF.** If you did that, MailMerge would read the GOTO command as "go to the next **.EF** command." In either case, with or without the label, MailMerge will skip everything between the conditional command and the end if command, assuming the proper conditions. The label, then, isn't needed in this case. Labels are necessary, though, in more complex files, where you have conditional commands overlapping one another.

OVERLAPPING CONDITIONAL COMMANDS

You might, for example, have three kinds of clients—CPA's who are also lawyers, CPA's who are not lawyers, and lawyers who are not CPA's. In that case, you might want to send substantially the same letter to all three sets of clients, but want certain sections to vary somewhat, depending on whether the client is a laywer or not and depending on whether the client is a CPA or not.

The body of your letter file might look something like the following.

FILE: CONDITIONAL BOILERPLATE WITH OVERLAPPING CONDITIONALS

For Creating Three Versions of a Letter

Dear &SALUT&:

    This is section one. It is included on all letters.
.IF &CLIENT& = "Lawyer" GOTO LAWONLY
.IF &CLIENT& = "Lawyer/CPA" GOTO LAWPLUS

    This is section two. It goes only to CPA's who are not lawyers.
.IF &CLIENT& = "CPA" GOTO CPA
.EF LAWPLUS

    This is section three. It goes only to lawyers who are also CPA's.
.EF CPA

    This is section four. It goes to all CPA's—lawyers or not.

    .EF LAWONLY

This is section five. It is included on all letters.

This file is a bit complicated to take in all at once, but if you run through it three times, once for each possibility, you'll see that it will produce three different letters, depending on which kind of client you're sending the letter to.

The important point here is that in this kind of file, with overlapping conditional commands, the label for the end if command becomes essential. Without it, you would have no way of telling MailMerge which **.EF** command line to go to, which means the overlapping itself would be impossible.

In using overlapping conditional commands, make sure that none of the labels is contained within another label. If, for example, you use LAWPLUS as a label, do not use LAW by itself as a separate label. Otherwise, if ".EF LAWPLUS" comes before ".EF LAW," MailMerge will match the first three letters of "LAWPLUS" when looking for "LAW" and will stop there.

KEEPING YOUR FILE SIMPLE

This last example also raises another point. You can put as many conditional commands as you like in your file, but they tend to complicate things, making the file difficult to understand. This, in turn, makes revisions difficult if you ever need to go back to the file to change it. It pays to keep this in mind when designing a file in the first place. Try to keep it readable and understandable, even if that means duplicating material. You could, for example, redesign this last letter so it looks like the following.

FILE: CONDITIONAL BOILERPLATE WITH OVERLAPPING CONDITIONALS

Alternate Design for Creating Three Versions of a Letter

Dear &SALUT&:

.IF &CLIENT& = "Lawyer" GOTO LAWONLY
.IF &CLIENT& = "Lawyer/CPA" GOTO LAWPLUS

..if client is a CPA only, MailMerge will print the following
    This is section one. It is included on all letters.
    This is section two. It goes only to CPA's who are not lawyers.
    This is section four. It goes to all CPA's—lawyers or not.
    This is section five. It is included on all letters.
.IF &CLIENT& = "CPA" GOTO END

.EF LAWONLY
    This is section one. It is included on all letters.
    This is section five. It is included on all letters.
.IF &CLIENT& = "Lawyer" GOTO END

.EF LAWPLUS
    This is section one. It is included on all letters.
    This is section three. It goes only to lawyers who are also CPA's.
    This is section four. It goes to all CPA's—lawyers or not.
    This is section five. It is included on all letters.

.EF END

    This version of the letter consists, essentially, of three complete letters, along with instructions to MailMerge telling it which one to use. In addition to being longer than the original version, it is also much easier to read. More important, it's easier to understand.

    These two files represent two extremes of organization, yet both will produce exactly the same letters given the same conditions. In either case, you have automated a decision. Instead of having three different letter files to remember for three different kinds of clients, you have only one file to remember; MailMerge will choose the proper version of the letter for you.

    The first file does all this in the most compact, least readable form. The second file does it in the most readable, least compact form. Which of these approaches is "best" is often a matter of personal taste. You might prefer an approach that lies between these two extremes. In this case, for example, you might enter the first and last sections only once because they are the same for each letter, but enter three separate versions of the middle sections.

    If the individual sections are each fairly long, finally, you can save a great deal of disk space, and improve the readability of this file at the same time, by putting each section in a separate file, and using file insert commands in this master file.

    In that case, the letter file would look like this:

FILE: CONDITIONAL BOILERPLATE

Second Alternate for Creating Three Versions of a Letter
Reading the Sections in from Other Files

Dear &SALUT&:

.IF &CLIENT& = "Lawyer" GOTO LAWONLY
.IF &CLIENT& = "Lawyer/CPA" GOTO LAWPLUS

..If client is a CPA only, MailMerge will print this.
.FI SECTION1
.FI SECTION2
.FI SECTION4
.FI SECTION5
.IF &CLIENT& = "CPA" GOTO END

.EF LAWONLY
..If client is a lawyer only, MailMerge will print this one.

```
.FI SECTION1
.FI SECTION5
.IF &CLIENT& = "Lawyer" GOTO END

.EF LAWPLUS
..If client is a lawyer and CPA, MailMerge will print this one.
.FI SECTION1
.FI SECTION3
.FI SECTION4
.FI SECTION5

.EF END
```

I've found that MailMerge will sometimes give me error messages on a conditional print command when nothing appears to be wrong. I've gone back and retyped the line character for character in those cases and found that it worked. As best as I can tell, the problems come from accidentally letting WordStar word wrap the command on first entry, thereby inserting soft spaces. MicroPro agrees that this is "probably so." If you're entering a conditional command, and it inadvertently gets word wrapped, play it safe and re-enter it.

USING THE FILE INSERT COMMAND
AS A CONDITIONAL COMMAND

Everything we've done up to this point with the conditional print commands can be very nearly duplicated by careful use of the file insert command. True, using the **.FI** command is not always as convenient as using the conditional print commands, but if you don't have the conditional commands to use, you should find this trick valuable. (If your release of WordStar includes the conditional print commands, you can skip this section.)

Let's start with the same simple example that we used in introducing the conditional print commands themselves. You're writing a short letter. There's a section in it that you want to include only in letters going to your lawyer clients. Here's how you do it with the file insert command.

FILE: CONDITIONAL
BOILERPLATE EXAMPLE

*Using the File Insert Command as a Conditional Command
for Creating Two Versions of a Letter*

Dear &SALUT&:
This is the first paragraph, which is included on all letters.

.FI &CLIENT&
This is the last paragraph, which is also included on all letters.

The trick here is almost ridiculously simple. Put the section for lawyers into a separate file named LAWYER. Make sure that there are no file names on the disk that match any other possibility. If the variable &CLIENT& is "lawyer," MailMerge will print the file LAWYER. If it is anything else, MailMerge will give you a warning message telling you that the file was not found, but will otherwise go merrily on its way, printing the rest of the letter without inserting anything.

This is almost as convenient as using the conditional print commands, but it does force you to worry about the names of your disk files.

If the situation is reversed—that is, if you want to insert the extra section for everyone but lawyers—you can still make the file insert command do at least some of the work for you, but not all of it. Specifically, you can use the ask for variable command to have MailMerge ask you whether the client is a lawyer, then have the file insert command set to read in a file or not, depending on your answer.

In this case, the one **.FI** command line is replaced with two command lines:

```
.AV "Is client a lawyer (Y/N)? ", ANSWER, 1
.FI &ANSWER&
```

In this example, the file to be inserted would be named N, and would only be inserted if the client were not a lawyer.

This second example is not as convenient to use as the first, but it does have the same advantage of guiding you into using the right version of the letter for each client. And of course, if you are entering all the data through **.AV** commands in the first place, the extra question makes for a trivial amount of extra work.

This same conditional file insert trick works just as well—if not better—with a longer, more involved file where you would otherwise use overlapping conditional commands. The trick is to break the file into a master file and series of related slave files. In this particular example, the slave files would be CPA.SLA, LAWYER.SLA, and LAWYER/C.SLA. ("LAWYER/C" because file names are limited to eight characters, and these are the first eight characters of the variable "Lawyer/CPA.")

The files themselves might look like the following.

CONDITIONAL BOILERPLATE EXAMPLE

Using File Insert as a Conditional Command for Creating
Three Versions of a Letter

Note: As before, the example shows only the body of the letter. Each of the slave files, though, is complete. Values would be assigned to the variables by adding appropriate commands to the top of the LETTER.MAS file.

FILE: LETTER.MAS

Dear &SALUT&:

.FI SECTION1
.FI &CLIENT&.SLA

Sincerely,

FILE: CPA.SLA

.FI SECTION2
.FI SECTION4
.FI SECTION5
#

FILE: LAWYER.SLA

.FI SECTION5
#

FILE: LAWYER/C.SLA

.FI SECTION3
.FI SECTION4
.FI SECTION5
#

If you run through these three files, you'll see that they will produce *exactly* the same letters as the earlier examples. In this case, you start with LETTER.MAS. MailMerge will enter the variable &CLIENT& into the **.FI** command, will automatically go to the proper slave file, then return to the master file to continue the letter. In either case though—whether using the conditional print commands or the file insert command—the files work the same way from the user's point of view.

These examples should be enough to convince you that you can often do virtually the same thing with the file insert command as with the conditional print commands. Throughout this book you'll find examples of how to do many things both ways.

This doesn't mean that conditional commands aren't useful. Aside from letting you do certain things a bit more conveniently than you can do them with the file insert command, they also have some additional capabilities that we haven't looked at yet.

A CLOSER LOOK AT THE CONDITIONAL PRINT COMMANDS

SIMPLE COMMANDS AND COMPLEX COMMANDS

Conditional commands come in two well-defined forms: simple and complex. The commands that we've looked at so far have all been simple commands. A *simple command* has only one condition, as in, "If this is true, then do that." A *complex command,* in contrast, contains more than one condition. One form for a complex command is, "If this is true *or* that is true, then do this." Another possibility is, "If this is true *and* that is true, then do this." In the first case, MailMerge will follow the command if either condition is met. In the second case, it will follow the command only if both conditions are met.

MailMerge uses the conditional print feature to link conditions together with either **.AND.** for or "and," **.OR.** for "or." These two MailMerge commands are *not* dot commands. They are in a class by themselves. Notice that they include a period after the command as well as before. In addition, unlike dot commands, they can show up anywhere in the line, and *they must be in upper-case letters.*

The total length of a conditional command must be 100 characters or less. Within that limit, though, you can use the **.AND.** and **.OR.** commands to link as many conditions together as you like.

Using complex conditional commands is an exercise in logic. The one point to remember is that MailMerge always evaluates the commands from right to left, opposite to the way you read them.

A command line that takes the form "a **.AND.** b **.OR.** c" will be obeyed only if condition "c" or "b" is met, *and* if condition "a" is met also. If the command line takes the form "a **.OR.** b. **.AND.** c," on the other hand, it will be obeyed only if both condition "c" and condition "b" are met, *or* if condition "a" is met.

One important use of complex conditional commands is to let you use either upper-case or lower-case letters in entering your variables. You can enter a complex command as

".IF &CL& = "LAWYER" .OR. &CL& = "Lawyer" .OR. &CL& = Lawyer".

In which case you can later use any of these variations of the variable, and still match the conditional statement.

COMPARISON CHARACTERS

When we first looked at the "condition" side of a conditional command, I mentioned in passing that MailMerge gives you other choices besides "equals" for comparing, or testing, the variable name. In fact, it gives you a total of six choices for comparison. They are:

=	Equal
< >	Not Equal
<	Less Than
>	Greater Than
< =	Less Than or Equal to
> =	Greater Than or Equal to

The two characters for "less than or equal to" can also be entered in reverse order. So can the characters for "greater than or equal to." The format of the conditional comparison is always the same, with the variable on the left side of the comparison character and the expression in quotes on the right side.

These additional comparison characters give you tremendous flexibility in what you can do and how you can do it. You might notice, for instance, that the conditional statement:

.IF &CLIENT& < > "Lawyer"

will give you the same results as:

.EX &CLIENT& = "Lawyer"

The point is that between **.IF, .EX, .AND., .OR.,** plus these six comparison characters, you can not only state any condition or set of conditions that you like, you can usually find more than one way to do it.

One other point about the comparison characters—the most obvious uses for comparisons like "greater than or equal to" are with numbers. If you have a form letter to customers, for example, asking for payment, these commands make it easy to tailor the letter according to the amount of money involved. One possible command might be:

.IF &AMT-OWED& > = "1000" .AND. &AMT-OWED& < = "5000" GOTO"

What may not be obvious is that alphabetical characters also have numerical values, which means you can use these comparison characters for text, if you need to.

WordStar uses a standard set of symbols known as ASCII, for American Standard Code for Information Interchange. **The ASCII values run, lowest to highest, from 0 through 9, then A through Z (in upper-case letters), then a–z (in lower-case letters).**

It should be clear by now that conditional commands provide an extremely flexible tool that can be used in any number of situations. Not only have we come nowhere near exhausting the possibilities as yet, but we will keep coming back to them throughout the rest of this book, using both the conditional print commands and variations on the conditional file insert trick.

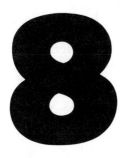

8

Creating a Data Entry Screen with MailMerge

AUTOMATING ADDRESSES

Commands Introduced
.DF (Data File)
.RV (Read Values)

Concepts Introduced
Data Files
Data Entry Screens

Uses Introduced
Printing Envelopes Automatically from Individual Letters
Printing Envelopes from Address Files
Automatic Printing of Labels

Up to this point, we have more or less assumed that when you're printing a letter, you're using single sheets of paper. If that's so, then printing an envelope along with the letter becomes trivial. All you have to do is tack an envelope section to the end of your letter, then add a prompt to remind you when to put an envelope in the printer instead of a piece of paper. This makes life easy, especially with form letters where you enter the address once, then let MailMerge print it out twice.

If you are using fanfold paper, though, and especially if you are using a tractor feed, life begins to get complicated. In particular, if you are sending a large number of letters, you will certainly prefer to print all the letters first, then remove the tractor feed and print the envelopes separately. If you do that, though, you then have to worry about how to get the envelopes printed.

In Chapter 4, we created an envelope file that made printing an address on an envelope roughly equivalent to typing it on a typewriter. But that's not acceptable. A computer isn't supposed to make things as easy as doing it on a typewriter, it's supposed to make them easier.

The fact is, you typed this information once already—in the letters themselves. There's no reason you should have to do it again. More than that, as far as the envelopes are concerned, you should be able to automate the whole process. You can of course. You just need two more commands. These are:

.DF (Data File)
.RV (Read Variables)

THE .DF AND .RV COMMANDS

The **.DF** and **.RV** commands are designed primarily to let you merge mailing lists with form letters (mail merging—with a lower-case "m"). Together they replace, and serve essentially the same function as, the **.AV** command that we've been using up to now.

Basically, the **.RV** or read variable command tells MailMerge to read the variables from a disk file, (rather than asking for variables on the screen, then looking to the keyboard for a response). The **.DF,** or data file command, tells MailMerge which disk file to read those variables from.

THE DATA FILE COMMAND

The data file command takes the form:

.DF FILENAME

As with the file insert command, you can use the data file command along with the CHANGE command, using the form:

.DF FILENAME CHANGE

MailMerge will then stop when it gets to the data file command and remind you to put the proper disk in your machine. Once MailMerge finds the proper file, it reads the variables from that file as instructed by the read variable command.

THE READ VARIABLE COMMAND

The read variable command is followed by a list of variable names—much as each **.AV** command is followed by a single variable name). Each of the variable names in the list is separated by a comma.

For a simple, three-line envelope file, then where the address block is:

&NAME&
&STREET&
&CITY&, &STATE& &ZIP&

The **.RV** command for the file would look like:

.RV &NAME&, &STREET&, &CITY&, &STATE&, &ZIP&

The actual data file, meanwhile, (the file referred to with the **.DF** command) contains the variables. Here also, the individual variables are (usually) indicated by separating them with commas. So the first line in the data file that goes with this envelope file would look like:

Big Bird, Sesame Street, New York, New York, 10021

If everything is set up right (a point we'll come back to), MailMerge will match the first variable (Big Bird) to the first variable name (&NAME&), the second variable (Sesame Street) to the second variable name (&STREET&), and so forth. It will keep doing that until it runs out of variable names to match variables to.

After printing an envelope with this first set of variables, MailMerge will then look for another line in the data file. If it doesn't find one, it stops. If there is another line (and there certainly will be if you're printing mailing lists), the program will then go through the same procedure again, except that this time it will start at the beginning of a new line.

Once again, MailMerge will match the first variable to the first variable name, the second variable to the second variable name, and so forth, ending by printing another envelope using the new set of variables. The program will keep going this way, printing a separate envelope for each set of variables, until it runs out of variables in the data file.

One last thing about the read variable command. MailMerge doesn't care if a line goes off screen or not; it will read the entire line regardless. This means you can list as many variables as you want on one line.

For human readability of the file, though, it helps to break the line into portions that will fit on the screen. MailMerge doesn't care about that either. This means you can set up the read variable command this way:

.RV &NAME&, &STREET&, &CITY&, &STATE&, &ZIP&

or this way:

.RV &NAME&, &STREET&
.RV &CITY&, &STATE&, &ZIP&

Either one will give you the same result.

SETTING UP DATA FILES

Null Variables—(Variables Without Values)

As you might expect, there are a few complications you have to consider when creating files for use with the **.DF** and **.RV** commands.

To begin with, if you want a useful envelope file, you need an all-purpose address block that can handle anything from a three line to a seven line address. In other words, you want essentially the same address block we developed in Chapter Four, complete with the omit commands. Basically, it should look like this:

```
&NAME/O&
&TITLE/O&
&DEPT/O&
&COMPANY/O&
&STREET&
&CITY&, &STATE& &ZIP&
&COUNTRY/O&
```

Or, if we use the same shorthand as before for the variable names (A1, A2, and so on), it will look like this:

```
&A1/O&
&A2/O&
&A3/O&
&A4/O&
&A5&
&A6&, &A7& &A8&
&A9/O&
```

In that case, your read variable command will look like this:

.RV &A1&, &A2&, &A3&, &A4&, &A5&, &A6&, &A7&, &A8&, &A9&

MailMerge will be expecting to find, and trying to match, nine variables in your data file for each envelope you print. What you have to do, then, is tell MailMerge when you want to give a variable a "null" value—that is, when you don't want to assign a value to the variable. You do that by putting extra commas in the data file.

When MailMerge sees a comma, it knows that this is the end of one variable and the start of the next. If the next character is another comma, MailMerge will assign a null value, meaning no value at all, to that variable and will then match the null value to the appropriate variable name.

Read that last sentence again. It's not easy. What it translates to, in practice, is this. In this example, in order to wind up with a three line address, the line in the data file has to look like this:

Big Bird,,,,Sesame Street, New York, New York, 10021,,

MailMerge will match "Big Bird" to &A1&, then read the commas, and match a null value to &A2&, a null value to &A3&, a null value to &A4&, "Sesame Street" to &A5&, and so forth.

Notice also the two commas after the zip code. The zip code itself is A8. If A9 had a value (USA in this case), the second comma would not be needed. When the last field is empty, though, MailMerge 3.0 (and 3.2) will go right past the hard carriage return if this last comma is not there. It will read the first variable on the next line ("C. Brown" as it happens), and print this variable as &A9& on the first envelope.

If this is the last record in the data file, moreover, and you leave this second comma out, MailMerge will not work properly. This final comma is important to keep in mind whenever the final field in each record may be omitted occasionally. You can ignore it if your final field will be given a value in every record. If the last field in an address file is STATE, for example, you know beforehand that there will always be something there.

MailMerge 3.3 seems to have cured this problem, but the manual says otherwise. Since it does no harm to include the extra comma, and since it can do a great deal of good, it's best to play it safe and include the extra comma regardless.

COMMAS WITHIN VARIABLES

While we're discussing commas, this would be a good time to talk about what happens when you use commas within a variable—or rather, it would be a good time to explain *how* to use commas within a variable.

Notice that in this address block, as opposed to earlier address blocks, we've broken "city and state" into two variables rather than keeping it as one. This lets us take the comma that goes after "city," and put it in the format section of the file, rather than in the data file.

The reason for this, of course, is that if we entered, for example, "Ridgewood, N.J." as a single variable in the data file, MailMerge would read the comma after "Ridgewood" and assume that it had just reached the end of the variable.

You can get around this problem by putting quotes either around the comma or around the entire variable so that it reads:

Ridgewood"," N.J.

or

"Ridgewood, N.J."

The quotes serve as instruction to MailMerge. Specifically, they tell MailMerge to treat any commas inside the quotes as text rather than as further instructions. In this case, they tell MailMerge to print the variable as "Ridgewood, N.J."—with the comma and without the quotes.

This is an important capability, since there will be times when you must use commas as part of a company name, or somesuch. The problem, though, is that you have to remember to put the comma in quotes in the first place. For the most part, if you are entering the data through Word-

Star's edit mode, you're better off sidestepping this problem whenever you can by designing the file so that the comma is part of the format file rather than part of the variable.

There is another way out of the "comma" problem, but a warning goes with it. In computer jargon, each variable in a data file is called a field. The commas, which are used to define the fields, are called field delimiters. If you want to, you can reinstall WordStar to change the field delimiters from commas to anything that you like. (See Appendix D for a discussion of how to do this.)

This means that if there is a character you never (or hardly ever) use in your data files, a bracket perhaps, you can make this symbol the field delimiter. If you do that, you will then be free to use commas within your variables without having to do anything, since they no longer have any meaning as an instruction to MailMerge.

Don't do this, though, without thinking about it carefully beforehand. The comma-as-field-delimiter is one of the more-or-less standard methods for defining fields in data files. You may eventually want to use MailMerge along with, say, a data base program. (This is a subject we'll get to in a later chapter.) If you choose a data base program that already uses commas, you will find that this particular customization of MailMerge will complicate matters.

Up to this point, we've been talking about data files in very general terms. (Notice that we haven't talked about how to create data files, much less the best way to create them.) Underlying this whole discussion, though, has been the assumption that we were dealing with mailing lists (with an assumed next line in the file for producing the next envelope). We still haven't looked at how to apply the read variable command and data file command to our original problem, which was automating the printing of individual envelopes separately from the letters they go with.

The "best" solution to this problem, meaning the most efficient, depends very much on whether you're dealing with one or two envelopes or one or two thousand. Let's solve the problem first for a situation where you need only a few envelopes at a time.

Automated Envelopes—Using the Letter as a Data File

One way to create envelopes from unique letters, surprisingly, is to get the address from the letter itself. Here is a MailMerge file that will do that for you—read a letter file, then print an envelope.

FILE: AUTOENV

For Printing Envelopes from Letter Files, Limited to Three Line Addresses

.DM This file prints envelopes directly from LETTER FILES
.DM It assumes

```
.DM  1) That there is only one comma in the address, namely
.DM      the one between City and State.
.DM  2) That there are 3 lines in the address.
.DM  3) That the DATE is the only text before the address.
.DM
.DM If any of these assumptions is wrong, this will not work.
.PL 26
.MT 0
.AV "NAME OF FILE TO GET ADDRESS FROM ", F1
.DF &F1&
.RV DATE1, DATE2, NAME, STREET, CITY, STATE
.DM Place Envelope in Printer (top of env at bail).
.DM Hit SPACE then P to continue printing
^C
.PO 40
#
#
#
#
&NAME&
&STREET&
&CITY&, &STATE&
.PA
```

What this file does, very simply, is treat the letter file as a data file. Take a look at the Read Variable command:

```
.RV DATE1, DATE2, NAME, STREET, CITY, STATE
```

The first thing MailMerge comes across in the letter is the date. Let's use March 1, 1985. Following the usual rules, MailMerge will match the month and day—March 1—to DATE1, and the year—1985—to DATE2. Since neither of these variables shows up in the format section of AU-TOENV, neither will be printed. Because MailMerge has four more variable names to match, it then bypasses the carriage returns until it gets to the address.

In this case, the address is set up in a "human readable" format, namely:

Big Bird
Sesame Street
New York, New York 10021

MailMerge matches ("Big Bird") to the first variable name (&NAME&), goes past the carriage return to match "Sesame Street" to the second variable name, and so on. Notice that state and zip code become a single variable here, since there is no comma between them in the address. Notice also that the file assumes preprinted stationery. If you include your own address, you'll have to add more unused variable names to the read variable command.

This file represents a perfectly acceptable, often convenient way to print envelopes automatically, but there are at least three drawbacks to it. First, this particular file can only deal with three line addresses. Second, this approach can't deal with commas within variables—in a company name, for example. Third, and finally, it requires some minor extra work to get MailMerge to stop after printing one envelope. (MailMerge wants to treat the rest of the letter as more data.)

ADDRESS FILES REVISITED

We'll tackle the third problem first. In Chapter Three, we discussed using address files as a way to help create unique letters in WordStar. A simple modification of the AUTOENV file will let you use those address files to print envelopes as well.

If we stay with a three line address for the moment, then all you have to do is delete the DATE variables (DATE1 and DATE2) from the read variable command in AUTOENV, so it reads:

```
.RV NAME, STREET, CITY, STATE
```

Don't forget to revise the reminders in the AUTOENV file while you're at it.

The second problem, dealing with commas, is also easy to solve. Simply make sure that whenever you create an address file, you put quotes around any commas that you put in the file. When you read the address into a letter, of course, you'll have to delete the quotes, but that's still much easier than typing an entire address.

You can solve the one remaining problem, the number of address lines, in either of two ways. The obvious choice is to create different files for addresses, so that you wind up with AUTOENV3 for three line addresses, AUTOENV4 for four line addresses, and so forth. This might be a problem if you have limited disk space, though, and besides, there's a more elegant way.

You can use MailMerge to create the address files in the first place. You can design the format of the address files so they will print correctly regardless of the number of lines in the address.

Briefly, you create a file that uses the ask for variable command to prompt you for data (the address). This file then stores the data on a disk (in the address files). These data files, or address files, are designed to work with a modified version of the AUTOENV file, so that together they will print the address correctly.

CREATING DATA FILES WITH MAILMERGE

The easiest way to understand what you need to do here is to work through the procedure backwards. If you want an AUTOENV file that will print anywhere from three to five lines, for instance, then the format section of that file has to look like this (note the omit commands):

```
&NAME/O&
&TITLE/O&
&COMPANY/O&
&STREET&
&CITY&, &STATE&
```

The read variable command in this file will look like this:

```
.RV NAME, TITLE, COMPANY, STREET, CITY, STATE
```

In order to print correctly even if there are, for instance, three lines in the address, the data file (or address file) can be set up in basically two different ways. It can look like this:

```
Big Bird,,,Sesame Street,New York,New York 10021
```

or like this:

```
Big Bird,

,

,
Sesame Street,
New York, New York 10021
```

Notice the comma at the end of each of the first four lines. If there is no variable in the line, it needs to be there. If there is a variable, it makes no difference.

Either one of these formats will work, but since we also want to be able to read these files into letters and use them for address blocks, let's stay with the second version.

We have to create a MailMerge file that includes this format section:

```
&NAME&,
&TITLE&,
&COMPANY&,
&STREET&,
&CITY&, &STATE& &ZIP&
```

In addition, if we want to free ourselves from having to worry about commas, we should enclose the first three variables in quotes. Finally, of course, we need the ask for variable commands to prompt for the variables.

Here then, is the file that will create the (address) data files. (The AUTOENV file should be easy enough to create by yourself.) To use this file, you turn off the file directory, call up MailMerge, answer "Y" to the "DISK FILE OUTPUT (Y/N):" prompt, then enter an appropriate file name, when asked.

FILE: CREATE

To Create Address Data Files

```
.DM This file creates address files from screen input.
.DM It will automatically enclose Name, Title, and Company
.DM in quotes.
.AV "Enter Name: ", NAME
.AV "Enter Title: ", TITLE
.AV "Enter Company Name: ", COMPANY
.AV "Street and Number: ", STREET
.AV "City: ", CITY
.AV "State: ", STATE
.AV "Zip Code: ", ZIP
.MT 0
.MB 0    Format commands are set for creating disk file without
.PO 0    unwanted blank lines or spaces.
.PL 5
"&NAME&",
"&TITLE&",
"&COMPANY&",
&STREET&,
&CITY&, &STATE& &ZIP&
```

Data Entry Screens

We have not yet solved the problem we started with at the beginning of this chapter—or rather, we have solved it only for a limited number of cases. What we haven't gotten to yet is how to print envelopes automatically when dealing with more than just a few. We'll look at that specific problem in the next chapter.

For the moment, though, there's a much more important point to make. What we've done here is much more significant than simply find a way to automate envelopes—in fact, we've demonstrated one of the hidden capabilities of MailMerge. What we have done, in effect, is create a data entry screen. We've created a file that will prompt you for information and record your answers on disk in a data file.

As a data entry program, MailMerge has some limitations that we'll cover later, but the fact is that it can be used that way. And the basic concept of what we've done here, using MailMerge to create a data entry screen, raises all sorts of possibilities that we'll come back to a little later.

Mass Mailings

PRODUCING ENVELOPES, LABELS, AND FORM LETTERS

Uses Introduced
Printing Envelopes (or Labels) from Mailing Lists
Printing Form Letters from Mailing Lists

One of the most powerful things that MailMerge can do is take a long list of names and addresses and use it to produce a large number of labels, envelopes, or form letters for a mass mailing.

If you regularly send mass mailings—a twice-yearly brochure to all your customers, perhaps, or an alumni newsletter, then using your computer to print the labels or envelopes can simplify life enormously. At its simplest, a mailing list is no more than that: a list of names and addresses. Once the list is on disk, sending out future mailings becomes a matter of telling MailMerge to print the addresses. Then you slap the labels on, or stuff the envelopes, and drop the whole batch off at the post office.

If you read the last chapter, then whether you realize it or not, you already know how to make MailMerge do all this. Let's go through the process once quickly, though, just to make sure.

THE MAILING LIST

To begin with, you need a mailing list. This can be any length right on up to the limits of your disk capacity, but in the interests of keeping things simple, let's stay with three names and addresses.

As before, you have a choice of two formats for the addresses in the file. They can look like this:

Big Bird,,,Sesame Street,New York,New York 10021

Or like this:

Big Bird,

,

,

Sesame Street,
New York, New York 10021

The first format is "MailMerge-readable." The second format is "human-readable." In the last chapter, we chose the human-readable format on the grounds that it was easier to adjust with WordStar after reading an address file into a letter. The MailMerge-readable format, though, is the preferred version, and is the format that MicroPro recommends. There are two arguments in its favor.

First, this is the norm for programs that use the comma-as-field-delimiter standard. MicroPro's DataStar, for example, stores and reads data in the first format only. Give it files in human-readable format, and it gets lost. What this translates to is that if you ever want to use DataStar (or some similar program) to maintain your MailMerge data files, those files must be in MailMerge-readable format. Or, to put it another way, if you use the human-readable format, you may find the files easier to read, but programs like DataStar will not.

Even if you plan to stay strictly with MailMerge, though, there is still one advantage to using the first format. Namely, it minimizes the damage if you have somehow left a comma out of an address, or have accidentally put an extra comma in.

If, for example, you are printing envelopes, and you have left one comma out of a line, MailMerge will ignore the hard carriage return at the end of that line, and go instead to the next line for the last variable of the address. It will then print that variable—a name presumably—where the state or zip code ought to be on the envelope.

At that point, MailMerge is in the middle of a line, and in the middle of an address. Instead of starting the next envelope with the next variable, though, it looks for a hard carriage return, and the beginning of a new line, before matching the next set of variables to the variable names.

The result is that you wind up with two envelopes to redo. If the file were in human readable format, in contrast, you would have to redo every envelope after the mistake. In the address files, where there is only one address per file, this is a moot point, but it becomes important indeed in a long mailing list, where a mistake at the beginning can lead to much wasted time and effort.

Here, then, is our three address data file, DATAFILE.1. It is designed to work with an envelope or label file that assumes a maximum of five lines in any one address:

```
Big Bird,,,Sesame Street,New York,New York 10021          <
Santa Claus,,,General Delivery,North Pole, Wisconsin      <
,MicroPro International Corp.,,,33 San Pablo Avenue        <
San Rafael,California 94903                               <
```

There are several things to notice here. First, each line ends with a hard carriage return. This is important since MailMerge looks for a hard carriage return—and the beginning of a new line—each time it starts matching a new set of variables to the variable names.

Second, notice that the third address—for MicroPro—has been broken into two lines. This is a compromise between a MailMerge-readable and a human-readable format. On the one hand, it will work with Mail-Merge, and it will let MailMerge recover quickly if there are too many or too few commas in a line (assuming most addresses are on lines by themselves). On the other hand, it will still confuse a program like DataStar. The benefit from your point of view is that it lets you read the whole address at once instead of having the line run off the edge of the screen.

Notice also in the MicroPro address that there is no comma after the STREET variable at the end of the first line. Instead, the hard carriage return serves the function of the missing comma. This is important to remember if you decide to break an address into two or more lines; the end of each line—with its hard carriage return—will be read as the end of the variable. The break in the line, then, must never come in the middle of a variable, or else MailMerge will treat the one variable as two.

Confusing the issue somewhat is that you can just as easily end the broken line with or without a comma. In other words, each of the following two records will be treated exactly the same way by MailMerge, even though the first one has a comma and the second one doesn't.

```
,MicroPro International Corp.,,,33 San Pablo Avenue,       <
San Rafael,California 94903                               <

,MicroPro International Corp.,,,33 San Pablo Avenue        <
San Rafael, California 94903                              <
```

In general, you're safer putting the comma in than leaving it out. If you reform the record into one line, for instance, the comma will already be there, and you won't have to remember to put it in.

Finally, there is a warning to keep in mind. When you create a data file simply by opening a file in WordStar, then typing it in, you *must not let WordStar word wrap the lines.* If it word wraps with right justification on, WordStar will insert soft spaces in the lines. These soft spaces will confuse MailMerge, which will wind up printing garbage. In addition, whether right justification is on or not, word wrap will insert soft carriage returns. If these soft returns show up in the middle of a variable, MailMerge will treat them as hard carriage returns and break the variable in printing.

Basically, there are two ways to avoid this problem when you create or modify a data file: Turn word wrap off, or open the file with WordStar's **"N"** command, for "Open a *Non*-Document file." If you use the **"N"** option, the file will automatically come up with both word wrap and right justification off.

PRINTING THE ENVELOPES

Assuming you have managed to enter DATAFILE.1 correctly on the disk, here is the envelope file that goes with it.

FILE: MASSENV.MAS

For Printing any Number of Envelopes from a Data File

```
.. This file prints addresses directly from files on disk.
.. It assumes 6 variables, and addresses with 3–5 lines.
.PL 30 (For envelopes mounted on continuous tractor feed
..          paper with 5" from top of one envelope to the next.)
.MT 0
.AV "Name of Data File to use: ", FILENAME
.FI MASSENV.SLA
```

FILE: MASSENV.SLA

```
.DF & FILENAME&
.RV NAME, TITLE, COMPANY, STREET, CITY, STATE
.PO 40




&NAME/O&
&TITLE/O&
&COMPANY/O&
&STREET&
&CITY&, &STATE&
.PA
```

This file should look familiar. Except for the fact that it is broken into a master and slave file, it is virtually identical to what you should have wound up with as AUTOENV in the last chapter. The point is that when using the data file and read variable dot commands, MailMerge doesn't care whether an address file has one address in it or one thousand addresses. It will keep repeating the file, and printing envelopes, until it runs out of data. The file has to be broken into two parts in this case because Mail-

Merge will repeat the entire file each time—including the **.AV** command. If you don't want to stop and reanswer the question after each envelope, then, the **.AV** command line must go in a separate file from the **.DF** and **.RV** commands.

Notice in passing, incidentally, that you could change the data file command line to read ".DF DATAFILE.1," in which case you could delete the **.AV** command and join the two files. You also wouldn't have to enter the name of the mailing list each time you used it. The advantage of using the **.AV** command, though, is that it lets you use this same file with any number of different mailing lists.

USING MAILING LISTS FOR LETTERS

As you've probably guessed already, it is a small step from using mailing lists for producing envelopes to using data files for producing individualized form letters.

Here's an example: You are the publisher of a new guide called *Public Benefactors*. This book consists of short biographies of people and companies who qualify as having made "substantial contributions to the public good." You've compiled a long list of potential benefactors to fill out the book. Now you need to contact everyone on the list, both to get the information you need and to sell them a copy.

As part of the mailing, you want to include an individualized letter to each prospect. The letter file (minus the format commands) might look like the following.

```
.DF DATAFILE.2
.RV NAME, TITLE, COMPANY, STREET, CITY, STATE
.RV SALUTATION, BENEFICIAL-HOW
.SV DATE, April 1, 1985

&DATE&

&NAME/O&
&TITLE/O&
&COMPANY/O&
&STREET&
&CITY&, &STATE&
```

Dear &SALUTATION&:

I don't write fan letters very often, but in this case I must make an exception. Your work has been so beneficial in &BENEFICIAL-HOW& that I feel it is truly deserving of special recognition.

Keeping that in mind, I thought you should be listed in the next issue of Public Benefactors. I am, therefore, sending along some information about this guide, along with a questionnaire so you can provide the biographical information.

Should you decide to be listed, for the nominal fee of $20.00, you will be entitled to buy a copy of the guide for only $49.50, a fifty dollar savings over the list price of $99.50.

I look forward to hearing from you.

Sincerely,

Malcolm Fitzgerald Jones
Hype Expert
.PA

Aside from the five line address block, the body of this letter contains two additional variables: &SALUTATION&, and &BENEFICIAL-HOW&. I've put these in a second Read Variable command line only because a single .**RV** line would be too wide to print in this book.

The date here is a side issue. In this case, I used the set variable command to give it a value. You could as easily call the letter up with a file that asks for the date, then asks for the name of the file to print (see Chapter Six).

All that remains before you can print this letter is to set up DATA-FILE.2. Basically, this consists of starting with DATAFILE.1, and adding more information—namely the additional two variables for each letter.

DATAFILE.2, then, might look like this (the new variables are in boldface):

```
Big Bird,,,Sesame Street,New York,New York 10021              <
Big Bird,helping educate children                            <
Santa Claus,,,General Delivery,North Pole,Wisconsin          <
Mr. Claus,making children happy at Christmas                 <
,MicroPro International Corp.,,,33 San Pablo Avenue           <
San Rafael,California 94903                                   <
Friends at MicroPro,making the writer's life easier          <
```

One note about the format of data files. For reasons that are not at all clear, MailMerge 3.3 will not print properly if a record has been broken into more than one line, and one of those lines has only one field in it. This record, for example:

```
Field one, Field two                                         <
Field three, Field four, Field five                          <
Field six                                                    <
```

will print perfectly well with release 3.0, but not with release 3.3. Change it to this, though:

```
Field one, Field two                                         <
Field three, Field four                                      <
Field five, Field six                                        <
```

and the problem disappears.

At any rate, once you have this data file on disk, you can call up the form letter with MailMerge, and it will print three personalized letters, beginning with:

Dear Big Bird:
I don't write fan letters very often, but in this case I must make an exception. Your work has been so beneficial in helping educate children that I feel it is truly deserving of special recognition . . .

Having printed three letters (or three hundred letters, for that matter), all on fanfold paper, you now need the envelopes to go with them. In fact, we've worked our way back to the question of how to print the envelopes separately from the letters.

With DATAFILE.2 already on disk, this is not a problem. You can use a slightly modified version of AUTOENV to print the envelopes from the same data file as the letters. Simply change the **.RV** command in AUTOENV so that it reads:

.RV NAME, TITLE, COMPANY, STREET, CITY, STATE
.RV SALUTATION, BENEFICIAL-HOW

This, of course, is identical to the **.RV** command lines in the letter, which is only reasonable considering that both format files are reading the same data file. Of course, the last two variables don't show up in the format section of AUTOENV, but that won't make any difference. MailMerge will match the unused variables to the unused variable names, and otherwise ignore them.

We're not quite finished with the subject of printing envelopes separately from the letters they go with. There is a major difference between the situation we just dealt with and the situation we started with at the beginning of the last chapter. Here, we started with a mailing list you already had on disk, which you planned to use over and over. This is not the same as writing a batch of letters for one-time-only mailing, where you didn't start with a mailing list, and have no intention of keeping one on disk.

Even so, if I've laid the groundwork well enough, the solution to the original problem should be reasonably obvious by now.

When setting up your format files, do not use the **.AV** (ask for variable) prompts as part of the letter file. Instead, use them to create a data entry screen, and have the file write your responses to disk. (This is not quite as straightforward as it sounds, unfortunately, but we'll skip the details for the moment.)

Once you've created the new data file, you design both your letter file and your envelope file so they will get their variables from the data file. Then all you have to do is stand back and let MailMerge do its stuff, printing one set of letters and one set of envelopes. When it's done, erase the data file—if you are sure that you'll never need it again. And now we're just about done with the subject.

Except that in the last two chapters, we've touched on a much more important point. You can use MailMerge to create your data files—not just temporary data files, but all your data files. And that's what the next chapter is about.

10
Creating and Maintaining Data Files
USING MAILMERGE AND WORDSTAR

Uses Introduced
Creation of Data Files
Maintenance of Data Files
  Adding New Data to Existing Files
  Altering Existing Data

In the WordStar manual, MicroPro suggests that for small to moderate size mailing lists, WordStar's non-document edit mode is adequate to enter or update data. Having said that, they say very little more, apparently assuming you can figure out what to do—not to mention the most efficient way to do it.

What the manual doesn't mention is that the most efficient way to enter or maintain the data is often not with WordStar's edit mode, but rather with MailMerge. In fact, using MailMerge for data entry, and for certain kinds of updating, not only results in fewer mistakes, it makes it possible to work conveniently with much larger data files.

CREATING A DATA FILE

DATA ENTRY SCREENS

We've already talked about creating data files with MailMerge. In fact, we've already done it; the address files we created in Chapter Eight are data files, even though they are very short ones.

We ended Chapter Nine, also, with a quick suggestion of how to use the **.AV** command to create longer data files. I added the warning then that the procedure wasn't as straightforward as it ideally should be.

If you set out to create a file to serve as a data entry screen—call it MAILIST.DES (for data entry screen)—you will probably wind up with something like the following.

FILE: MAILIST.DES (Incomplete Version)

For creating mailing list data file

```
.AV "Name of Addressee: ", A1
.AV "Title: ", A2
.AV "Company Name: ", A3
.AV "Street and Number: ", A4
.AV "City and State: ", A5
.AV "Zip Code: ", A6
.AV "Salutation (Include Mr. or Ms. if using last name): ", A7
.PF off
.PL 1
.MT 0
.MB 0
.PO 0
"&A1&",&A2&,"&A3&",&A4&,"&A5&",&A6&,&A7&
.FI MAILIST.DES
#
```

This file consists of three sections: the **.AV** command lines, the format section, and a file insert command.

"City and State" are reunited as one variable (A5) in the first section, because there is a strong tendency to type the information that way (city, comma, state). The format section of the file, meanwhile, includes quotation marks around the variable so that MailMerge will automatically put quotes in the data file, without your having to remember to add them. This automatic entry of the quotes eliminates the problem that made us separate city and state to begin with. The format section also includes quotes around the variables for name, title, and company name, for the same reason.

There are several other important commands in the format section.

The page length is set to one line, so the file we end up with will consist of lines of data without any blank lines between them.

With this page length setting, the top and bottom margins must be set to zero to keep MailMerge from getting confused. (Setting the top and bottom margins to zero when printing to disk is generally a good idea anyway. It keeps WordStar from inserting unnecessary blank lines in the file.)

Page offset is also set to zero so that WordStar will start printing in column one instead of the default setting of column eight.

Finally, print-time line-forming is turned off so that MailMerge will not wrap a line in printing and run the risk of breaking a variable into two parts.

The file insert command at the end seems simple enough. It tells MailMerge to go back to the top of the file and start over again.

By all rights, this file should work. Unfortunately, it doesn't. Or, rather, it works, but only to a point.

The basic idea is right. To use this file, you turn off the file directory, then call up the file with MailMerge, answer "Y" to the "DISK FILE OUTPUT (Y/N):" prompt, and give an appropriate name for the data file when prompted for the "OUTPUT FILE NAME."

MailMerge then prompts you for the variables, you supply the answers, and MailMerge writes the responses to disk, following the instructions in the format section of the file.

Unfortunately, for our purposes MailMerge does not write to disk as you enter each response—or even each set of responses. Instead, it holds those responses in memory until, every so often, it writes a batch of information to disk.

This would not be a problem, except that when you're finished entering your data, and you abort the printing process by using the "P to Stop Printing" option, you also lose whatever data hasn't been written to disk yet.

TELLING MAILMERGE WHEN YOU'RE FINISHED ENTERING DATA

What you need to do is find a way to tell MailMerge not to abort printing, but to finish printing, so it will write the remaining data to disk rather than have it disappear into the jaws of forgetfulness.

There happens to be a simple way to do this.

If you have the conditional print command, you need only to replace the file insert command line with these four lines:

```
.AV "More Data (Y/N)? ", DATA, 1
.IF &DATA& ="N" .OR. &DATA& ="n" GOTO END
.FI MAILIST.DES
.EF END
```

If there is more data to enter, you answer "Y," MailMerge reads the File Insert command, and you are back to the beginning of the file.

If you answer "N," MailMerge will jump to the **.EF END** command line, write the remaining data to disk, and close the file.

If you do not have the conditional print commands, you can get the same effect with a variation on the conditional File Insert trick. In bare bones form, you need these three lines:

```
.AV DATA          M (Flag for MailMerge Command)
&DATA/0&         —(Flag for Overprint next line)
.FI MAILIST.DES   < (Flag for Hard Carriage Return)
```

Take a careful look at the flags in the right hand column. The **.AV** command line (the first line) shows the MailMerge flag, as you would expect. The **.FI** command line (the third line) does not. Instead, it shows the flag for a hard carriage return. What's happening here is that because of the overprint command in the middle line (entered with **^PM),** WordStar is not recognizing the dot of the **.FI** command as falling in the first column of a line.

Notice, though, that the variable on the second line is entered with the **"/0,"** or omit command. This means that if you are printing this file with MailMerge, and you hit RETURN in response to the "DATA?" prompt, this second line will be omitted. At that point, MailMerge will suddenly recognize the **.FI** as a dot command, and will obey it.

With these lines in the file, then, if you want to enter more data when you get to the "DATA?" prompt, you enter RETURN, and MailMerge will read and obey the file insert command. If you're finished, though, you enter any random character plus RETURN, and MailMerge will close the file.

There's one additional twist to this trick. If you enter "any random character" plus RETURN, MailMerge will—with one exception—print the character plus .FI MAILIST as the last two lines in the data file. This is a small enough price to pay, and can always be deleted, but there's also a way to avoid it. If you enter a period as the character, MailMerge will read the last two lines as an invalid dot command. It will then put an error message on the screen ("Invalid Dot Command Ignored"). But it will not put the extra lines in your file.

The following shows MAILIST.DES in a workable form, complete with instructions reminding you how to use it. (Notice also the clear screen command (**.CS**) at the top of the file to minimize visual confusion.)

FILE: MAILIST.DES (Complete Version)

For Entering Addresses into a Data File

```
.CS
.AV "Name of Addressee: ", A1
.AV "Title: ", A2
```

```
.AV "Company Name: " A3
.AV "Street and Number: ", A4
.AV "City and State: ", A5
.AV "Zip Code: ", A6
.AV "Salutation (Include Mr. or Ms. if using last name): ", A7
.PF off
.PL 1
.MT 0
.MB 0
.PO 0
"&A1&","&A2&","&A3&",&A4&,"&A5&",&A6&,&A7&
.AV "More Data (Y/N)? ",DATA,1
.IF &DATA& ="N" .OR. &DATA& ="n" GOTO END
.FI MAILIST.DES
.EF END
```

Here is the alternate ending for releases without the conditional print feature:

```
.DM If there is more data, hit RETURN
.DM Otherwise enter a PERIOD plus RETURN
.AV "to close the file and write all information to disk", DATA
&DATA/O&
.FI MAILIST.DES
```

Whichever version of MAILIST.DES you use, the file will work essentially the same way. You tell MailMerge to print it to disk, give it a file name to use, answer the prompts, tell MailMerge when you're finished, and you wind up with a data file in MailMerge readable format.

There are a few hints you should keep in mind when using MailMerge to create a data file.

First, and most important, when MailMerge asks you for the output file name, you have to be careful to pick a name that does not already exist on the disk. As I've pointed out elsewhere, unless you have release 3.3 or later, MailMerge will not only overwrite the already existing file, but it will overwrite without telling you about it. This is a good way to lose your data files—something you want to avoid.

Of course, if you have a later release of MailMerge, you don't have to worry about this; the program will warn you when you are about to overwrite a file. Still, a good habit to get into is to reserve a name strictly for the creation process, then rename the file immediately after you're finished. I use the file name TEMP for this. Not only is it easy to remember, as an abbreviation of "temporary," but if a file TEMP is already on disk I won't mind losing it, since the only other time I use this name is on files that are truly temporary.

Double Checking Data on Screen

Another important point is that you ought to double check your data after you've entered it. You can do this by adding a few lines to your file so it will show you what the address will look like. If you spot an error, Mail-Merge won't let you back up and correct it, but there is a way you can mark the incorrect entries. This makes it easier to find them later.

The format section of the file, then, becomes:

FILE: MAILIST.DES (Partial Example)

For Checking Data on the Screen, and Entering an Error Marker

```
.DM This is what your address will look like in printing
.DM except that blank lines within the address will be deleted
.DM
.DM      &A1&
.DM      &A2&
.DM      &A3&
.DM      &A4&
.DM      &A5&      &A6&
.DM
.DM      &A7&
.DM
.DM If this is correct, enter "RETURN"
.DM Otherwise enter "xxx RETURN" to mark the entry as incorrect.
.AV "Correct? ", A8
&A8/0&,"&A1&","&A2&","&A3&",&A4&,"&A5&",&A6&,&A7&
```

Once the incorrect entries are marked in the file, there are several ways to use them in making corrections. The obvious choice is to wait until you're finished entering the data, then open the data file in edit mode, use the search function to find the error markers, then make the corrections directly on the data file itself. If you do this, though, you run the risk of making further mistakes while mucking around with the data file.

The second choice is the safer one. Re-enter the data immediately on the next pass through the data entry screen. You can use **^R,** or recall, to re-enter the correct answers, which means you only have to retype the incorrect ones. Correcting the data file with WordStar's edit mode then becomes a simple matter of finding the error markers and deleting the incorrect records. This means less mucking around in the file, and less opportunity to accidentally destroy your data.

If you have the conditional print feature, there's an even safer and more elegant way to delete the incorrect records later—by letting the conditional print command do the work for you. Here is a file that will run through the data file, copying correct entries to another file, and skipping over any records that start with the error marker.

FILE: ERROR.FIX

For Deleting Incorrect Entries from a Data File

```
.DF DATAFILE
.RV A8, A1, A2, A3, A4, A5, A6, A7
.IF &A8& = "xxx" .OR. &A8& = "XXX" GOTO END
.PF Off
.PO 0
.PL 1
.MT 0
.MB 0
"&A1&", "&A2&", "&A3&", "&A4&", "&A5&", "&A6&", "&A7&"
.EF END
```

This file should be self-explanatory.

You could also use the conditional file insert trick to do much the same thing manually, having MailMerge display each record on the screen, then ask you whether to delete it or not. If your files are large, however, you are likely to make mistakes. If you don't have the conditional print feature, you are better off using WordStar's search function in the edit mode.

DOUBLE-CHECKING DATA ON PAPER

In addition to double-checking your entries on the screen at entry time, it's also a good idea to check them by printing them on paper. Not only does the printed version serve to check the file, moreover, it also serves as a last ditch backup. If your computer is down and you need to find an address, the printout will provide it for you. If something disastrous happens so that your data disks and their backups are ruined, the hard copy will at least keep you from losing the information entirely.

At any rate here's a MailMerge file that will read DATAFILE and print the data on paper in address format.

FILE: PRINT.DTA

For Printing a Data File in Human Readable Format

```
.DF DATAFILE.3
.RV A1,A2,A3,A4,A5,A6,A7
.CP 7
&A1/0&
&A2/0&
```

```
&A3/0&
&A4&
&A5&      &A6&

&A7&
#
#
```

This file needs the two additional blank lines after the salutation line (A7), so the addresses will be separated on the paper. The conditional page command insures that MailMerge will not break an address that falls at the end of a page.

MAINTAINING A DATA FILE

Creating a data file is one thing. Maintaining it is something else again. There will be times when you need to add information to the file, or change what's already there, or even delete something altogether. All these possibilities come under the heading of "Maintaining the File." Some kinds of file maintenance are simple with WordStar or MailMerge, others are not.

ADDING INFORMATION TO A FILE

Let's start with adding data to a file. This can mean one of two things.

Each line in the data file—that is, each set of variables—is known as a *record*. Adding data to a file may mean adding new records, or it may mean adding new variables to records that are already there.

Adding new records is certainly easy. The first step is to use MAILIST.DES to create a data file that contains the new records only. Then, after correcting errors, you only need to combine the new file with the old one. You can do this in WordStar (by opening either file and reading the other into it using the read a file command), or you can go to your operating system and use PIP or an equivalent copying utility to join the two files. (In CP/M, the command would take the form PIP NEWFILE=OLDDATA,NEWDATA. If your data file is named MAILING.DTA, for example, you could use the command:

```
PIP MAILING.DTA=MAILING.DTA[V],TEMP
```

This would give you a new version of MAILING.DTA that joins the old version with the new file TEMP. The [V], for "verify," tells CP/M to double check the new copy. Details will vary with different operating systems, but regardless of the details, make sure you have a backup copy of the original MAILING.DTA file and the TEMP file in case something goes wrong in the copying.)

Adding new fields, or variables, to records that already exist is nearly as easy as adding new records. You may need to do this if, for instance, you've written a form letter that you want to send to everyone on your mailing list, but have included some variables in it that don't exist in your data file as yet.

You might, for instance, have included this sentence: "We believe that as a &WORK-DESCRIPTION& you will be particularly interested in our new product." Now you have to add the variable &WORK-DESCRIP-TION& to each record in the data file.

What follows is a file that will add the new field for you.

FILE: MODIFY.DTA

For Adding New Fields to Already Existing Data Files

```
.CS
.DF DATAFILE.OLD
.RV A1, A2, A3, A4, A5, A6, A7
.DM This is the Data as it is currently on Disk
.DM
.DM     &A1&
.DM     &A2&
.DM     &A3&
.DM     &A4&
.DM     &A5&     &A6&
.DM
.DM     &A7&
.DM
.DM
.AV "Describe Prospect's Work: " WORK-DESCRIPTION
.PL 1
.MT 0
.MB 0
.PO 0
.PF off
"&A1&","&A2&","&A3&",&A4&,"&A5&",&A6&,&A7&,&WORK-DESCRIPTION&,
```

This file does the work in four steps. It reads the data from the old file, a single record at a time, it shows you the data on screen so you know which record is being read, it asks you for the additional information, and finally, it writes all the information—old and new—to a new file. It will keep repeating this cycle until it runs out of data in the original file.

REWRITING A FILE: ADDING, DELETING, OR REARRANGING FIELDS

What we just did, in adding fields to a file, was rewrite the file. This is a powerful trick. You can use it not just to add fields, but to delete fields or rearrange them as well.

To *delete* fields in a data file, just eliminate the unwanted variables from the format section of the file. (But not from the read variable command.)

Similarly, to *rearrange* the fields in a data file, you only need to rearrange the variables in the format section.

You can add, delete, and rearrange fields, moreover, all in one pass.

If you are not adding any fields, you can skip the part where you display data on the screen. MailMerge will simply rewrite the data, reading from the one file, and writing to the other.

DELETING OR CHANGING RECORDS IN A DATA FILE WITH THE CONDITIONAL PRINT COMMANDS

Changing data in your files is a common need. A company folds, and you need to delete it from the file. Somebody moves, and you need to change an address. A contact at some company changes, and you need to change a name.

If you have the conditional print commands available, any of these changes can be done with surprising ease.

Let's try a specific example.

Bob Jones has just left the firm JJ&B, and is being replaced by Bill Martinson. You need to find the appropriate record, and change two fields: the NAME field, and the SALUT field.

What you have to do, then, is tell MailMerge what record to find, and how to change it. If you know each field in the record, or at least enough fields to identify it unambiguously, you can write a short file to do that.

In this case, the name Bob Jones, might not be enough to identify the record; it's a common enough name so that it might show up elsewhere in the data file. "Bob Jones" and "JJ&B" together, though, should do the trick.

Here is the file you might write for MailMerge. To make it easier to follow, I've interspersed comments (in boldface) between sections of the file.

FILE: CONVERT1

For Finding a Specific Record, and Changing One or More Fields in That Record

.PO 0
.MT 0
.MB 0
.PL 1
.PF Off
First, tell MailMerge to read the file.
.DF DATAFILE
.RV NAME, CO, STREET, CITY-AND-STATE, ZIP, SALUT

Next, tell MailMerge what record it's looking for.
.EX &NAME& = "Bob Jones" .AND. &CO& = "JJ&B" GOTO WRITE-TO-DISK
The following message will be displayed when the record is matched.
.DM   *******R E C O R D   M A T C H E D********
The following changes will only be made on the record (or records) that match the conditional statement.
.SV NAME, Bill Martinson
.SV SALUT, Mr. Martinson
.EF WRITE-TO-DISK
"&NAME&", "&CO&", &STREET&, "&CITY-AND-STATE&", &ZIP&, &SALUT&

Putting the message on the screen telling you that the record has been matched isn't absolutely necessary, but it is a nice touch. If the message does not show up, you know that something has gone wrong. Similarly, if the message shows up more than once, you know that the record has been matched more than once. This may mean that you have a duplicate record, or it may mean that you inadvertently changed additional records. Either way, you should go back to your file and check it out, using WordStar's search command in the edit mode.

If you'd rather avoid the possibility of having to use WordStar's edit mode, though, you can—with only a slightly more complicated file.

This next file will display records on the screen when a match is made, then ask you for permission before making any changes. If you don't give permission, it then asks you if you want to delete the record. If you say no, the file writes the record to disk as is.

Because this file shows you the record before doing anything to it, you can use the file to change or delete records even when you can't identify them conclusively in the conditional statement. You can also use the deletion option to eliminate duplications.

Once again, the file is broken into sections with added comments in boldface.

FILE: CONVERT2

For Finding a Specific Record, to Change One or More
Fields in That Record, or Delete the Record Entirely

.PO 0
.MT 0
.MB 0
.PL 1
.PF Off
First, tell MailMerge to read the file
.DF DATAFILE
.RV NAME, CO, STREET, CITY-AND-STATE, ZIP, SALUT
Next, tell MailMerge what record it's looking for.
.EX &NAME& = "Bob Jones" .AND. &CO& = "JJ&B" GOTO WRITE-TO-DISK

When the record is matched, MailMerge will display the following:

```
.DM      *******R E C O R D   M A T C H E D********
.DM
.DM              Name: &NAME&
.DM           Company: &CO&
.DM            Street: &STREET&
.DM    City and State: &CITY-AND-STATE&
.DM               Zip: &ZIP&
.DM         Salutation: &SALUT&
.DM
.AV "Do you want to change this record (Y/N)? ", CHANGE, 1
.EX &CHANGE& = "Y" .OR. &CHANGE& = "y" GOTO DELETE
```

The two changes that come next will only be made if the record matches the original conditional statement, and if the answer to the above question is YES.

```
.SV NAME, Bill Martinson
.SV SALUT, Mr. Martinson
.IF &CHANGE& = "Y" .OR. &CHANGE& = "y" GOTO WRITE-TO-DISK
.EF DELETE
```

The next question will only be asked if the record matches the original conditional statement, and if you told MailMerge not to change the fields.

NOTICE that if you answer the question with anything but "Y" or "y", the record will not be deleted. The way the file is designed, the current value of CHANGE is NO, or else you would not be asked whether you want to delete the record.

```
.AV "Do you want to DELETE this record (Y/N)? ", CHANGE, 1
.EX &CHANGE& = "Y" .OR. &CHANGE& = "y" GOTO WRITE-TO-DISK
```

Now, if the answer is yes, the file will double check before DELETING the record. But first it will reset the value of CHANGE to "N", so the default here will once again be "do not delete."

```
.SV CHANGE, N
.DM Are you sure you want to delete this record?
.DM Enter Y for Yes.
.AV "Any other entry will prevent deletion. ", CHANGE, 1
.IF &CHANGE& = "Y" .OR. &CHANGE& = "y" GOTO END
.EF WRITE-TO-DISK
"NAME&", "&CO&", &STREET&, "CITY-AND-STATE&", &ZIP&, &SALUT&
.EF END
```

Once you've created a CONVERT file for any given data file, you can use it as a format file for future CONVERT files. In fact, if you're ambitious enough, you can create an all purpose CONVERT file for any given data file. You can even design it so it will ask you which fields to match in the conditional statement, go on to create the conditional statement for you, and will then show you the matches, ask which fields to change, and ask what to change them to. The file that does all that is a bit too long and complicated to go into here, but you can do it if you want to, with the techniques you already know.

DELETING OR CHANGING RECORDS IN A DATA FILE
WITHOUT THE CONDITIONAL PRINT COMMANDS

If you don't have the conditional print commands available, you could use the conditional File Insert trick to create a file that was more or less equivalent to CONVERT2. You could then "page" through the file, record-by-record, looking for matches. As with the ERROR.FIX file we looked at before though, there is just too much opportunity for making mistakes this way. Here again, if you don't have the conditional print commands, you are better off using WordStar's edit mode to make the changes.

Before we get to the details of how to do that, let's back up a bit and take another look at the possibilities for rewriting a file.

The fact that you can rearrange data when rewriting files not only means that you can change the order of the variables within a given record, it means you can easily change a data file from one format to another. And that raises a question about whether you really need to keep files in the MailMerge-readable format in the first place. It certainly eliminates the compatibility argument, since it means you can convert your files to the standard MailMerge-readable format at any time. And you can do it easily.

Here is a file that will convert any format at all into the MailMerge-readable format.

FILE:HUMANTO.MM

For Converting a Human-Readable Format to
a MailMerge-Readable File

```
.DF DATAFILE.OLD
.RV A1, A2, A3, A4, A5, A6, A7, A8
.PL 1
.MT 0
.MB 0
.PO 0
.PF off
"&A1&","&A2&","&A3&","&A4&","&A5&","&A6&","&A7&","&A8&"
```

This is an all-purpose conversion file. You need only make sure that the number of variables matches the number of fields in the file being converted. Also, notice the quotes around each variable in the format section, rather than selected variables only. This insures that the conversion will work properly with any data file, regardless of what's in it.

The question of data file format is important because it affects the maintenance of the file. Specifically, it affects the ease with which you can make changes using WordStar's edit mode.

Of course it's easy enough to open any data file with WordStar (using the "N" option).

WordStar's find command (^QF), moreover, makes it easy to find the proper record, so that's not a problem either. The problem comes in typing the corrections.

If you are using the MailMerge-readable format, your data will look like this:

```
Big Bird,,,Sesame Street,"New York, New York",10021,Dea+
Santa Claus,,,General Delivery,"North Pole, Wisconsin"+
,MicroPro International Corp.,,33 San Pablo Avenue,"San+
```

except that it will fill the entire screen. Unfortunately, the human brain has trouble making sense out of so many bits and pieces of unconnected information. Also, notice the + flags in the right hand column, indicating that the lines continue off screen. The horizontal scroll, bouncing back and forth, is an added complication in trying to make sense out of the file.

All this makes it easy to make mistakes—accidentally deleting a comma, a word, or even an entire line without realizing it. This format also makes it hard to see the mistake once you've made it. Even if you realize you've made a mistake, the fact that these are unconnected bits of information may make it close to impossible to undo it. It is very easy, for instance, to hit ^Y twice and delete two lines when you meant to hit ^T to delete two words. Assuming you realize you've done this, there is no easy way to recover the lost lines.

One way to minimize the problem is to use the find and replace command (^QA) whenever possible rather than the find command. This can be used for changing or deleting a field. It cannot be used, though, for deleting an entire record.

This command must also be used with care. If you're changing "Mr. Jones" to "Bob," you want to be sure that you're replacing the correct "Mr. Jones" in the correct record. Here again, the MailMerge-readable format makes mistakes more likely by making it harder to read the screen.

Another way to minimize the risk of errors is to format the information in a more human-readable form. This doesn't necessarily mean formatting the records as if they were names and addresses on envelopes. It does mean breaking each record into two or three lines, so that, most of the time at least, the entire record will show on the screen at once. It also means putting a blank line between the records, so you can see all the fields in any given record as a related unit of information.

The format section of your data entry file, then, might look like this:

```
&NAME&,&TITLE&,&COMPANY-NAME&,
&STREET&,"&CITY-STATE&",&ZIP&,
&SALUTATION&,&KIND-OF-WORK&,
#
```

In which case your data file would look like this:

```
Big Bird,,,
Sesame Street,"New York,New York", 10021,
Mr. Bird, Performer,

Santa Claus,,,
General Delivery,"North Pole, Wisconsin",,
Mr. Claus, giver of gifts,
```

,,MicroPro International Corp.,
33 San Pablo Avenue,"San Rafael, California",,
Friends at MicroPro, producers of computer software,

Clearly, this format is much easier to read, which makes it much easier to correct without adding new mistakes.

What you've given up here is the ability to recover automatically from errors if too many or too few commas somehow get in the file. But you can get that back too.

Automatic recovery from errors will reappear whenever you use the one-line, MailMerge-readable format. You can use the format as often as you like, in the form of a "null record"—a record containing nothing but null variables.

In this case, a null record would consist of eight commas (to mark the end of each of the eight variables in each record). The easiest way to get this into the data file is by adding it to the format section of the data entry file, so that the format section reads:

&NAME&,&TITLE&,&COMPANY-NAME&,
&STREET&,"&CITY-STATE&",&ZIP&,
&SALUTATION&,&KIND-OF-WORK&,

,,,,,,,,

This line of commas will show up between each entry in the data file.

Please note that in order for this to work, the MailMerge file that uses this data file to print from should ideally contain a conditional command telling it to skip printing when it finds a null record.

If you don't have the conditional print commands, another possibility is to make sure that the MailMerge file doesn't contain any text but the variable names—not even a comma or period. Those variable names, moreover, must each include the omit command. Otherwise, each time MailMerge reads a null record, it will obediently print a form, or letter, or label, or whatever, complete with null variables.

If the format file must have additional text, though, and if you don't have the conditional print commands, a good compromise might be to use a null record every ten or twenty records. (You can either enter these manually, or set up the data entry file with the appropriate format.) This guarantees a certain percentage of bad printouts, but it also guarantees against total disaster.

SELECTING RECORDS WITH MAILMERGE

There is one other file maintenance function that you can do with MailMerge: Selection.

There are times when you need to select a particular set of records from your data file. You might, for example, want a list of all architects on your mailing list—or all architects who live in New Jersey. With the conditional print command, generating the list would be trivial. The file for it would look like the following.

FILE: SELECT

For Selection Operations with the Conditional Print Command

(NOTE: The conditional commands are broken into two lines in this file only because they would be too wide to fit here otherwise. You can join them into one line with **.AND.** Notice, though, how you can string conditional statements together this way when they would otherwise go beyond the one hundred character maximum length.)

```
.DF DATAFILE
.RV A1, A2, A3, A4, A5, STATE, A7, WORK-DESCRIPTION
.EX &WORK-DESCRIPTION& = "Architect" GOTO END
.EX &STATE& = "N.J." GOTO END
&A1&  &A2&  &A3&  &A4&  &A5&  &A7&
.EF END
```

Here again, you can do nearly the same thing with the conditional File Insert trick.

FILE: SELECT.MAS

*For Selection Operations Using the **.FI** Command*

(This is the master file; notice it will only pass control to the next file if &WORK-DESCRIPTION& is, in fact, "Architect." Otherwise it will read the next record.)

```
.DF DATAFILE
.RV A1, A2, A3, A4, A5, STATE, A7, WORK-DESCRIPTION
.FI &WORK-DESCRIPTION&.SLA
#
```

FILE: ARCHITEC.SLA

(This file will only pass control to the next file if &STATE& is "N.J." Otherwise, it will pass control back to SELECT.MAS, which will go to the next record.)

```
.FI &STATE&
```

FILE: N.J.

(This file will only print the information if the record has passed through the sieve of the last two files.)

&A1& &A2& &A3& &A4& &A5& &A7&

This is a little clumsier than using the conditional print feature, but it will work. Be aware, though, that there are some things you cannot do with the File Insert command. You cannot, for example, imitate this selection command:

.IF &AMT-OWED& $>=$ 5000 GOTO

MAILING LISTS AS DATA BASES

You've probably noticed that in the last chapter or so I've stopped referring to "mailing lists" and "names and addresses," and have started talking instead about "data files" and "records."

The point is, there is no real difference between a mailing list and any other data base. If you can use WordStar and MailMerge to create and maintain mailing lists, then, you can also use them to create and maintain data bases in general.

This brings us to the hefty subject of data base management.

11

Using WordStar/MailMerge as a Data Base Program

Concepts Introduced
"Index Card" Programs
    vs.
"Real" Data Base Programs

Uses Introduced
Using WordStar/MailMerge to Enter,
   Maintain, and "Index Card" Data
   Base—Quote File Example
Index Files

At this point, you already know quite a bit about data bases, just from what we've gone over in the last two chapters. You should, for instance, have a good sense of what fields, records, and files are, and what a data entry screen is. It won't hurt, though, to start with some basic definitions.

    To begin with, a data base is a collection of information, pure and simple. The term legitimately applies to any collection of information: a mailing list, a stack of letters, an encyclopedia, or your last ten years' worth of tax records.

Similarly, a data base management system is any organized approach to handling the information in a data base. Here again, you can apply the term to any approach to handling information. (Or any organized approach, at least. If it's not organized, it's not a system.) Here again, it doesn't matter what the information is or how it's stored. It can be on disk, paper, or index cards. It can be kept in a file cabinet, a card catalog, or a shoe box.

Finally, a data base program, for our purposes at least, is any computer program that helps you organize and manage information.

(A short warning: These are very basic, all-encompassing definitions. As such, they simplify things tremendously. Data base aficionados talk about "data base management systems" and "file management systems." This is a distinction that's not worth going into for our purposes, but you should know that such distinctions exist.)

DATA BASE PROGRAMS

What we've been doing up to this point—working with a mailing list—is a reasonably typical approach to handling information. Most microcomputer data base programs—including dBASE II, The Formula, and MicroPro's InfoStar, for instance—work in much the same way.

This doesn't mean that there is no difference between using Word-Star/MailMerge and using a "real" data base program. It's just that the differences lie in the ease with which you can handle the data—not in the way the data is organized.

To change entries with a data base program, for instance, you don't have to rewrite the entire data file as you make each change. The program finds the record you're looking for and displays it for you, along with the data entry screen. You make the change, or changes, and the program modifies the data file. Because it does not have to rewrite the entire file each time you make a change, though, the process is much faster than doing the equivalent with conditional print commands in MailMerge.

The point, though, is that whether you are using WordStar/Mail-Merge or a "real" data base program, the information itself is organized the same way. The approach to handling that information (as opposed to the implementation of that approach) remains the same.

In each case, you start by designing a form, or data entry screen. These forms include questions (prompts), and blank spaces (fields). You answer the questions for each item in your data base, and the set of answers for each item becomes a record.

Retrieving a particular record becomes a matter of picking a key field to search through—a name, perhaps, or a record number—and finding the record that matches the key word you're searching for.

USING WORDSTAR/MAILMERGE AS A DATA BASE PROGRAM: LIMITATIONS

Basically, you already know how to use WordStar/MailMerge as a data base program. If you want to organize some other information besides mailing lists—personnel records, medical claims, or whatever—all you have to do is create an appropriate MailMerge file to serve as the data entry screen. Before you do that, though, you should also know what the limitations are in using WordStar and MailMerge alone.

To begin with, you should find that you can handle a reasonably large data file without much trouble—especially if you have the conditional print commands available. "Reasonably large" is a relative term. You'd probably like something more specific. The problem is, the maximum size file that you can conveniently maintain depends on two things. First, it depends on your computer's speed, memory size, and disk access time. Second, it depends on what you need to do with the information.

In general, if you're using floppy disks and do not have the conditional print feature, the "maximum-sized convenient file" is whatever will fit in your computer memory at one time. With anything larger, the time involved in reading from and writing to disk makes search operations intolerably long. Even so, this can still translate to a file with anywhere from several hundred records to over a thousand records in it—depending on how much memory is in your computer and how long each record is.

At the other extreme, many systems are now equipped with disk emulators. These emulators use the same kind of electronic memory that you'll find in your computer's main memory, but they are set up so that your computer will treat them as if they were disks. Because they are fully electronic, though, they cut down disk access time by a factor of about one hundred.

A factor of one hundred means that something that would ordinarily take you ten minutes to do with a floppy disk will take you six seconds with a disk emulator. This is a tremendous advantage whenever you're doing something that is disk intensive—meaning that most of the computer's time is spent reading from or writing to disk. If you have one of these on your system, your maximum-size convenient file may be long indeed.

No matter how fast your system is, though, there is the second factor to consider. There are certain things that you cannot do conveniently with WordStar and MailMerge, and other things that you cannot do at all.

In particular, you have no way to sort your data file.

Sorting is simply a matter of putting your records in some kind of order, alphabetically or numerically. A good data base program will let you sort your data by any field, so you can put it in alphabetical order by last name, or by state, or numeric order by zip code—whichever you happen to need at the moment. It will also let you sort on more than one field at a time, so you can put your data in order alphabetically by name within each state, if you need to.

The only way to do this with WordStar and MailMerge files is to buy (or write) a separate sorting program.

Of course, there are some applications where you may never need the ability to sort, and if you don't need it you won't miss it. If you find yourself running up against limitations, though, then you know it's time to get another program. Which program and which kind of program, depends very much on your individual needs.

There's another capability that you don't have with MailMerge unless you have the conditional print commands—the ability to retrieve your records along with the data entry screen (or something that serves the same purpose, as with CONVERT2 in Chapter Ten). On a short, self-explanatory record (like the name and address on a mailing list) this is not a problem. On a long or complicated record, though, this can be confusing. If you can't match the fields to the questions they go with, it's hard to do anything useful with the information.

Of course, you can always create a MailMerge output file that contains the original questions. This can read the data file with .DF and .RV commands, then print a series of completed forms. But that means you have to work with the printed forms, not with the data file. This pretty much defeats the purpose of putting the information in your computer in the first place.

Finally, you should be aware that many data base programs have capabilities to do things automatically that you have to do manually with WordStar/MailMerge.

In entering data, for instance, many programs will do some simple math for you. This means you can enter a price on an invoice, and the program will automatically compute the tax. Most data base programs also do simple error checking. You can tell them, for example, not to accept letters for a field that is supposed to contain only numbers. In some of the more sophisticated programs, you can even change the same data in two different files at the same time. You set up a master data file and a subset data file. Make a change in the master file, and the program automatically makes the same change in the subset file.

This is just a sampling of some of the features that you will find in "real" data base programs that you won't find in WordStar/MailMerge. But here again, if your application is a simple one, you may never need these more sophisticated capabilities, and never miss them.

"INDEX CARD" PROGRAMS

The "standard" data base programs that we've been discussing represent one approach to handling information. The most important feature of that approach, for our purposes, is that it uses fields: It both stores and retrieves information in terms of field. There are other programs available, though, that use a different approach altogether. These are often sold as

"Index Card" programs, because they do essentially what an index card filing system does.

With an index card program you don't use fields at all. Instead, you are free to enter the information in any form that's appropriate—a paragraph of text, for instance. More important, you are also free to enter a series of key words, without worrying about which words go in which fields. (A note of warning here to avoid confusion. There are programs on the market that store and retrieve information in fields, but call themselves index card programs because they hold about as much information as an index card. For our purposes, these are not index card programs—they are "standard" data base programs with limited capability. What we are interested in here are programs with free-form entry, and no fields. The term "index card program" may not be the ideal one, but it seems to be the best available.)

It might be helpful here to compare the typical index card program with a real index card filing system. You might, for instance, keep a quote file on index cards. Whenever you run across a quote that you like, you write it down, along with the source and the name of the person being quoted. Then you pick a key word, and file the card alphabetically.

The problem comes in picking the key word.

As a rotten speller, for example, I've always been partial to this quote:

Any man who can't think of more than one way to spell a word can't have too good an imagination.

Thomas Jefferson

Would you file this under "Jefferson," or "Spelling," or "Bad Spelling?"

Or what about Einstein's famous quote objecting to quantum theory:

God does not play dice with the universe.

Would you file this under "Einstein," or "Science," or "Quantum Theory," or "Quantum Mechanics?"

The point here is that if you use real index cards, and you want to index an entry under more than one key word, you need to write a separate index card for each key word.

With an index card program, though, you can enter as many key words as you like, and retrieve the quote under any one of them.

It would be essentially impossible to put a quote file on a standard, field-oriented data base program. The problem is twofold. First, the quotes will each be different lengths, but a standard data base program requires that field sizes be the same for all records in the data base.

Even more of a problem, though, is the question of data retrieval. To retrieve an entry with a standard data base program, you not only have to tell it the key word to look for, you have to tell it which field the key word is in. This works nicely if you are looking for a company name in a mailing list, or a social security number in a personnel record. It does not work on something like a quote file, where there is no way to know beforehand which key words will go in which fields—and no easy way to keep track of what you did afterwards, much less be consistent about it.

With index card programs, though, this doesn't matter. You simply enter the key words in any order as they occur to you. You then can retrieve the quote under any one of the words, or any combination of them. This gives you the ability to find all related quotes at once by subject, or find any individual quote you're looking for under any of several subjects.

Using WordStar/MailMerge as an "Index Card" Program

WordStar and MailMerge can be used as an index card program as well as a "standard" data base program. In some ways, in fact, they are better suited for use as an index card program.

In particular, since index card data files generally follow free form entry, the lack of a data entry screen is rarely a problem in making sense out of the information later.

The simplest way to create and use an index card data file is to enter the information using WordStar's edit mode, then use the find command (^QF) when you find something.

With the quote file, for instance, you might create a data file that looks like this:

Any man who can't think of more than one way to spell a word can't have too good an imagination.

Thomas Jefferson

JEFFERSON / SPELLING / BAD SPELLING

God does not play dice with the universe.

Albert Einstein

EINSTEIN / SCIENCE / QUANTUM THEORY / QUANTUM MECHANICS

It's important to include key words and phrases separately, since many of the keys don't show up in the quote being indexed. I've capitalized the key words to make them stand out from the quotes themselves, and separated individual words and phrases with a slash to make them easier to read. By being consistent about capitalizing the key words, incidentally, it also becomes slightly easier to use WordStar's find command. You can answer the "FIND?" prompt in uppercase and not have to tell WordStar to ignore case.

Index Files

The obvious problem with this approach is that the data file will tend to get much too large much too quickly. The length of an average quote is much longer, for instance, than the length of the average record in a mail-

---

ing list. Yet the maximum convenient size of the data file will be the same. This means that if your system can deal conveniently with two or three hundred names on a mailing list, it may only be able to deal with seventy or eighty quotes in a quote file.

There's a way to ease this restriction on the size of your data file, though. Change it from a data file to an index file. Paradoxically, this means leaving the quotes out of the file. You can put them in another file (or files). You can even put them on index cards. But whatever you do with the quotes themselves, you identify them with an index number (or record number, or card number, or whatever else you want to call it), and you include the index number along with the key words in the index file.

In this particular case, it's probably easiest to put the quotes themselves on index cards. If you do that, your index/data file (entered with WordStar) would look like this:

Card 1/JEFFERSON / SPELLING / BAD SPELLING

Card 2/ EINSTEIN / SCIENCE / QUANTUM THEORY / QUANTUM MECHANICS

To use this index file, you open it in WordStar, then use the find command (^QF) to look for your key words. Each time you make a match, you can either mark down the card number, or thumb through your index cards to look at the quote. Then you use the ^L command to move to the next match.

If you're searching for a specific quote, you'll find that the other key words in any given entry function as a timesaver. If, for instance, you're looking specifically for the spelling quote from Jefferson, you can search for "Jefferson," and ignore any matches that don't also have "spelling" listed as a key word.

Although we've wound up putting the quotes back on index cards in this particular example, we could also have left them on disk in a separate file. If, for example, you were indexing letters that were written on the computer in the first place, you might want to cut down the number of entries in the disk directory by joining several letters in each of several data files. When you wanted to retrieve a letter (or letters) on any given subject, you could then use the index file to tell you not only which letter to look at, but which data file to find it in—and even which disk to find the data file on.

At the other extreme, you could use the index file to keep track of books, for example, using the key words to remind you which book or books to look in when searching for information. (You may recognize this as an electronic version of a library card catalog.)

This basic concept of using an index file, then, does much more than simply increase the number of entries you can deal with in a single disk file. It gives you a way to index correspondence, articles, books, research notes, or anything else where the information you need to keep track of is much longer than you can type into a data file.

If you create an index file for something like books or articles, you will find that the entries tend to be longer than they would be in something like a quote file. For instance, with an article, in addition to including key words, you have to identify the article, the magazine it's in, its page number, and possibly include a sentence or two describing the article.

This, of course, brings us back to the limitation on the maximum convenient size for a data file. Once again, the number of entries you can conveniently deal with depends on your computer system.

This also brings us to the end of the road as far as the possibilities for using WordStar and MailMerge as a data base program. By now we've pretty well covered both the capabilities and limitations of using WordStar/ MailMerge alone. You should have a good idea of what they can do and can't do, and you should have a sense of what's worth doing on your own system, and what's not worth the effort.

It's time to move on to a slightly different subject.

12

Creating a Screen for an Index Card Program

Uses Introduced
Using MailMerge with Another Program
Using MailMerge with an Index Card Retrieval System
A Photo File Data Base
Using an Index Card Program with MailMerge to Provide Selection Capability

---

Until now, we have dealt exclusively with MailMerge and WordStar. Some of the most intriguing applications for MailMerge, though, involve other programs. In many cases you can effectively increase the capabilities of both MailMerge and of whatever other program you are using.

One possible use of MailMerge is in combination with an index card program. Up to this point, it's been enough to talk about these programs in general. If we're going to talk about details, though, we need to use actual examples, and that means using a specific program for the examples.

For the rest of this chapter, then, we are going to look at how you might use MailMerge with a specific program—Superfile from FYI, Inc. Most of the concepts in this chapter will work for other index card programs as well, though details will vary of course.

A Quick Look at Superfile
as an Index Card Program

FYI does not bill Superfile as an index card program. They call it a "free format information filing and retrieval system." This is somewhat more than just a matter of semantics. The implication in calling something an index card program is that each entry is limited to what could fit on an index card. With Superfile, the only limits on the length of any individual entry are your good sense and, ultimately, your disk capacity.

Our definition of an index card program, though, does not include any mention of length for the entries; it is concerned instead with the approach to handling the information. Superfile, with free-form entry, no fields, and retrieval by key words, certainly qualifies on that score.

Using Superfile to manage a quote file, for example, is not all that different from using WordStar alone to manage a quote file, just more convenient.

To begin with, Superfile has no editing capabilities, which means you have to use WordStar (or some other word processor) to create the data file in the first place. For a quote file, this means typing the quotes, just as you would if you were planning to use WordStar alone to retrieve them afterwards.

One thing Superfile does insist on in the way of format is that the key words come at the end of the entry, and that the individual key words and phrases be separated by slashes. This is exactly the format we used before in creating a quote file to use with WordStar alone. When we did it before, though, it was a matter of choice and convenience. We could just as easily have put the key words before each entry, and separated the keys with some other symbol. When using Superfile, we don't have the choice.

The only additional constraints with Superfile are that the beginning of each entry must be marked with ***C,** the beginning of the key words must be marked with ***K,** and the end of the entry must be marked with ***E.**

Here, then, is the same quote file we used before, but this time set up for Superfile:

*C
>   Any man who can't think of more than one way to spell a word can't have too good an imagination.

>   Thomas Jefferson

*K JEFFERSON / SPELLING / BAD SPELLING
*E

*C
God does not play dice with the universe.
>   Albert Einstein

*K EINSTEIN / SCIENCE / QUANTUM THEORY / QUANTUM MECHANICS
*E

So far, we haven't done anything very differently than we would do if we were using WordStar alone to build a data file. All we've done, in fact, is add markers to designate the beginning and end of each entry, and the beginning of the key words within each entry.

The next step in using Superfile is to build an index file. Here again, the concept is pretty much the same as creating an index file for use with WordStar by itself. In both cases, the idea is that by eliminating the data from the file, the index file becomes shorter, and searching through it takes less time. In both cases also, the point of the index file is that it tells you where to find the information you want. The difference, in part, is that Superfile creates its own index. The rest of the difference is that Superfile's index is meant to be read by Superfile, not by you.

When you tell Superfile to index a file, it asks for the name of the disk that the file is on. When you go to retrieve information, Superfile will tell you which disk to put in the machine. This lets you put your quote file in any number of different disk files on any number of different disks (quotes1, quotes2, and so forth). As long as the disks themselves are labeled, you should never have trouble finding the proper disk.

Retrieving information from Superfile is also similar in concept to what you would do with WordStar alone, except that you use Superfile's search capabilities instead of WordStar's.

Superfile lets you search for a combination of key words. "JEFFERSON **AND** SPELLING" for instance, will retrieve the Jefferson spelling quote and ignore any other Jefferson quotes in the file. "JEFFERSON **NOT** SPELLING" will ignore this quote but will retrieve any other Jefferson quotes you may have. "JEFFERSON **OR** EINSTEIN" will retrieve both of the sample quotes, "JEFFERSON **AND** EINSTEIN" will retrieve neither of them (since neither has both Jefferson *and* Einstein as key words).

When you're using WordStar and you match a key word in an index file, you read the index entry, then go to the disk file, or physical index card, or whatever to read the data.

When you're using Superfile and you match a key word (or combination of key words), Superfile reads its own index, tells you which disk to put in, then finds the entry by itself, and displays the data for you.

This is by no means a complete description of what Superfile does, but it should give you a feel for what Superfile can do that WordStar by itself cannot do. It should also give you some sense of how Superfile works—enough, at least, so you can follow the examples in the rest of the chapter.

LIMITATIONS OF FREE-FORMAT ENTRY

The free-format entry of Superfile is one of the real advantages of using this program, or one like it, for a certain kind of information.

There are times, though, when an index card program like this could benefit tremendously from using a data entry screen like a "standard" data base program. You might, for instance, be a photographer with a large number of stock slides that you want to index. The usual way to do this is to set up a series of subject headings, then file each slide under an appropriate heading. This approach works, but more often than not, a given photo could be filed under more than one heading. It would be nice if you could number the photos arbitrarily, then cross index them with appropriate key words.

This is clearly a case where an index card program is called for rather than a field-oriented data base program. Even so, there is some data that should go in each record. You might, for instance, want to put in the date, the place you took each picture, the subject, whether a release was signed, and so forth. It would be helpful to have a data entry screen that will remind you to enter that information.

One approach to the problem is to use what FYI calls "templates." These are essentially the same thing as format files. The idea is that you create a file with all the "background" text. Then, each time you make an entry, you read the "template" into your working file, and fill in the blanks.

This works well enough, but it leaves you with extra work to do. You will probably want at least some of your standard entries to be listed as key words. If you're using templates, that means you have to type those entries twice: once as an answer to a prompt, and once as a key word.

By using MailMerge, though, you can create a data entry screen that will fill in both the blanks and the key words with a single entry.

DESIGNING A MAILMERGE ENTRY SCREEN FOR AN INDEX CARD PROGRAM

The basic idea of using MailMerge to create a data entry screen for Superfile is simple. For each item you want to remind yourself to include, you enter an ask for variable command. You then include the variable in the format section of the file. If you also want the variable to function as a key word, you include it a second time, in the key word section. In addition, you might like to label the items that will automatically become key words, so that you'll know which ones they are when you enter the data later.

If you want to use the location of the shooting as a key word, then, your file would include these lines:

```
. . . . .
.AV "Location (AUTO KEY): ", LOCATION
. . . . .
. . . . .
*C
. . . . .
Location: &LOCATION&
. . . . .
. . . . .
*K. . ./ &LOCATION&/ . . ./. . .*E
```

All this is straightforward. The complications in designing a data entry screen of this sort come from other considerations. There are, for instance, a few reminders that you should include in the beginning of the file.

One of those reminders should tell you what version of the entry screen you're about to use. This is important. If you ever revise an entry screen, you want to make sure that you don't accidentally use the old version later. By including this note, you're more likely to realize your mistake if you somehow wind up with the wrong version.

Another note you might like to include is a reminder to set your keyboard for all uppercase letters so you can quickly distinguish background text from data when retrieving information later.

The complication here is that you only need to see these reminders once at the beginning of a session. You can avoid the bother of having to read them before each entry by putting them in a separate "sign-on" file, FOTOFILE.MAS. This sign-on file calls up the file with the data entry screen, FOTOFILE.SLA, which is the only part of the file that repeats.

There is another factor to consider—when you're entering a large number of photos into your data base, odds are that many of the pictures were taken at the same session, which means they have identical answers to many of the prompts. You can use the ^R command (recall last entry) to avoid having to type the answer each time, but even that can be tedious. A better approach would be to bypass these questions altogether, so Mail-Merge will remember your previous answers without your having to do anything.

The trick here is to identify the questions that are likely to remain the same for large numbers of photos within any given batch. Then you can use either the conditional print command or the conditional file insert trick to skip over them or not.

PRINTING INFORMATION FROM AN INDEX CARD DATA BASE

There is yet another complication that we have to keep in mind in designing this file.

If you're keeping slides in your own files, strictly for your own personal use, it's probably enough to number them by hand. If the slides are going to a photo research agency, though, you'll also need to label each one with a picture description. In that case it pays to set up your data files so you can print the picture description and photo number automatically on labels—without having to reenter the information.

This brings up a more general point—the importance of being able to retrieve information from your data base in ways that are useful to you. Otherwise there's no point in setting up the data base in the first place.

Superfile gives you two basic choices for retrieving information, or generating reports, to use standard data base jargon. You can retrieve each entry from start to finish, or you can retrieve partial entries. The partial, or short form, version of each entry has to be designed into the data file. The marker is a single asterisk. If you then tell Superfile to retrieve the short-form version, it will give you everything up to the asterisk in each entry, and ignore the rest.

All this means that you can design your photo file to print labels by treating them as a partial entry in your file. You could, for instance, include the variables PIC1 (picture description, line 1), PIC2 (line 2), and NUMBER (slide number) as the first three variables in the file, followed by an asterisk to mark the end of the partial entry.

If you did that, the format section of your MailMerge file might start like this:

```
*C
&PIC1&
&PIC2& &NUMBER&*
```

If you also add a batch name in your entry screen, then each time you enter a batch of slides into your data base, you can have Superfile retrieve the entire batch (using the batch name as the key word). All that remains is to put your labels in your printer, and tell Superfile to print the short version of each entry.

There's a problem though: In printing the labels this way, you are stuck with whatever line height and pitch your printer is set for. In many applications this won't matter. In many other applications, including this one, it will.

Slides, and the labels that go on them, are fairly small. The labels measure $\frac{7}{16}$ inch by just under 2 inches. At 10 pitch and 6 lines per inch, this gives you room for 2 lines of 19 characters each. Depending on the photo, this may or may not give you enough room to fully describe the slide. Worse, the labels will quickly get out of sync with the printer.

Slide labels come on a continuous roll with no space between them, so they measure $\frac{7}{16}$, or $\frac{21}{48}$ inch from the top of one label to the top of the next.

Printing at six lines per inch translates to $\frac{8}{48}$ of an inch per line.

This means that when you get to the end of the first label (at $\frac{21}{48}$ of an inch), you're in the middle of the third line ($\frac{8}{48}$ plus $\frac{8}{48}$ plus $\frac{5}{48}$, with $\frac{3}{48}$ of an inch to go).

And this, in turn, means that you have to stop after every second label to readjust the labels in the printer.

Notice, though, that if you could change the line height setting to $\frac{7}{48}$ inch, you could solve both these problems at once. At $\frac{7}{48}$ inch per line, you can fit exactly three lines on each label. This would not only give you an extra line for describing the picture, it would also keep the printer and the labels in sync.

Assuming that your printer is capable of varying the line height in the first place, then, you can solve these problems simply by printing the labels with MailMerge instead of Superfile. Or, to put it another way, what you need to do is turn WordStar/MailMerge into a report generator for Super-file.

You do that by setting up your variables in MailMerge-readable format. (Notice in passing that this MailMerge-readable line will often be wider than your screen. If you want to make sure you can read these variables on retrieval with Superfile, you need to enter them in your format file a second time as well, in human-readable format.) The short-form section in FOTOFILE.SLA, then, might look like this:

```
*C
.PF off (To prevent breaking the next line)
&PIC1&, &PIC2&, &PIC3&, &NUMBER&*
```

As before, each time you enter a batch of slides into your data base, you retrieve them by using the batch name as the key word. This time, though, you tell Superfile to send the short form entries to a disk file, not to the printer. Once you have the MailMerge-readable disk file, printing the labels becomes a simple straightforward process, using this two part MailMerge file:

FILE: SLIDELAB.MAS

For Printing Slide Labels

```
.LH 7 (For 7/48 inch/line, or 3 lines = 21/48 inch)
.CW 8 (for 15 pitch)
.PL 3
.PO 0
.MT 0
.MB 0
.AV "File to get Data From? ", FILE
.FI SLIDELAB.SLA
#
```

SLIDELAB.SLA

```
.DF &FILE&
.RV PIC1, PIC2, PIC3, NUMBER
&PIC1&
&PIC2&
&PIC3& &NUMBER&
```

Here, finally, is the MailMerge file—or two MailMerge files linked together as Master and Slave—that function as the data entry screen for a photo file.

Notice how the Master file uses the clear screen and ask for variable commands to create a double reminder to set your keyboard properly.

FILE: FOTOFILE.MAS

A Data Entry Screen for a Free-Format Index Card
Data Base Program

```
.PO 0
.MB 0
.MT 0
.PL 17
.CS
.DM This is the original version of FOTOFILE.
.DM
.DM Many of the Prompts in this entry screen contain the
.DM notation (AUTO KEY). Whatever you enter in response to
.DM those prompts will automatically show up as key words.
.DM In addition, there are five prompts for key words that will
.DM show up in the file ONLY as key words.
.DM
.DM Please note:
.DM     For maximum readability, ALL ENTRIES SHOULD BE IN CAPS.
.AV         "Hit Return to clear screen.", return
.CS
.DM          Is ALL CAPS on?
.AV "Hit Return to clear screen.", return
.FI FOTOFILE.SLA
#
```

FOTOFILE.SLA

(This is written for use with the conditional print commands. Lines that would have to be revised for use with the conditional file insert command are in boldface. Batch questions would also have to be removed from this file and placed in a separate file.)

```
.CS
.AV "Photo Number (AUTO KEY): ", NUMBER
.AV "Pix Description 1 (AUTO KEY): ", PIC1, 29
.AV "Pix Description 2 (AUTO KEY): ", PIC2, 29
.AV "Pix Description 3 (AUTO KEY): ", PIC3, 24
..NOTE: The maximum length commands above are based on two inch
..labels printing at 15 pitch.
.CS
.DM The current answers for the batch questions are:
.DM     Batch Name: &BATCH&
.DM       Subject: &SUBJECT&
.DM Release Signed: &RELEASE&
```

```
.DM      Date Taken: &DATE&
.DM          Location: &LOCATION&
.AV "Change answers to Batch questions (Y/N)? ", SKIP
.IF &SKIP& = "N" .OR. &SKIP& "n" GOTO SKIP
.DM
.DM Name of batch (use "C" prefix for Color)
.AV "     (AUTO KEY): ", BATCH
.AV "Subject (AUTO KEY): ", SUBJECT
.AV "Release Signed: ", RELEASE
.AV "Date Taken: ", DATE
.AV "Location (AUTO KEY): ", LOCATION
.EF SKIP
.AV "Comments 1: ", C1
.AV "Comments 2: ", C2
.AV "Key Word : ", KEY1
.AV "Key Word : ", KEY2
.AV "Key Word : ", KEY3
.AV "Key Word : ", KEY4
.AV "Key Word : ", KEY5

*C
.PF off (To prevent breaking the next line)
&PIC1&, &PIC2&, &PIC3&, &NUMBER&*
.PF on
&PIC1&
&PIC2&
&PIC3& &NUMBER&
Batch Name: &BATCH&.
Subject: &SUBJECT&
Release Signed: &RELEASE&
Date Taken: &DATE&
Location: &LOCATION&
Comments: &C1/0& &C2/0&
.PF off (To prevent breaking a key phrase into two sections)
*K &PIC1&/ &PIC2&/ &PIC3&
&NUMBER& / &BATCH&
&SUBJECT&/ &LOCATION&/ &KEY1&
&KEY2&/ &KEY3&/ &KEY4&/ &KEY5&
.PF on
*E
.AV "Is there more data to enter (Y/N)? ", DATA, 1
.IF &DATA& = "N" .OR. &DATA& = "n" GOTO END
.FI FOTOFILE.SLA
.EF END
```

If you're using the File Insert command rather than the conditional print command, the batch questions (meaning everything between the first

.IF command and the first .EF command) should be put in another file (FOTOFILE.SL2). In addition, the boldfaced lines in the above file should be replaced by these lines:

```
. . . . .
. . . . .
.DM To CHANGE answers to batch questions, hit RETURN
.DM Otherwise enter a PERIOD plus RETURN
.AV "to skip batch questions and retain previous answers", B
&B/0& Followed by ^PM for overprint flag
.FI FOTOFILE.SL2 (Contains the batch questions)
. . . . .
. . . . .
.DM If there is more data, hit RETURN
.DM Otherwise enter a PERIOD plus RETURN
.AV "to close the file and write all information to disk", DATA
&DATA/0& Followed by ^PM for overprint flag
.FI FOTOFILE.SLA
#
```

In addition, if using the file insert command, a blank line should be added before the first line in the file FOTOFILE.SLA. Otherwise the first **.CS** command will be printed instead of being interpreted as a dot command. Similarly, a blank line should be used as the first line in FOTO-FILE.SL2, so that the first **.DM** command will be interpreted correctly. Finally, you will need to add a blank line between the **.FI FOTOFILE.SL2** command line and the **.AV** command line that follows it.

Except for one or two minor points, this file should be self-explanatory (in either version). It's designed in such a way that if you simply answer the questions, it will produce an appropriate data file, complete with background text, data, key words, and the markers that Superfile needs so it can find the beginning and end of each entry, and the key words within each entry. (A reminder: this file will run much faster if you remember to turn off the file directory before calling up MailMerge.)

In addition to the prompts that produce both data and key words, some prompts produce data only, and other prompts produce key words only. This last set of prompts lets you add key words and phrases on a picture-by-picture basis.

In looking at the "data only" prompts, notice the comment lines in particular. These let you add one or two lines of notes to the entry. You can, of course, put as many of these comment lines in the file as you like.

WordStar/MailMerge as a "Universal" Report Generator

One last comment on the photo file: There is one unnecessary limitation built into it. In considering the problem of printing information, we started with a specific need—the labels. We then designed the MailMerge-readable, short-form version of the file to include only those variables that we needed for that one format. If you ever need to generate a report that uses additional variables, you're out of luck.

There's an obvious way around this limitation. Don't design the short-form version of the file around a specific report. Instead, include all your variables in it, in MailMerge-readable format, of course.

If you do this, then once you create your MailMerge-readable data file, you'll be able to generate any report at all from it—not just the ones you thought of when you designed the original data entry file.

There is a cost involved in this. Extra entries mean longer disk files, but file length is still at a premium. Any changes in the entries still have to be made with WordStar's edit mode. The longer the files are, the less convenient that will be.

In general, though, unless you are absolutely sure that you will never need more than a limited number of report formats, you're better off including all variables in your short-form version of the file. Otherwise you may find yourself having to re-enter information to produce an unforeseen report.

To change FOTOFILE so that you can generate other reports, you only need to change the beginning of the format section, which would look like this:

```
*C
.PF off (To prevent breaking the next line)
&PIC1&, &PIC2&, &PIC3&, &NUMBER&, &BATCH&, &SUBJECT&, &RELEASE&+
```

This line, of course, would continue off screen to include the rest of the variables.

OTHER APPLICATIONS

What we have just done, in effect, is to create a hybrid—a data base program with some of the benefits of a field-oriented program, and some of the benefits of a field-independent program. We did that by using WordStar and MailMerge to create a data entry screen on the one hand, and a report generator on the other.

This hybrid is well-suited for handling a certain kind of information—namely, information which is best entered with a data entry screen, but which requires field-independent keys for retrieval. If, in addition, the information requires little or no updating once it's been entered, this hybrid is nearly ideal.

All this should be reasonably obvious by now. What may not be obvious is that you can use these same techniques to handle other kinds of information as well.

You could, for instance, use this approach with a mailing list. Your data entry file might look like the following (this file assumes four address lines in the interests of simplicity).

FILE: MAILIST2

A Data Entry Screen for Use with Superfile

```
.CS
.AV "Name of Addressee. Last Name Only: ", LST
.AV "First Name, Middle Initial: ", FRST
.AV "Company Name: ", CO
.AV "Street and Number: ", STR
.AV "City: ", CTY
.AV "State: " STATE
.AV "Zip Code: ", ZIP
.AV "Salutation (Include Mr. or Ms. if last name: ", SAL
.AV "Type of Business: ", BIZ
.PL 10
.MT 0
.MB 0
.PO 0
.PF off
..Beginning of format section
*C
..Short-form retrieval—ALL variables in MailMerge format
&LST&, &FRST&, &CO&, &STR&, &CTY&, &STATE&, &ZIP&, &SAL&, &BIZ&*
> > > >
..Now, All Variables once again — in human readable format
&FRST& &LST&
&CO&
&STR&
&CTY&, &STATE& &ZIP&
Salutation: &SAL&
Type of Business: &BIZ&
> > > >
*K &LST&/ &FRST&/ &CO&/ &CTY&/ &STATE&/ &ZIP&/ &BIZ&
*E
.AV "Is there more data to enter (Y/N)? ", DATA, 1
.IF &DATA& = "N" .OR. &DATA& = "n" GOTO END
.FI MAILIST2
.EF END
```

Alternate Ending for Use with the File Insert Command

```
.DM If there is more data, hit RETURN
.DM Otherwise enter a PERIOD plus RETURN
.AV "to close the file and write all information to disk", DATA
&DATA/0& Followed by ^PM for overprint command
.FI MAILIST2
#
```

Note: Here again, if using the file insert command, the first line in MAILIST2 must be a blank line, or the **.CS** command will be printed rather than interpreted.

With this data entry file, each entry in your data file will look something like this:

```
*C
Jones, Bob, Jones Associates, 1013 13th Ave, New York, N.Y.+
> > > >
Bob Jones
Jones Associates
1013 13th Ave
New York, N.Y. 10022
Salutation: Bob
Type of Business: Management Consultant
> > > >
*K Jones/ Bob/ Jones Associates/ New York/ N.Y./ 10022/ Man+
*E
```

Once you've indexed this data with Superfile, you can use Superfile to manage the list and use WordStar and MailMerge to print it.

If, for instance, you've just written a form letter you want to send to all management consultants on your mailing list, you tell Superfile to retrieve all entries with the key phrase "Management Consultant." You then create a disk file with the short-form entry—meaning the MailMerge-readable data—for each management consultant.

If you want to send the mailing only to management consultants in New York, you tell Superfile to retrieve all entries with the key words "Management Consultant" and "New York," and so on.

The point is, you can use Superfile to select specific sub-groups from your master mailing list, if you like, instead of using MailMerge. This is not particularly important if you have the conditional print feature in your MailMerge, but it can simplify life enormously if you otherwise have to rely on the file insert command to do selections.

Much more significant is that Superfile can also sort data files. This means you can, for instance, put a mailing list in zip code order or alphabetical order.

This sorting capability can be important. If you're doing a bulk mailing for instance, the post office insists that your mail be sorted in zip code order. Sorting can also make it easier to maintain your files.

Superfile lets you index any number of different disk files into a single data base. If your mailing list grows too long to allow convenient updating with WordStar, then, you can break it into two or more data files. This presents another problem though. Before you can update any given entry, you need some way to know which file the entry is in.

If you sort your file in alphabetical order before you divide it you have a simple way to solve that problem too. You can even name your files for their alphabetical contents (MLISTAB). Thanks to the sorting capability, then, you can create any number of short, easy to update files, and still know which file to go to when you need to update any given record. (Once you make the changes, incidentally, you then have to reindex your files to update the indexes as well.)

This quick look at handling a mailing list should be enough to make the point. You can use this hybrid approach to substitute for a field-oriented program, if necessary.

But notice that hedge: "if necessary."

There are some real limitations in using this approach as opposed to a standard, field-oriented program. In entering data, for instance, you have to cope with MailMerge's refusal to let you back up and correct mistakes in earlier fields. In addition, your data base will take up more disk space, records will take longer to retrieve, and updating records will be a more difficult proposition.

Keep in mind, then, that for field-oriented information, this is a make-do substitute, not the preferred choice. Still, it is a real improvement over using WordStar and MailMerge alone to maintain that information. If you find that your needs have outgrown the capabilities of WordStar and Mail-Merge, and if you already have Superfile or some similar program for other reasons, you might like to try this approach before spending the money on yet another program.

13

Using MailMerge as a Report Generator

DATASTAR, INFOSTAR, dBASE II, THE FORMULA II, AND OTHER FIELD-ORIENTED PROGRAMS

Free-format information retrieval systems are not the only data base programs that you can use WordStar and MailMerge with. In fact, you can use WordStar/MailMerge as a report generator for just about any data base program. The benefits are always real, and are often enormous.

We touched on reports and report generators in the last chapter. I didn't define the terms then, mostly because the basic concept of a report is reasonably obvious.

Just about any time you extract information from your data base by printing that information on disk or paper, the printed output qualifies as a report. It doesn't matter what form the output takes: mailing labels, form letters, alphabetized lists, or anything else you can think of—they all qualify.

A report generator, in turn, is that part of a data base management system that produces reports.

Of course, all data base programs must have at least some capacity for producing reports; without it they would be largely useless. When it comes to creating a new format for the report, though, nearly all these programs are limited in one way or another—often severely limited.

Capabilities cover a broad range. In some cases, it is impossible to design a new format to print with. In other cases, it is possible but difficult. In still other cases, designing a new format is nearly as simple as typing it in—much as you would create a format file in WordStar.

In all these cases, though, you can put WordStar and MailMerge to good use. The more limited the program, the greater the benefits, but the point is that there are benefits to be gained over even the best built-in report generators.

Here's a look at how to use WordStar/MailMerge with four specific data base programs: DataStar, dBASE II, The Formula II, and InfoStar. Taken together, these four programs represent a fair sampling of the kinds of report capabilities that are found in data base programs in general. They range from DataStar, with extremely limited report capabilities, to Formula II and InfoStar, each of which has a report generator that is almost as easy to use as WordStar when designing new formats.

USING MAILMERGE WITH DATASTAR: A MARRIAGE MADE AT MICROPRO

We'll start with an easy one: DataStar. DataStar is easy, in part, because it keeps its data files in MailMerge-readable format. It was designed that way, of course. The program is sold by MicroPro and is meant precisely to be used along with WordStar and MailMerge. In fact, DataStar is part of the InfoStar package and is also designed to be used along with Report-Star, the other part of InfoStar. Since DataStar is sold separately, though, and since there are other programs available that are comparable to it, we'll look at it by itself first, and save InfoStar for later.

DataStar is also easy in the sense of being an easy-to-learn, easy-to-use program, with somewhat limited capabilities for managing information.

The program has two basic functions: one module lets you create data entry screens, or forms; a second module lets you use those forms to enter, delete, search for, or change information.

DataStar's entry screens are a vast improvement over the MailMerge data entry screens we've been using. To begin with, DataStar will let you back up and make corrections when entering information, without having to design any special tricks into the file. More significant, though, is that in creating the form, DataStar lets you assign one or more "attributes" to each of your fields.

The attributes cover a wide range of choices. They include error checking features, so that you can, for example, tell DataStar to accept only letters for a given field, or only numbers, or even some limited range of numbers.

They also include formatting features. If a given field is a dollar amount, for instance, you can tell DataStar to automatically add a dollar sign and two decimal places, so that all you have to enter are the numbers themselves.

The attributes let you designate derived fields. You can enter a formula as an attribute and have DataStar use that formula to calculate the value for the field. This can be valuable on an invoice, for example, where you might use one set of fields to enter the prices of specific items, use a second set of fields to enter the quantity of each item being ordered, then use a third set of fields to let DataStar calculate prices, the total, and even the tax.

Another advantage that DataStar has over MailMerge is in finding information in a data file, whether to change it or just look it up. Unlike MailMerge, DataStar doesn't have to run through the entire data file and write it back to disk every time you want to look up a record or change it. This speeds things up considerably. What's more, DataStar keeps a separate index file that tells it where to find records. The records are indexed by one or more key fields. If you search the data file by key field, DataStar can find the record by reading the much shorter index file instead of reading the data file itself—a trick that speeds up record retrieval even more.

All this, and more, is reasonably typical of field-oriented data base programs. It is not meant as an exhaustive list of DataStar's capabilities, but rather as just enough to give you a taste of the possibilities.

As I've already pointed out, DataStar has some limitations, especially in each of three areas: sorting, selection, and formatting of reports.

DataStar's sorting ability is strictly limited to sorting on the key field or fields. MailMerge can't do anything to improve that, but it can do quite a bit to improve DataStar's selection and formatting functions.

The program's selection capabilities are limited in two ways. First, complex conditional selections in DataStar can only be linked together with "and." If, for example, you need a list of all architects in your data file who are in New York, you can obtain the list by telling DataStar to retrieve all records that contain "New York" in the "STATE" field *and* "Architect" in the "TYPE OF BUSINESS" field. If you need a list of all architects from either New York *or* Colorado, though, you can't get it—at least not in one step.

In this case you could go through the file twice, generating two lists: one for architects from New York and one for architects from Colorado. You can then join the two. If you need a list of architects from each of fifteen different states, though, you'd have to go through the file fifteen times.

If you need a list of architects from every state *except* New York, there is simply no convenient way to get it with DataStar.

The second limitation on DataStar's selection capabilities is that it will not let you select for anything but an exact match. This means with a personnel file, for example, that you can list everyone who has worked for you for exactly 8 years; you can even list everyone who's worked for you for anywhere from 10 to 19 years (by matching the "1"), but you cannot list everyone who has worked for you for "8 years or more," except by running through the file 2, or possibly 3, times.

It should be obvious that you can improve on DataStar's selection capabilities very easily by using MailMerge to select the set of records—especially if you have the conditional print feature. The data files are already in MailMerge readable format. All you need to do is create a MailMerge format file with the appropriate data file and read variable commands, along with the conditional print commands or the conditional file insert commands as appropriate (see Chapter 10 for details).

DataStar's report formats are also severely limited, more so than its selection capabilities. The program is, in fact, limited to two formats. It can print each selected record exactly as entered on screen—background text and all—or it can print each record exactly as entered on screen, but without the background text.

That's all it can do. It can't even send the output to a disk file instead of the printer.

Here again, it should be obvious that you can use MailMerge with the DataStar data files to create reports in just about any format you like. Once again, all you need to do is create a format file, add the necessary .**DF** and .**RV** commands, then print your report.

You can also combine the selection function and the formatting function in the same MailMerge file to generate reports in a single step.

None of this should be surprising. After all, as I pointed out in the beginning of this section, DataStar was designed to work along with Mail-Merge. The possibility of using MailMerge as a report generator for Data-Star is even hinted at in the MicroPro manuals.

What may be surprising is that the same basic idea works with other data base programs as well—even when the data files are not kept in Mail-Merge readable format. Consider, for instance, dBASE II.

USING WORDSTAR/MAILMERGE WITH dBASE II

Ashton-Tate's dBASE II is one of the better known data base programs for microcomputers. There's no point in going into the details of what it can do, except to say that it is a "heavy duty" data base program in the same sense that WordStar is a "heavy duty" word processing program. In each case, the program can do just about anything you might want of it.

For dBASE II, that means, among other things, that it can include as many as thirty-two fields per record, and as many as one thousand characters per record (not including background text). It also means that the program can sort on any field, retrieve records, and select for sub-groups of records based on various combinations of AND, OR, and NOT.

As you may know, dBASE II contains what amounts to its own programming language. This is a sophisticated command language complete with the ability to do loops and conditional statements. You can use these commands to manipulate data directly, or you can string them together in a batch file, in which case the batch file functions as a program by itself.

Once you learn this language, you can use it to do just about anything you want. Until you learn it, though, your options are limited.

When it comes to producing reports, for instance, the program includes a "quick and easy" report generator. This makes it relatively simple to produce any number of variations on a standard columnar format. If you want any other format, though, you have to write a program in the dBASE language. In theory this means you can produce any format you like—including complete form letters if necessary. In practice it means that anything besides the standard columnar format is an effort often left undone.

This is precisely the kind of situation where using WordStar/Mail-Merge can do the most good. You can manage a mailing list, for instance, with dBASE II, then use WordStar to create a form letter, use MailMerge to print it, and ignore the programming altogether.

There's a catch, though. Before MailMerge can function as a report generator, it has to be able to read the data. But before it can read the data, the file must be in MailMerge-readable format. With dBASE II, it's not. And that means you have to convert the data file first, using dBASE to do it.

Converting dBASE II Data Files to MailMerge Data Files

Fortunately, there's a way out of this particular catch-22. You can write a single, all-purpose dBASE II program that will convert any dBASE II data file to MailMerge format, complete with commas between fields and quotes around each field. Having written this one program, you'll never have to write another. You will find this all purpose conversion program at the end of this chapter. (The program was written by John Schnell, who has graciously allowed me to use it.)

When you run the conversion program, it will ask you the name of the data file to convert. It will then look to the file, and show you the fields one-by-one, asking in each case whether to include the field in the Mail-Merge output file. All you have to do is answer "Y" for yes or "N" for no. The program will then ask you to provide a name for the MailMerge-readable file, and present you, finally, with the converted data file. After that, you're in familiar territory. Use WordStar to create a format file, and Mail-Merge to print it.

All this is obviously a lot easier than writing a new program every time you need a new report format. If you don't want to write even one program, though, and if you want greater speed and flexibility than you can get from the dBASE program, there's also another way out of this catch-22.

Like WordStar, dBASE II has been around for some time. Like Word-Star also, it has sold enough copies so that other companies have begun writing and selling programs that are specifically designed to work with it. Inevitably perhaps, at least one of those programs, DBPlus from Human-soft, Inc., is designed, among other things, to convert dBASE II data files to MailMerge data files.

DBPlus

If you have dBASE II, DBPlus is worth looking at. It functions, in effect, as a dBASE utility—or set of utilities. In addition to converting files to MailMerge-readable format, the program has several other uses.

Briefly, it can sort dBASE II files, compress and decompress them, and transform them to a new file structure for use within dBASE II.

The advantage of the compression and decompression utility is that it lets you store your backup files or archive files in less disk space. Also, if you transmit your data files to another computer by phone, you can speed up the process—and cut down the phone bill—by compressing the files before sending them, and decompressing them on the other end of the phone line.

The sorting capability of DBPlus outdoes the dBASE II sort utility in two ways. It's faster, and it will let you sort on as many fields as you like—right up to the maximum of thirty-two fields per record.

dBASE users please note: dBASE II will sort your files based on as many fields as you like, but it will only sort on one field at a time. If, for instance, you want your file sorted alphabetically by company name within each state, you can sort once by company name, and a second time by state. When doing this kind of multiple sorting, you start with the least important field and work your way to the most important. In this example, for instance, if you were to sort by state first, and company name second, the file would be sorted by state within company name—which is not likely to be useful. One other thing: instead of sorting the data file with dBASE II, you can sort the index to the data file, in which case you can sort on as many as thirty-two fields at a time. As your data file gets more and more out of order in relation to your index, though, data retrieval begins to slow down more and more.

The most impressive capability of DBPlus is its ability to transform data files from one form to another. This can be useful if, for instance, you have a large data file, and have decided you need to add a new field to each record. If you create a new data entry screen with the extra field in it, you'll find that the new screen will be able to read the old data file, but not be able to write the new field into the file. Before you can use the new field, you have to modify the data file to take the new field into account. With dBASE II by itself, you need a working knowledge of the command language before you can do this. If you don't quite know what you're doing, you risk losing the file. With DBPlus, though, the transform utility will do the work for you.

USING DBPLUS TO CREATE
MAILMERGE-READABLE DATA FILES

When using DBPlus, it doesn't much matter from your point of view as a user, whether you are transforming a file into a new form for use within dBASE II, or transforming it to MailMerge format. The procedure is the same.

Everything in DBPlus is done through menus. When you call up the program, the main menu gives you four choices: sort, compress, decompress, or transform.

If you choose "transform," the program leads you through the process in a series of simple, straightforward steps. It asks you to choose the input file to use, whether the output file is going to be a dBASE II data file or a MailMerge data file, the name of the output file, and so forth.

When it comes to designating the fields for the output file, DBPlus is remarkably helpful. First it shows you the fields as they are defined in the input file. At that point you not only choose which fields to keep, but you can change the order they'll show up in simply by choosing them in the order you would like. The program then lets you insert new fields and modify old fields—changing field lengths, field names, and so forth, however you like. Here again, it prompts you at each step in the process.

DBPlus will even let you create a new field that is derived from one of the old fields. This is a particularly nice touch. You might, for instance, be dealing with personnel records, and want to send a letter to all salaried employees, telling them what their Christmas bonus is going to be. All you have available in your data file, though, is a field, SALARY, that lists the yearly salary of each employee.

Let's assume it's been a good year; the bonus for each employee will be ten percent of the yearly salary. DBPlus will not only let you create the new field BONUS, it will let you define that field as ten percent of the old field (BONUS equals 0.1 times SALARY). It will then calculate the new field for each record, automatically adding the new values to the output file as it creates the new format.

Assuming you started by telling the program to keep the fields for LAST NAME, FIRST NAME, STREET, CITY, STATE, and ZIP CODE, you will wind up with a MailMerge-readable file that contains the name, address, and amount of bonus for each employee on the list. All that remains is to write the form letter with WordStar, and print it with MailMerge.

That form letter might start like the following example.

```
.DF BONUS.WS
.RV LASTNAME, FIRSTNAME, STREET, CITY, STATE, ZIPCODE, BONUS

&FIRSTNAME& &LASTNAME&
&STREET&
&CITY&, &STATE& &ZIPCODE&

Dear &FIRSTNAME&:

    Merry Christmas. We're happy to say that the company has
had a very good year. We thought you'd like to know that
you're due for a bonus of $&BONUS&. This is the best way we
know to thank you for your work . . .
```

And here again, you're in familiar territory.

ANOTHER LOOK AT THE dBASE CONVERSION PROGRAM

As I've already pointed out, this last capability of DBPlus is a nice touch. Don't cross off the dBASE II conversion program from your list just yet, though. Although the conversion program will not do quite as much quite as easily in transforming files, it will come close to doing as much.

In this last example for instance, you wouldn't be able to create the BONUS field with the dBASE conversion program. On the other hand, you would be able to create a MailMerge file that contained the name, address, and salary of each employee. At that point you could produce the same final letter by using a format file that started this way:

```
.DF BONUS.WS
.RV LASTNAME, FIRSTNAME, STREET, CITY, STATE, ZIPCODE, SALARY
.CS
.DM Salary is $&SALARY&
.AV "How much is bonus? ", BONUS
&FIRSTNAME& &LASTNAME&
&STREET&
&CITY&, &STATE& &ZIPCODE&
```

Dear &FIRSTNAME&:
    Merry Christmas. We're happy to say that the company has
had a very good year. We thought you'd like to know that
you're due for a bonus of $&BONUS&. This is the best way we
know to thank you for your work . . .

This file should be self explanatory. Before printing each letter, Mail-Merge will stop, show you the yearly salary of the employee, then ask you to enter the correct bonus. This is not as convenient as having DBPlus compute the bonus for you, but unless you are sending out an enormous number of letters, it is still much more convenient than writing a program in the dBASE programming language.

More to the point, this problem usually won't show up. The vast majority of the time your dBASE II file will already contain all the variables you need. In fact, if you run across this situation very often, you should take it as a sign that you need to redesign your files. They are supposed to include all—or at least most—of the information you want in your reports. That's the whole point of keeping a data file.

In any case, it doesn't really matter whether you use DBPlus to convert your files, or the dBASE conversion program, or some other program altogether. What does matter is that it is both possible to convert your files to MailMerge format, and convenient to do it. And that means you can use dBASE II to manage your data, and use WordStar/MailMerge to format and print your reports.

OTHER DATA BASE PROGRAMS

dBASE II is only one example of a data base program that forces you to learn programming in order to use it efficiently. There are similar programs that do essentially the same thing. Because they are similar, though, the approach to using them with WordStar and MailMerge is also similar—almost by definition.

With any of these "programming-oriented" data base programs, the most important advantage of using MailMerge as the report generator remains the same: Instead of writing a program to produce the report format, you can type the format in. This means you get to watch the report take form on the screen, and you can even make adjustments as you go, based on what you see.

Translated into computer jargon, what WordStar does for you is give you a full-screen text editor. This is just another way of saying that you can move the cursor anywhere you like on the screen, enter any text you like, join two lines if necessary, and do all the other usual editing functions you've grown used to with WordStar.

There are other data base programs available, however, that already have full-screen text editors for their report generators. It may not be immediately obvious, but even these programs can benefit from using Word-Star/MailMerge.

WORDSTAR/MAILMERGE AND THE FORMULA II

The Formula II, from Dynamic Microprocessor Associates, is one example of a data base program that already contains a full-screen text editor as part of its report generator.

Like dBASE II, Formula II qualifies as a "heavy duty" data base program. Unlike dBASE II, The Formula requires essentially no programming, except in the broadest possible sense of designing applications. Here again, there is no point in going into details, except to mention that The Formula can handle one hundred fields per record, and one billion records per file—more than you're likely to need.

One thing also worth pointing out is that because The Formula does not require programming to use efficiently, it is generally much easier to learn and use than a program like dBASE II. This, combined with the fact that it is comparable to dBASE II in terms of the applications it can handle, makes it worth looking at if you are in the market for a data base program.

For our purposes, the really interesting part of The Formula is the report generator. Like dBASE II, Formula II has a quick and easy report generator that will produce reports in columnar format. Unlike dBASE II, The Formula also has a more sophisticated report generator that includes a full-screen text editor.

Basically, using The Formula's text editor is very much like using WordStar. You enter the edit mode, and start typing. One nice touch for WordStar users, in fact, is that most of the commands are identical to WordStar commands: ^E moves the cursor up a line, ^X moves it down a line, ^Y deletes a line, ^N inserts a line, and so forth. An even nicer touch is that DMA has made it easy to redefine the commands. This lets you use arrow keys and even function keys, if you have them. (It also gives non-WordStar users the option of using the commands that they are familiar with.)

There are differences, of course, between using The Formula and using WordStar. For one thing, The Formula's text editor is nowhere near as powerful as WordStar's; the program is, after all, a data base program, not a word processor. Also, the conventions for designating variables are different from MailMerge conventions. Finally, and most important, the actual report generator (as opposed to text editor) can do things that Mail-Merge cannot do. (It can, for example, merge data from several different data files at once.) Still, all things considered, creating a report format with The Formula is similar to creating a format file with WordStar.

If you think of using WordStar, but limiting yourself to just those commands that show up on the Main Menu, you'll have a pretty good idea of what Formula's edit mode is like. It may not let you do anything fancy, like moving a block of text, or reading in text from another file, but it is certainly efficient enough for entering an invoice or a form letter.

The Christmas bonus letter would look like this example if typed with The Formula's editor.

```
c# # # # # # # # # # # # # # # # # # # # # # # # # #
# # # # # # # # # # # # # # # # # # # # # # # #
c# # # # # # # # # # # # # # # # # # # #, c# # # # # # # # # # # # # # # # # #
Dear c# # # # # # # # # # # # #:
    Merry Christmas. We're happy to say that the company has
had a very good year. We thought you'd like to know that you're
due for a bonus of $ # # # # # #. This is the best way we know to
thank you for your work . . .
```

Briefly, without getting into unnecessary details of how The Formula works, there are three major differences between this file and the equivalent WordStar/MailMerge format file.

First, there are no data file or read variable commands, or anything to replace them. Formula's report generator includes a separate series of prompts that ask you the name or names of the data files to use. (You can read data from up to six different files.)

Second, you can hardly overlook the use of number signs instead of variable names. When you designate a variable, The Formula asks you which variable to use, and which file to get it from. It then stores that information separately from the text. The number of number signs indicate the maximum length of the field. The lower-case "c," which appears in some of the variables, is a command to "compress" the field when appropriate. This will eliminate blank spaces in printing when the variable is shorter than the maximum length of the field. (Using this with the variable marker for city, for example, prevents gaps from showing up between city and state.)

Third, notice the "bonus" field. In the WordStar file, we had to enter this manually. The Formula, though, like DBPlus, will let you designate derived fields, and will do the calculations for you.

So much for the differences. The really important thing to notice is the similarity. That's why I included this example in the first place.

Once again, the point is that with The Formula II, as with WordStar, you can create this letter—this report format—simply by typing it in, and designating the variables to use. This brings us back to where we started in discussing The Formula. Given that The Formula will let you design a report format this easily, it is not at all obvious that there's anything to be gained by using WordStar and MailMerge.

In fact, though, there are several benefits to be gained.

The Formula's limitations as a word processor don't stop with its editing functions. They also extend to its print controls and formatting capabilities.

Certain print enhancements—boldface, double strike, and underlining—are available with The Formula II, but they are somewhat clumsy to use. What you can do in WordStar with two keystrokes—^PB, for example, to turn boldfacing on or off—takes four keystrokes in The Formula. This is a minor inconvenience though. The real problem is with The Formula's format capabilities.

The report generator has a format section that will allow you to change the page length, the page width, and a few other parameters fairly easily, but the program does not give you a simple way to change the number of lines per inch, or the spacing between characters, much less vary them at different points within the report.

It's not that you can't do these things, just that it is difficult. What The Formula will let you do is embed the decimal values of ASCII characters in your file—not just the standard printing characters, but the control codes. If you know the control sequences for your printer, then, you can use this embedding capability to adjust character width and line height.

The overall effect in printing is the same as if you used a character width or line height command in WordStar. The amount of work involved, though, is significantly different. To tell WordStar to change to 15 pitch, for instance, you only have to enter the command **.CW 8.** Entering the same command in The Formula is much more complicated.

If you're using a Diablo 630, to take a specific example, the ASCII control code for adjusting character width is **ESC US (n).** The decimal value for **ESC** is 27. The decimal value for **US** is 31. The **n** is the character spacing. This is measured the same way as it is in WordStar's **.CW** command—namely, in increments of $\frac{1}{120}$ of an inch.

The embedded command for 15 pitch, then, is "**27 31 8.**" In order to embed any ASCII character into The Formula's report file, though, you have to start by telling The Formula to embed the character instead of treating your entry as text. You do that by entering the command **ESC Z** followed by the ASCII character, followed by a carriage return. You have to do this, moreover, for each character in the control sequence. In other words, what comes out in WordStar as **.CW 8,** comes out in The Formula as **ESC Z 2 7 RETURN ESC Z 3 1 RETURN ESC Z 8 RETURN.** Four keystrokes have been transformed into fourteen.

All of this assumes that you know the control codes for your printer in the first place.

The reason for going through these details is to make a point: It may be possible to control character width and line height with The Formula, but it is not easy.

An additional complication is that The Formula does not display the embedded commands on screen the way WordStar does. This makes it impossible to simply look at your file and see what print controls are in it. (You can find out what print controls are in the file, but not just by looking at it.)

All this makes it difficult, at best, to match your printed output to odd size labels, or to someone else's randomly designed report forms. It will also tend to discourage you from adding that final polished look to your reports.

There are other inconveniences in using Formula as opposed to WordStar, but this should be enough to make the point: The Formula's text editor is impressive for a data base program, but it is still no match for a full-function word processor like WordStar. When it comes down to the final touches—the formatting and print controls that can give your report a polished professional look, or simply make it fit on a label—WordStar and MailMerge can outperform Formula's built-in text editor hands down. That means that by using WordStar and MailMerge as your report generator, you can improve the capabilities of even this program.

Put it another way—if you convert the data to MailMerge-readable format, you can get all the additional WordStar conveniences. And there's not a single reason not to do it.

Converting Formula Data Files to MailMerge Data Files

The concept in converting Formula data files to MailMerge data files is much the same as it is in converting dBASE II data files. The difference is that the execution of the concept is much easier. In particular, you don't have to buy or write a program to do the conversion for you. Instead, The Formula's report generator makes it easy to do the conversion on a case-by-case basis.

The file for converting Formula data files to MailMerge data files is almost embarrassingly simple. Typically, it will look something like this:

```
"c########","c######","c#########","c######"
```

The names of the data files are stored elsewhere. So are the names of the particular fields to use, as well as any calculations needed for derived fields. This format, though, is the key. It will tell The Formula to put the variables all on a line, separated by commas. The "c" in each variable will tell The Formula to drop extra spaces if the variable is shorter than the maximum length of the field. The quotes around each variable, finally, are needed for fields that might contain commas. When in doubt, you're better off using them.

Once you've created your MailMerge data file you're back in familiar territory, working with WordStar and MailMerge format files.

One last thing about Formula II: As of this writing, DMA expects to incorporate printer control features into The Formula in the near future. These features will make it easier to use The Formula itself to produce a final polished look. Even so, there still are advantages to using WordStar/

MailMerge as the final report generator. We'll get to these additional advantages shortly, in discussing InfoStar.

USING WORDSTAR/MAILMERGE WITH INFOSTAR

InfoStar comes in two varieties: InfoStar and InfoStar+. Both of these are "packages" of closely related programs. InfoStar consists of DataStar plus ReportStar. InfoStar+ consists of DataStar plus ReportStar plus StarBurst.

StarBurst is a kind of umbrella that will let you link programs together through a single master menu. If there are people using your system who are less knowledgeable than you are about computers, you can use StarBurst to custom-design menus and help screens for them. You can also use StarBurst to automate what is known as a job stream. A job stream, if the term is new to you, is simply the series of steps involved in completing a given task.

What we've been discussing in this chapter, for example, is a job stream. The idea in each case is that you begin by creating a disk file with a data base program. You then use WordStar to create a MailMerge format file, and finally, you use MailMerge to print the file.

You can follow this job stream manually, going from one stage to the next by calling up the appropriate program at each step, or you can use a program like StarBurst. In that case, you choose the appropriate option from a menu that you've previously created, and StarBurst will automatically take you from one program to the next as needed.

Most "heavy-duty" data base programs have modules that are more-or-less equivalent to StarBurst, meaning they will let you create master menus to control job streams.

So much for the StarBurst part of the package. As for DataStar, of course, we already covered that at the beginning of the chapter. All of which brings us to ReportStar, which consists of several modules, including a sorting module and a report generator.

For the most part, InfoStar's report generator is comparable to The Formula's. Like Formula II, InfoStar includes a quick and easy report generator. Like Formula II also, InfoStar contains a full-screen text editor for producing reports in any format you care to create.

Using InfoStar's full-screen text editor is very much like using the Formula's text editor. Details are different, of course; where the Formula uses number signs to mark variables, for example, InfoStar uses underlinings. Even so, the two are similar, in general terms at least. Both allow you to define more than one file to get data from, both ask which file to use for each field, both allow you to designate calculated fields, and so forth.

For our purposes, in fact, there is only one important difference between these programs when it comes to formatting reports: InfoStar will let you enter format commands and print enhancements nearly as easily as you can enter them in WordStar. More than that, the print enhancements use essentially the same commands as WordStar, and the format commands use exactly the same dot commands.

ReportStar recognizes ten dot commands:

.CW Character Width
.PO Page Offset
.BP Bidirectional Print On/Off
.MB Bottom Margin
.LH Line Height
.OP Omit Page Number
.PL Page Length
.PN Set Page Number
.SR Subscript/Superscript Roll
.MT Top Margin

The first three in this list (character width, page offset, and bidirectional print), can be placed anywhere in the file. The rest can only be used before the first printing line. This is a minor restriction. For most purposes these commands will let you tailor the format of your report in any way that you like. They will also allow you to accomplish that task almost as easily as if you did it in WordStar.

Yet with all this, there are still benefits to be gained from using WordStar (not MailMerge) as the final report generator. The trick is to write the report to disk, then print the file with WordStar. If the printed report isn't quite perfect, it's much easier to open the file with Wordstar and do some simple editing than to go back to InfoStar's report definition and change it.

I am not talking here about things that are obviously wrong, and that ought to be changed in the report definition anyway, such as a missing **^B** to turn off boldfacing. I am referring to subtle problems that are likely to change each time you generate the report. The number of records, for example, may change from one time to the next. This may leave you with a page that looks out of balance unless you add a few lines, or change the top or bottom margins. This kind of problem cannot be taken care of in the report definition except by clumsy trial and error each time you produce the report.

Using WordStar for this kind of fine tuning is simply a more elegant solution to the problem and you can use it, of course, with any data base program at all.

APPENDIX

INFOSTAR: A SHORT NOTE

If you have InfoStar with ReportStar 1.00, be aware that there is a bug in it that can be fixed fairly easily. The bug is in FORMSORT, which sometimes fails to put an end-of-file marker on the file when it finishes sorting. Once that happens, DataStar will stop working properly, occasionally erasing records, or even refusing to open the data file.

To fix this problem on the CP/M version, use DDT to go into FORMSORT.COM and change Address 0880 from 00 to 10.

For the MS-DOS version, use DEBUG to go into FORMSORT.OVR and change Address 099E from 00 to 10.

Notice that the fix in the CP/M version is in the COM file, while the fix in the MS-DOS version is in the OVR file.

Here's a step-by-step description of the fix, if you're not familiar with DDT or DEBUG.

DDT first:

From the A> prompt, the command is:

        X:DDT Y:FORMSORT.COM

where "X" is the drive that DDT is on and "Y" is the drive that FORMSORT.COM is on.

DDT will respond with a sign-on message, ending with its prompt, a minus sign.
You enter: S0880 <RETURN>
DDT will respond with: 0880 00
You enter: 01 <RETURN>
DDT will respond with: 0881 2A
You enter: . <RETURN>
DDT will respond with its prompt: —
You enter ^C.
You will be returned to the CP/M prompt: A>
You enter: SAVE 69 FORMSORT.COM

With that, your computer will write the fixed version to disk, and you're done.

Here's the DEBUG version of the fix for MS-DOS:

From the A> prompt, once again, the command is:

        X:DEBUG Y:FORMSORT.OVR

where "X" is the drive that DEBUG is on and "Y" is the drive that FORMSORT.OVR is on.

DEBUG will respond with a sign-on message, ending with its prompt, a minus sign.
You enter: E 99E 10 <RETURN>
DEBUG will respond with its prompt once again: —
You enter: W <RETURN>
DEBUG will write the corrected file to disk, then respond with its prompt: —
You enter: Q <RETURN>

That's it. DEBUG will send you back to the operating system, and the A> prompt. You're back in familiar territory.

If you still don't feel comfortable using DDT or DEBUG, call your dealer or MicroPro, and let them walk you through the change.

A dBASE II Conversion Program for Converting dBASE II Files to MailMerge-Readable Format

If you don't have dBASE II, there's no point in reading this section. If you do have dBASE II, though, and don't have DBPlus, you should be able to make good use of this conversion program. As I've already pointed out, this will not do quite as much as DBPlus in converting files. It will not, for instance, let you modify fields or add new ones. It will also work more slowly than DBPlus.

Even so, this program will convert any dBASE II file into a Mail-Merge-readable format, complete with commas between fields and quotation marks around them. It will also show you each field and ask whether you want to include it in the output file.

This will work with any release of dBASE II. You will find some comments about using it at the end of this section.

```
*****************************************************************
** DBASE-MM.PRG - JOHN SCHNELL - 1983                        **
** program to convert dBASE.DBF files to MAILMERGE.TXT files **
**                                                           **
** Datafile needed: TEMPLATE.DBF (zero records)              **
**    One fieldname: CONCAT,C,100 (can increase size up to   **
**                   a maximum of 254 characters to equal    **
**                   maxlength field)                        **
*****************************************************************
**                   This program was written by and is included **
**                   here Courtesy of John Schnell           **
*****************************************************************


ERASE
SET TALK OFF
SET ECHO OFF
SET BELL OFF
SET CONFIRM ON
SET DEFAULT TO B:
CLEAR
STORE 100 to maxlength
*************************
*get name of file to convert*
*************************
STORE F to ok
DO WHILE .NOT. ok
   STORE '      ' TO filename
@ 01,05 SAY 'Enter name of dBASE file to convert to MAILMERGE file';
   GET filename
   READ
   ERASE
   @ 01,05 SAY 'insert diskette with .DBF file into drive B:, push any key'
   SET CONSOLE OFF
```

```
        WAIT
        SET CONSOLE ON
        IF     FILE('&filename')
          STORE T TO ok
        ELSE
          ERASE
          ?CHR (7)
          @ 01,00 SAY'!!Sorry, only these .DBF files are on this disk,';
             + 'please try again!!'
        ?
        LIST FILES LIKE *.dbf
        STORE 100 TO delay
        DO WHILE delay > 0
          STORE delay-1 TO delay
        ENDDO delay > 0
        ERASE
        ENDIF FILE('&filename')
      ENDDO .NOT. ok
      ***********************************************************
      *READ FILE STRUCTURE AND GET FIELDS TO CONVERT*
      ***********************************************************
      ERASE
      SET CONFIRM OFF
      ? '=== Retrieving database record structure ==='
      USE &filename
      COPY STRUCTURE EXTENDED TO tempstru
      USE tempstru
      STORE F TO ok
      DO WHILE .NOT. ok
        STORE 0 TO count
        STORE 2 TO offset
        STORE 0 TO length
        GOTO TOP
        ERASE
      @ 01,01 SAY '    FIELDNAME / TYPE / LENGTH';
        +'-Please identify fields you wish to convert.'
      DO WHILE .NOT. eof
      STORE 'N' TO include
      @ # +(offset),01 SAY str(#,2)+'. '+field:name+' '+field:type+' ';
          +STR(field:len,3)+'    —Include in MailMerge file (Y/N)    ';
        GET include
      READ
      IF     !(include) = 'Y'
        IF     field:type = 'C'
          STORE 'var'+STR(count+10,2) TO variable
          STORE field:name TO &variable
          STORE length+field: len TO length
          STORE count+1 to count
        ENDIF field:type ='C'
```

```
          IF      field:type = 'N'
            STORE 'var'+STR(count+10,2) TO variable
            STORE 'STR('+field:name;
              +','+STR(field:len,2);
              +','+STR(field:dec,2)+')' TO &variable
            STORE length+field:len TO length
            STORE COUNT+1 to count
          ENDIF field:type = 'N'
        ENDIF !(include) = 'Y'
      SKIP
      IF      # = 20
        ERASE
        STORE -19 TO offset
      ENDIF # = 20
      ENDDO    .NOT. eof
      @ 24,10 SAY 'Is the above correct ???';
      GET ok
      READ
      IF length > maxlength
        STORE F TO ok
        ERASE
        ? CHR(7)
        ? 'Concatenated string too long, ';
          +'eliminate'+STR(length - maxlength,3);
          +' characters from selected fields'
        STORE 100 TO delay
        DO WHILE delay > 0
          STORE delay-1 TO delay
        ENDO delay > 0
        ERASE
        ENDIF length > maxlength
      ENDDO    .NOT. ok
      USE
      DELETE FILE tempstru
      ****************************************************************
      * CONVERT FIELDS INTO ONE CONCATENATED FIELD IN TEMPFILE *
      ****************************************************************
      ERASE
      ? '=== Creating tempfile ==== '
      ?
      USE template
      COPY STRUCTURE TO tempfile
      USE
      ERASE
      ? '=== Creating concatenated records ==== '
      ?
      SELECT PRIMARY
      USE &filename
```

```
SELECT SECONDARY
USE tempfile
SELECT PRIMARY
GOTO TOP
DO WHILE .NOT. eof .AND. count > 0
  STORE '"'TO m:concat
  STORE 0 TO loop
  DO WHILE count > loop
    STORE 'var' +STR(loop+10,2) TO variable
    STORE &variable TO variable
    STORE m:concat-&variable TO m:concat
    STORE loop+1 TO loop
    IF    count > loop
      STORE m:concat-' ",''' TO m:concat
    ELSE
      STORE m:concat-' " ' TO m:concat
    ENDIF count > loop
  ENDDO count > loop
  SELECT SECONDARY
  APPEND BLANK
  REPLACE concat WITH m:concat
  ?m:concat
  SELECT PRIMARY
  SKIP
  ENDO    .NOT. eof .AND. count > 0
SELECT PRIMARY
USE
*******************************************************
* COPY CONCATENATED .DBF FILE TO .SDF/.MM FILE*
*******************************************************
STORE F to ok
DO WHILE .NOT. ok
  ERASE
  STORE "          " TO mmfilename
  SET CONFIRM ON
  @ 01,05 SAY 'What name do you want for the MailMerge .TXT file ? ';
  get mmfilename
  READ
  SET CONFIRM OFF
  @ 03,05 SAY 'Is ' +! (mmfilename)-'.TXT correct (Y/N) ' GET ok
  READ
ENDO    .NOT. ok
ERASE
@ 01,05 SAY !(mmfilename)-'.TXT file now being created. Please standby'
SELECT SECONDARY
COPY TO &mmfilename SDF delimited with ,
USE
DELETE FILE tempfile
```

```
ERASE
@ 05,05 SAY 'dBASE to MailMerge file conversion is complete'
SET INTENSITY OFF
CLEAR
RELEASE ALL
```

COMMENTS ABOUT THE dBASE II-TO-MAILMERGE CONVERSION PROGRAM

There are one or two additional considerations to keep in mind before using this program. First, before you use it, you have to create a dBASE data file called TEMPFILE.DBF. This file must contain a single field with the name CONCAT. The field must be designated as a character field with a length of one hundred characters.

This brings us to the second point. Notice that the maximum length—"maxlength" in the eighth line of the file—is also set to one hundred characters. This one hundred character maximum should be long enough to handle most conversions. It will certainly handle all the characters in a name and address, for instance. On the other hand, the maximum length was chosen more or less arbitrarily and can easily be changed, up to a maximum length of 254 characters. Just make sure that the maximum length as defined by "maxlength" matches the length of the field CONCAT in TEMPFILE.DBF. In general, the shorter the maximum length, the less chance you have of running out of disk space while running the conversion.

14

MailMerge as a Bridge
MOVING DATA FROM A DATA BASE TO VISICALC (AND OTHER CALC PROGRAMS)

Data base programs are nice to have, no doubt about it. Once you get the hang of them they make it exceedingly easy to store and retrieve information. They even let you manipulate that information, as long as you know exactly how you want it manipulated.

There are times, though, in playing with numbers, when you don't know beforehand what you want the final result to look like—when what you really need to do is play with your data, to massage the numbers in various ways, to ask "what if" questions. There are times, in short, when what you really need is to have your data entered in a calc program—VisiCalc or one of its imitators.

If you find yourself in this position, you have three choices. Enter the data into the calc program by hand, forget the whole idea on the grounds that it takes too much work, or let MailMerge do the work for you, transforming your data base file into a calc file.

Of course setting up the transformation file also takes some work. In fact, if the file is short enough, it may be faster to enter the data manually. Still, designing the transformation file is generally worth the effort. It is certainly worth it if your data file is long, if you expect to use the same worksheet again, or if you simply can't afford the possibility of introducing errors in the process of manually re-entering the data.

The transformation takes two steps. First you transform your data base files to MailMerge-readable format. Then you transform your Mail-

Merge-readable data file into a calc data file. You already know how to do the first step. This chapter will show you how to do the second.

The Transformation File: The Concept

The key to the transformation trick is simple. WordStar, as I've mentioned earlier, writes its files in a standard computer code known as ASCII. If the calc program you're using also writes its data files in ASCII, then you should (in principle at least) be able to use MailMerge to create data files for the calc program.

All you have to do, basically, is create a worksheet with the calc program. Instead of entering data in the worksheet though, you enter variable names. If you then go into the worksheet's data file with WordStar, you can add a data file command and a read variable command to the top of the file, at which point the worksheet's data file becomes a MailMerge format file. This format file is the transformation file. It will read a MailMerge data file, and write a calc program data file.

Of course, there are some complications—there always are. The one real limitation to this transformation trick is that it won't work with all calc programs. After a random sampling of half-a-dozen programs I wound up with three that can use the trick and three that can't. VisiCalc, I'm happy to say, is among those that can, and will serve as an example in this chapter. As for the rest, you'll have to check the individual programs yourself. In fact, even if you're using VisiCalc, you should double-check, since almost anything may change from one revision to the next. (Two of the programs I looked at, for example, were two different releases of the same program—Execuplan from Vector Graphic. Version 1.1 can't use this trick. Version 2.1 can. Moral: don't assume anything.)

One other thing: I did this on an IBM PC, with both VisiCalc and WordStar running under MS-DOS. If you're using an Apple II, with Visi-Calc running under Apple DOS and WordStar running under CP/M, you will have problems. CP/M and Apple DOS use different file formats. Even though both operating systems store information in ASCII, you still won't be able to read a file written in one format with a program that uses the other format. It is possible, though, to convert the files back and forth between the two formats. You'll have to decide whether it's worth the extra work or not.

Checking Out Your Calc Program

Determining whether your calc program uses ASCII data files is easy enough. Take any data file that's been created by the program, and browse through it with WordStar. If you can read the file, it's ASCII. If you can't, it's not.

If, in addition to the data, there is "garbage" in the file that you can't read, or if there is nothing but garbage in the file, you will not be able to use this method of transforming the data. The garbage characters represent information stored in non-ASCII format. WordStar/MailMerge will not be able to copy this part of the file faithfully.

The browsing part is important, by the way. There is nothing in principle to keep a program from storing data in ASCII format, and storing other information in a compressed format. In fact, this is done all the time. If you open a dBASE II data file with WordStar, for instance, what you will see on the screen, mostly, is four lines of garbage characters, with one or two readable words mixed into the second line. If you explore further, you'll find that all the data is neatly stored in ASCII code.

A little hint here may be helpful—WordStar gets painfully slow when trying to move a cursor through an exceptionally long line. In fact, if the line is long enough, you may get the impression that the keyboard has locked up on you. You will often get a quicker response by doing a paragraph reform (^**B**), thereby converting the one long line into a series of short lines.

After you're finished browsing through the file, you should leave it by way of the quit command (^**KQ**), rather than a save command. Otherwise, if you've made any changes to the file—purposely or not—your calc program may no longer be able to read it.

DIVINING THE FILE STRUCTURE

Assuming you can read the data file, the next step is to learn how the file is structured.

Before you can design the transformation file, you need to find out how the calc program knows whether a given entry is supposed to be text or is supposed to be a numerical value. In particular, you need to find out how the program tells the difference between a number entered as text and a number entered as a value.

This takes a little detective work. You have to take a data file that's been produced by the calc program and examine it, looking for patterns in the way it designates text as opposed to values. If the file structure is simple, the patterns will be easy to find. If the structure is more complicated, the patterns may be somewhat hidden.

In the interest of simplicity, it makes sense to create a data file just for this purpose. That way you can keep it as short and as simple as possible, but still make sure you've entered enough information to tell you what you need to know.

Here's an example of what your test file might look like when you create it with your calc program.

	A	B	C
1	TEXT	VALUES	VALUES2
2			
3	43	13	23
4	44	14	24
5	45	___	25
6	46	27	___
7	Ab		72
8	Bc		

Notice that everything entered in column A, including numbers, is entered as text. The numbers in columns B and C, though, are entered strictly as values (except for the totals, which are the result of formulae). When looking at the data file, this will make it relatively easy to compare numbers entered as text with numbers entered as values. Notice also that the entries were designed to make them easy to identify in the data file. In each of the columns the last digit of the number matches the row number, so that 43, 13, and 23, for example, are all in row three. Similarly, the first digit in each number is the same for all numbers in any given column. The columns are each a different length, meanwhile, to see what effect, if any, that will have on the structure of the file. (In some programs it will make a difference, while in others it won't.)

From this point on, details will differ, depending on the program you're using.

Once you have created this worksheet, you need to save it to a data file—call it TESTDATA. With VisiCalc you have two basic choices. You can either use the VisiCalc format, in which case the file will be named TESTDATA.VC, or you can use the Data Interchange Format, in which case the file will be named TESTDATA.DIF. (You have three additional choices as well within the DIF format, but they all look substantially the same, varying only in details.)

If you have a similar choice with the program you're using, save the worksheet in both formats, or all possible formats. Odds are that one of them will be significantly easier to work with than the others.

Before leaving the worksheet, it's also a good idea to print a copy so you can have it in front of you when you're looking at the data file. In fact, in looking at the data file itself, it will also be more convenient to deal with a printed copy. That way you can make notes on the paper, right next to the data.

With VisiCalc, TESTDATA.DIF will look like this:

```
TABLE
0,1
""
VECTORS
0,9
TUPLES
0,4
DATA
0,0
""
-1,0
BOT
1,0
"TEXT"
1,0
""
1,0
```

"43"
1,0

The file will go on like this for several pages.

TESTDATA.VC is more encouraging. When you print it, it will look like this:

```
>A8:"Bc
>C7:@SUM(C3. . .C5)
>A7:"Ab
>C6:"———
>B6:@SUM(B3. . .B4)
>A6:"46
>C5:25
>B5:"———
>A5:"45
>C4:24
>B4:14
>A4:"44
>C3:23
>B3:13
>A3:"43
>C1:"VALUES2
>B1:"VALUES
>A1:"TEXT
/W1
/GOC
/GRA
/GC9
/X>A1:A1:
```

This is the entire file.

Even a quick glance at these two data files should convince you that the second format will be easier to work with. Not only is it more compact than the data interchange format, but the entries are clearly labeled in terms of the cells they go in. This will make it easy indeed to match each entry in the worksheet to the same entry in the data file.

The VisiCalc format uses an exceedingly simple file structure. You might notice in passing that it lists only those cells that contain data, and that it lists them in descending order. The cells, in fact, are sorted by row—from the highest number to the lowest—and within each row by column—from the "highest" letter to the "lowest."

As for the differentiation between text and numerical values, a quick comparison of the worksheet with the data file shows that text is always indicated the same way. A8, C6, and A6, for example, include letters, symbols, and numbers, yet all three follow the same format:

CELL NAME:"text entry

What's more, the only difference between these entries and numbers entered as values is the presence or absence of the quote sign after the colon. Text has the quote sign, while values do not.

In designing the transformation file, then, you have to find a way to make the quote sign show up where you want text, or numbers treated as text, and keep it from showing up where you want numbers treated as values.

The first part is easy. The second is not.

When you enter a variable name into the worksheet, you have no choice but to enter it as text. VisiCalc will automatically mark that entry with the quote sign in the VisiCalc data file. When MailMerge uses this as a format file, it will replace the variable name with data, and the quote sign will remain.

This automatically puts the quote marker on entries that are meant as text. Unfortunately, it also puts a quote marker on the entries that you want treated as values.

The simplest way to get rid of the unwanted quote markers is to add a marker of your own when you enter your variable names that represent values. "V," for "value," would be one possibility.

Whatever marker you use though, the point is that variable names for text should have one format (&Text&) while variable names for values should have another (V&Value&). When you open the file later in WordStar, this will let you do a global search and replace with the ˆQA command—searching for and deleting the "V."

The procedure is right out of basic WordStar, but it's important enough to be worth going through it here step-by-step.

When you do the search and replace, WordStar will ask you what to find. You type "V RETURN. (That's a quote sign followed by the "V" marker, followed by a RETURN.)

When WordStar asks you what to replace it with, you enter RETURN. This tells WordStar to replace it with nothing, or, in effect, to delete the quote sign and the V.

If you also choose the options "N" (replace without asking) and "G" (global search and replace), WordStar will go through the entire file and automatically change the format of all "value" entries from

CELL NAME"V&Value&

to

CELL NAME:&Value&

This will remove the quote markers from each "value" entry while leaving them on each "text" entry—both in the format file itself, and in the VisiCalc readable data file that MailMerge will create from this format file.

CREATING THE TRANSFORMATION FILE

All the details in the last section apply strictly to VisiCalc. I've included them less for VisiCalc users, though, than for users of other calc programs. Seeing this step-by-step example of how to decipher one program should help in deciphering whatever you happen to be using. Once you've reached this point in understanding your calc program's data files, you're ready to create a transformation file.

Here again, we'll use VisiCalc as the example.

The first step in creating the transformation file is to design the worksheet. This means deciding beforehand exactly which fields from your data file you want to use, where you want to use them, and just how you want to play with them.

Let's go back to the Christmas bonus example from the last chapter. But let's back up a bit from the letter, and see how you might figure out the bonus percentage.

You might, for example, have a standing policy to calculate the Christmas bonus at the end of each year on the basis of the profit for that year. If everyone is getting the same bonus in terms of percentage, then all you have to do to compute the proper percentage is take the total bonus amount and divide it by the total salary of all employees.

But a more complicated arrangement might be used. Employees might, for example, get different percentage bonuses, depending on how many years they've been with the company. In that case, once you know the total bonus, you have to calculate the amount for each person. You can do this easily with a calc program.

Your worksheet needs four columns: Column A for the name of each individual, Column B for his or her salary, Column C for the number of years he or she has been with the company, and, finally, Column D with the formula for computing the bonus. Each of these formulae will be based on increments of the same unknown value. The idea is that you keep plugging in numbers for this unknown value until the total sum of all bonuses—that is, the total sum of Column D—equals the total bonus that you want to pay. (This is not the most elegant way to solve the problem, but it will work.)

Your transformation file, then, should start out as a worksheet that looks like this:

	A	B	C	D
1	NAME	SALARY	YEARS WITH	BONUS
2			COMPANY	
3				
4	&N1&	V&S1&	&Y1&	
5	&N2&	V&S2&	&Y2&	
6	&N3&	V&S3&	&Y3&	
7				——
8			TOTAL	0

There are several things to notice here. First, the zero in cell D8 indicates the presence of a formula there. This is the sum of all the individual bonuses. This file assumes that you will enter the rest of the formulae in Column D manually based on what shows up in Column C. This assumption was made in the interest of simplicity. If you were really setting up a file like this, you would probably make use of conditional commands in either your data base program or your MailMerge file to load the proper formulae into Column D for you.

In the interests of simplicity I've kept this short, but note that you must enter a set of variable names for each employee, or more generally, for each record in your data base. Otherwise MailMerge will write a separate worksheet for each record. On the other hand, if you are dealing with many records, you'll have to make sure your worksheet is short enough so it will still fit in your computer's memory even after you've loaded in the data. That way, if MailMerge can't fit all the records into a single VisiCalc data file, it will automatically generate two or more VisiCalc files, continuing until it runs out of data.

Finally, note that you can have more sets of variable names in the worksheet than you have records in your data file. MailMerge will simply complete the VisiCalc data file using null values.

When VisiCalc reads the worksheet, it will ignore these null values. When it saves the worksheet back to disk, it will eliminate them from the file.

It generally makes sense, then, to put extra sets of variable names in the transformation file. In this example, for instance, the extra variables will let you use the same transformation file from year to year without changes even though the number of employees may vary from one year to the next.

Once you've created the basic worksheet complete with variable names, the next step is to save the file to disk, then open it up in WordStar's edit mode. (To play it safe, you should use the "N," or "non-document" mode. This will guard against accidentally introducing garbage that might later confuse your calc program.)

We've already covered most of what you have to do at this point, namely, enter an appropriate data file command, enter an appropriate read variable command, and do a global search and replace to delete all the "V" markers from cells that should be values.

In addition, you have to add a few more format commands to prevent WordStar from adding extra lines and spaces that will confuse your calc program. Specifically, you have to add commands to set the top and bottom margins to zero, and set the page offset to zero. You may also have to turn print-time line-forming off, depending on the width of your lines—which depends, in turn, on the structure of your data file. (In this example you don't need to bother.)

An example of what the final transformation file will look like follows.

FILE: SAMPLE MAILMERGE TO VISICALC TRANSFORMATION FILE

```
.DF PERSONNEL.REC
.RV N1, S1, Y1, N2, S2, Y2, N3, S3, Y3
.MT 0
```

```
.MB 0
.PO 0
> D8:@SUM(D4. . .D6)
> C8:"TOTAL
> D7:"————
> C6:"&Y3&
> B6:&S3&
> A6:"&N3&
> C5:"&Y2&
> B5:&S2&
> A5:"&N2&
> C4:"&Y1&
> B4:&S1&
> A4:"&N1&
> C2:"COMPANY
> D1:"BONUS
> C1:"YEARS WITH
> B1:"SALARY
> A1:"NAME
/W1
/GOC
/GRA
/GC10
/X > A1: > D8:
```

One more hint on this transformation file. Typing the read variable command can be tedious, particularly if you have many variables in the data file. Thankfully, you can usually avoid most of the typing.

Most calc programs, including VisiCalc, will let you write the worksheet to disk using the worksheet format. This capability is there mainly so you can go into the worksheet with a word processor and add a few final touches before printing.

If the variables in your MailMerge data file are in the same order in which they show up on the worksheet, though, you can save some work here. Printing the worksheet to disk will give you a list of the variables in the same order that you need them in for the read variable command.

In this case, for instance, if you print the file to disk, then delete everything before and after the variables, you'll wind up with this:

```
4    &N1&    V&S1&    &Y1&
5    &N2&    V&S2&    &Y2&
6    &N3&    V&S3&    &Y3&
```

You can then use manual commands to delete the row numbers, ampersands, the V's, and the extra spaces. All that remains then is to add an **.RV** at the beginning of each line, and add commas after each variable. Don't forget, also, that you're free to either join all the variables in one line, or to leave them in three different lines, as long as each line starts with the read variable dot command.

In a longer file, you can use global search and replace to do the same thing much more easily. To close up the space between the first column and the second column, for instance, you could tell WordStar to find the sequence: "&   V&" and to replace it with a single comma. To delete row numbers, you could use column mode (^KN) and delete all the numbers at once. Finally, if you want to join all the variables into one line, you can use global search and replace again to look for a carriage return (entered as ^PN), and replace that with a comma as well.

A word of warning if your spreadsheet is wider than your screen: WordStar 3.00 has a tendency to freeze up when trying to scroll horizontally while in column mode. Not only that, but it has this problem whether the block markers are displayed or not. Any time you are working on something that's wider than your screen, you should make sure that you are not in column mode when moving the cursor. This means that if you have to do a column delete, for example, on a wide spreadsheet, you should mark the beginning and end of the block, turn the column mode on, delete the block, and, finally, switch column mode back off before you do anything else. Similarly, if you are doing a column move or column copy, you should:

1. mark the block
2. turn column mode off
3. move the cursor to the column destination
4. turn column mode back on
5. move or copy the column
6. hide the markers
7. and, finally, turn the column mode back off before you do anything else

This bug, incidentally, appears to have been fixed in release 3.30.

Notice that to use this trick for writing the **.RV** command, the variables in your MailMerge-Readable data file have to be in the same order as you want them to show up in the worksheet. This provides a good argument for designing your spreadsheet before extracting the MailMerge data file from your data base.

Notice also that aside from saving yourself the work of typing all the variable names into the file, this approach has the added advantage of guarding against typos. Even if your data is already in MailMerge readable format, then, these two benefits, taken together, provide a good argument for generating a new data file for use with the spreadsheet, when necessary.

Once you have the transformation file, you're essentially done. All that remains is to run MailMerge, and produce a calc data file.

Don't forget to use an appropriate ending for the file name (.VC for VisiCalc). If you did everything right, you should wind up with a usable, and useful, calc data file.

15

MailMerge as a Programming Language

BIBLIO: A BIBLIOGRAPHIC GENERATION PROGRAM

In previous discussions of MailMerge, I pointed out that the program was, for all intents and purposes, a simple programming language. We didn't pursue the thought then. It's time now, though, to go back and develop this idea further.

PROGRAMMING WITH MAILMERGE

In a very real sense, every MailMerge format file that we've looked at, in fact every MailMerge format file ever written, is a program.

Whether you accept that statement or not depends mostly on how you define "program." I choose to define it as any set of computer-readable instructions that will cause a computer to behave in a more-or-less predictable manner. (If you've done much programming, you know why I'm hedging the predictable part.)

By this definition, MailMerge format files are clearly programs. To run them, you call them up from within MailMerge, and MailMerge interprets them, sending instructions to the computer. This is just what a BASIC interpreter does when running a program written in BASIC.

All this, by definition, makes MailMerge a language program. That means that the set of all MailMerge commands is a computer language.

Of course, this is all semantics. You can just as easily use a definition of "program" that eliminates MailMerge format files from that category.

The fact remains, however, that you can create MailMerge files for some fairly sophisticated, non-trivial applications. Consider, for instance, a MailMerge file—or series of files—that will generate a bibliography for you. This application is complicated enough so that it will take the rest of this chapter to examine just a part of the program. In the process, we're going to look at some of the best-hidden, and some of the most surprising, capabilities of MailMerge.

A WORD ABOUT BIBLIOGRAPHIES

Most writers I know hate typing bibliographies. I, for one, consider it a mechanical, non-creative, and above all, time-consuming chore. Every time I write a bibliography, I waste a great deal of time checking to see if I'm using commas, periods, quotes, and underlinings properly—not to mention the time I waste checking the order that the information is supposed to go in.

Part of my problem in remembering the correct format for bibliographies is that I don't use them very often, so that I tend to forget from one time to the next. A much more basic problem, though, is that the format varies from entry to entry, depending on the precise nature of the reference. Entries for articles, for example, follow a different format than entries for books. Entries for articles in a magazine follow a different format than entries for articles in a newspaper. Both of these follow a format different from entries for articles in a scholarly journal. Even if you stay strictly with one kind of entry, such as articles in scholarly journals, the formats will still change slightly from entry to entry depending on whether the journal uses series numbers, volume numbers, issue numbers, or any combination of these.

Yet for all my complaining, the rules for bibliographic entries are straightforward—even if the various permutations and combinations of those rules are not.

What this all adds up to is that generating a bibliography is just the sort of thing that computers are best at.

The ideal program—for me at least—would be menu driven, so I wouldn't have to remember any commands from one time to the next. In addition, it would prompt me for information, show me how to enter that information, then automatically write each bibliographic item to disk. The program would not only add periods, commas, quotes, and underlining where called for, it would modify the format depending on the entry itself. In other words, it would automatically take the permutations and combinations of the various rules into account. That's the program we are going to write.

DESIGNING THE PROGRAM

The first step in writing any program is to decide exactly what you want the program to do. We've just defined the goal in general terms, but before we can actually write anything we have to be more specific.

There are, as it happens, several "standard" bibliographical formats. The first thing we have to do is decide which one to use. For the examples in this chapter we are going to stay with the format suggested in the *MLA Style Sheet,* 2nd edition. (Or with my understanding of that format, at least.) This one decision tells us most of what we need to know before we can design the program. Specifically, it tells us exactly what we want the final output to look like. All that remains is to figure out how to produce that output.

Let's add one more specific to help simplify the job. Assume that you have completed a project—a book, a thesis, or whatever—in which you've used nothing but newspapers for research. This means you can limit the program to dealing with newspaper articles.

Here, then, is a program that will do precisely what you need it to do: generate the correct entries for newspaper articles, using the MLA format.

PROGRAM: NEWSPAPER BIBLIO

A Limited Bibliography Program

FILE NAME: NPAPER.MAS

```
.MT 0
.MB 0
.PO 0
.OP
.PF off (To make sorting easier.)
        The following file is unformatted.
        To Format, first sort the file.
        Once sorted, Format the entries with ^Q^Q^B
        Then delete this instruction.
.DM This is NPAPER.MAS. It is the master file for generating
.DM Bibliographic Entries for ARTICLES in NEWSPAPERS.
.DM
.AV "Do you need further instructions (Y/N)? ", HELP, 1
.IF &HELP& = "N" .OR. &HELP& = "n" GOTO BEGIN
.FI HELPFILE
.EF BEGIN
.FI N.SLA
#
```

Alternate ending for use with file insert commands only:

```
.DM Do you need further Information or Instructions?
.DM "If so, Enter [RETURN]
.AV "If not, enter [. RETURN]", HELP
&HELP/0&
.FI HELPFILE
#
.FI N.SLA
#
```

This is the master file. The first five dot commands control the format MailMerge will use in writing the bibliographic entries to disk. The reasons for at least four of these commands should be obvious: margins and page offset are set to zero, and page numbering is omitted (**.OP**). A bit less obvious, perhaps, is the reason for turning off print-time line-forming.

The note in the file points out that the **.PF off** command is there to make sorting easier. The presumption is that when you're finished entering the bibliography, you will need to put the entries in alphabetical order by last name of author. Whether you're doing the sorting manually or with a sorting program, the single line entries will make the job easier. If you're sorting manually, the last names will be easier to pick out, and the beginning and end of each entry will be easier to mark before moving. If you're using a sorting program, you'll usually find that the single-line format is the easiest approach to telling the program where each entry starts and stops. There are some programs, in fact, that won't sort any other format.

The lines of text immediately after the first five dot commands are instructions for turning the generated bibliography into a finished product. They will show up in the bibliography file itself.

After the instructions comes a sign-on message, telling you what program you're in, and what it's for. This is followed by a question, giving you the choice of reading further instructions or not. The mechanics of setting up this conditional choice should be familiar by now, whether you are using the conditional print commands or the conditional file insert command. Just remember, if you are using the file insert command, to enter the &HELP& line with an overprint command (^PM), rather than with a RETURN. Notice, by the way, that if you are using the conditional print command you can put the instructions into the master file and still be able to skip over them in using the program.

The last command in this file is a file insert command that will take you to the file N.SLA. N.SLA contains the questions and format for the bibliography entries.

In either version of NPAPER.MAS, the blank line at the end of the file is important. In the version that uses the conditional File Insert command, the blank line between the two **.FI** commands is also important. If you leave either of these lines out, the file insert commands will not work properly.

N.SLA also has a blank line at the beginning of the file. This is not necessary if you are using the conditional print commands. It is necessary if you are using the conditional file insert command. With the **.FI** command, MailMerge will write the first line of N.SLA in your bibliography. By putting a blank line there, you minimize the need for editing later.

If you are using the conditional file insert trick, MailMerge will also put the overwrite command in your bibliography. This will show up as a minus flag.

Both of these unwanted items—the extra line and the overwrite command—can be deleted easily enough when editing later.

Before looking at N.SLA, take a look at the instructions for using it. These will tell you most of what you should look for in reading the N.SLA file.

There isn't too much to say about the instruction file itself. You might note how it uses the ask for variable and clear screen commands to divide the instructions into a series of "pages."

Also note the blank line at the end of HELPFILE. This line is, once again, extremely important. Without it, the file insert command will not work properly.

You'll probably notice, also, that comment number four describes a trick for marking errors that we've used earlier, and that you presumably already know. You'll also find a reminder to turn off the file directory so the program will run faster—another point you presumably already know. In fact, although we're talking in terms of writing this program for your personal use, all the instructions are written as if they were for someone who knew nothing about the program. This is good procedure, and not just because you may wind up giving the program to someone else to create your bibliography for you. Any time you write a program, you have to think in terms of coming back to it six months or six years later, at which point you may not remember anything about it. Tricks that seemed obvious when you wrote the program may no longer be obvious. Or, you may have discovered new tricks and expected them to be in the program, and they did not appear.

The point is this: When in doubt about how much documenting to do, do more, not less.

FILE NAME: HELPFILE

```
.DM
.DM
.DM        This file contains the instructions for using NPAPER.MAS
.DM
.DM        This program will generate Bibliographic entries for
.DM        Articles in Newspapers only.
.DM
.DM
.DM        It will run MUCH faster if you have turned the file
.DM        directory off.
.DM
.DM
.DM
.DM
.AV  "          Please Hit < RETURN > ", X
.CS
.DM        Some comments:
.DM
.DM            1) NPAPER.MAS uses the Bibliography format
.DM        suggested by The Modern Language Association of America
.DM        in the The MLA Style Sheet, Second Edition.
.DM
.DM            2) Some entries—such as long titles—may
.DM        require more than 1 line. I have therefore included
```

```
.DM     extra lines where it seemed appropriate. These will
.DM     show as prompts whether you need them or not. Don't
.DM     let them throw you. If you don't need them, simply
.DM     hit RETURN. They will not show up in your
.DM     bibliography.
.DM
.DM         3) I have also included lines for comment about
.DM     the entries. Once again, if you don't need them,
.DM     simply hit RETURN and ignore them.
.DM
.AV "        Hit <RETURN> to continue", X
.DS
.DM         4) MAILMERGE will not let you back up and make
.DM     corrections. Be sure each answer is correct BEFORE you
.DM     hit RETURN. If you make a mistake, this program
.DM     provides some help in correcting it. After you finish
.DM     each bibliographic item, the program will show you what
.DM     you've just entered. If it is not exactly correct, you
.DM     can enter an error marker (the program suggests @@@).
.DM         At that point, you can immediately enter the same
.DM     item again using ^R for each prompt. This will re-
.DM     enter your answers automatically. Later, when you open
.DM     the bibliography file in WordStar's edit mode, you can
.DM     use the search command to find the error markers, then
.DM     delete the incorrect entries.
.DM
.AV "        Hit <RETURN> to continue", X
.CS
.DM
.DM         5) The program is designed to be self-explanatory,
.DM     whether you are familiar with bibliography formats or
.DM     not. Along with the prompts, you will find
.DM     instructions on how to enter the information. You will
.DM     also find sample entries to act as a guide. These
.DM     should be particularly helpful in those cases where the
.DM     information varies from one bibliographical reference
.DM     to the next. Sample entries are always labeled, and
.DM     are always contained in brackets.
.DM         You should always type exactly what's in the
.DM     brackets, including punctuation and spaces. If the
.DM     example is, [Late City Ed.,], then you would type
.DM     "Late City Ed.," followed by a space, followed by a
.DM     RETURN.
.DM
.DM
.DM
.DM
.AV "        Hit <RETURN> to continue", X
```

```
.CS
.DM
.DM          6) When you finish entering the bibliography with
.DM      this file, your entries will still need to be sorted
.DM      and formatted. Do not forget to do that. Also, do the
.DM      sorting first.
.DM
.DM
.DM
.DM
.AV "        Hit <RETURN> to continue", X
.CS
#
```

The file that actually generates the bibliography is presented in the following.

FILE NAME: N.SLA

(This file must start with a blank line if using the conditional file insert commands. The line can be left out when using the conditional print commands.)

```
#
.DM
.DM Author or Authors
.DM Generally this will be entered Last name, First name.
.DM You must enter commas between names.
.AV "Author Name: ",A1
.AV "Name (Cont): ",A2
.DM
.DM Article Title in Full. (Including Subtitle, if any).
.DM Title and Subtitle are Separated by a Colon and Space.
.DM Usually you will end this entry with a Comma.
.DM Exception 1:
.DM   If Subtitle ends with a question mark, do not use a comma.
.DM Exception 2:
.DM   If subtitle contains a quotation and ends with quotation
.DM marks, the comma goes INSIDE the internal quotes.
.DM Examples: [Title: Subtitle,] or [Title: Subtitle?]
.DM                  or [Title: 'Subtitle,']
.AV "       Title: ", T1
.AV "Title (Cont): ", T2
.DM
.AV "Newspaper Name: ", M1
.AV "Name (Cont): ", M2
.DM
```

```
.DM Enter edition if available.
.DM   (Different editions are laid out differently.)
.DM End this entry with COMMA and SPACE, if used.
.DM Example: [Late City Ed., ]
.AV "Edition: " , E
.DM
.DM Date (Volume and Issue can be substituted here,
.DM   but date is preferred.)
.DM Also note: Preferred format is Day Month Year.
.DM Example:    [12 December 1982] (Date)
.DM           or [3, No. 12 (1982)] (Volume and Issue)
.AV "Date: ", D
.DM
.DM Section, if appropriate.
.DM NOTE: End this entry with comma and space, if used.
.DM Example: [Sec. 5, ]
.AV "Section: ", S
.DM
.DM Page Number.
.DM NOTE: Enter this as "p." for a single page
.DM   or "pp." for more than one page.
.DM Omit "p." or "pp." if you used vol. & issue instead of date.
.DM Example: "12 December 1982, [pp. 16–18]"
.DM         But "3, No. 12 (1982), [16–18]"
.AV "Page: ",P
.DM
.DM Columns.
.DM Column numbers are optional, but can be helpful.
.DM NOTE: If you use this entry,
.DM   be sure to START with a comma and space.
.DM Examples: [, col. 4] or [, cols. 6–7]
.AV "Column(s): ", C
.DM
.DM The Following Lines are for any comments you want to add.
.DM They will show up as continuous text in the bibliography.
.AV C1
.AV C2
.AV C3
.AV C4
.AV C5
.CS
.DM
.DM THIS ITEM WILL APPEAR IN YOUR BIBLIOGRAPHY AS FOLLOWS
.DM   (Except for format):
.DM
.DM This is your chance to note any mistakes for correction
.DM
```

```
.DM
.DM &A1&&A2/0&.
.DM "&T1&&T2/0&" ^S &M1&&M2/0&. ^S
.DM &E/0&&D&, &S&&P&&C/0&.
.DM &C1/0&&C2/0&&C3/0&&C4/0&&C5/0&
.DM
.DM If the above entry is correct, enter RETURN.
.AV "If the entry is NOT correct, enter @@@ return: ", ERROR, 3
.DM
&ERROR/0&&A1&&A2/0&. "&T1&&T2/0&" ^S &M1&&M2/0&. ^S
&E/0&&D&, &S/0&&P&&C/0&.
&C1/0&&C2/0&&C3/0&&C4/0&&C5/0&
```
NOTE: The above three lines should be one line in the file. They are broken into three lines here for readability only.
```
#
.CS
.AV "More entries (Y/N)? ", MORE, 1
.IF &MORE& = "N" .OR. &MORE& = "n" GOTO END
.FI N.SLA
.EF END
```

Alternate ending for use with conditional File Insert command.
```
.DM If this is the last entry, enter [. RETURN]
.AV "If there are more entries, enter [RETURN]", MORE,
&MORE/0&     This must be entered with ^PM
.FI N.SLA
#
```

    If there is anything at all surprising about this file, it's simply that there are no new tricks in it—no ideas that we haven't already used elsewhere. Yet we have created a usable, useful program.

    As it stands, the program is fairly long (in comparison to what we've been doing), but still straightforward; if you read the instruction file first, you should have no problem following it. Basically, it asks you for specific information, and tells you exactly how to enter that information, item by item. When you finish, it shows you what the whole entry looks like, and gives you a chance to mark the mistakes. Finally, it gives you the choice of adding more entries or not, courtesy of either the conditional print commands or the conditional file insert trick that we've put to such good use in so many applications.

    To run this program, then, you call up MailMerge, and tell it to Merge-Print NPAPER.MAS. After that, you only have to follow the instructions on the screen.

    Two final points about the format: The variable names in the format section should all be on one continuous line. In order to show all the variables, I've been forced to break the line in the example. Notice also the extra line after the variables. This puts a blank line between entries in the bibliography, making it easier to read the file later if you are sorting manually, and also making it easier to read the final bibliography.

Making Full Use of the
Conditional Print Commands

The partial bibliography program as written will work on any version of MailMerge. If you have the conditional print feature, though, there are a few changes you might like to make. There are, in fact, several places where you can use the conditional print command in interesting ways.

If you look through the program, you'll see several instructions that give you, as the user, a conditional command. On the entry for "edition," for example, the instructions say, in effect "*If* you use this entry, *then* add a comma and space. Anytime you see a statement like this, odds are you can find a way to make MailMerge do the work for you.

Ideally in this case, as the user you should be able to enter the edition, if you know it, without having to worry about adding the additional punctuation. As a programmer, then, you have to find a way to tell the program to add the comma and space for you—but only if you entered an edition.

One way to accomplish that task follows.

PARTIAL EXAMPLE:
AUTOMATIC PUNCTUATION

```
.DM Enter Edition if Available.
.DM (Layout Changes from one edition to the Next)
.DM Example: [Late City Ed.]
.AV "Edition: ", E
.EX &E&   > = "A" GOTO NOEDITION
.SV E,&E&,
.EF NOEDITION
```

The **.EX,** or "EXcept" command here says, in effect: Unless E is greater than or equal to "A," go to the line that reads **.EF NOEDITION.** In other words if you as the user entered nothing here (E is less than "A"), MailMerge will skip to the **.EF** line. If you entered a response (E is greater than or equal to "A"), it will not skip.

The next line is the one that adds the comma and space. This one's a little tricky. It is entered as <PERIOD>, S, V, <SPACE>, E, <COMMA>, <AMPERSAND>, E, <AMPERSAND>, <COMMA>, <SPACE>, <RETURN>.

The space between the "SV" and the "E" is not important. The space that doesn't show though—the one between the second comma and the return—is critical. The Set Variable command, remember, will set the value E *exactly* to whatever is on the right side of the comma. In this case, that means the old value of E followed by a comma, *followed by a space.* Since the space doesn't show on your screen, you have to be especially careful to include it when writing the command line. And just as careful not to put any extra spaces in.

There you have it. If you enter an edition, MailMerge will automatically adjust the format for you. If you enter a RETURN to bypass the question, MailMerge will leave the format untouched.

Most of the other possibilities for using the conditional print command in this program are variations on this example. There is one other possibility, though, that deserves special mention.

As it stands, the user has to enter the error marker manually for incorrect entries. By taking advantage of the conditional print command, though, you can have the program ask whether the entry is correct, let the user answer with "Y" or "N," and have MailMerge automatically enter the marker or not, as appropriate. Aside from saving two keystrokes, this also guarantees that the marker will be entered correctly each time, making it essentially impossible to miss it later when using the search command in WordStar.

The application looks like this:

PARTIAL EXAMPLE:
AUTOMATIC ERROR MARKING

```
.DM Is the above entry correct (Y/N)? If you answer "N",
.AV "an error marker (@@@) will be added to the entry.", ERR, 1
.EX &ERR& = "N" .OR. &ERR& = "n" GOTO NOERROR
.SV ERROR, @@@
.DM
.EF NOERROR
&ERROR/0&&A1&&A2/0&. . . . (followed by the remaining variables)

.SV ERROR,
```

The prompt here is self-explanatory.

The conditional command will accept either "N" or "n" as a proper answer, in which case it will read the first set variable command and set the variable "ERROR" to "@ @ @." On any other response—including a RETURN or an incorrect letter—the program will skip to the **.EF NOERROR** command line. This means, in effect, that the default for this answer is "Y."

Notice, finally, the last line here, setting the variable "ERROR" back to a null value. (Here again, be careful not to include an extra space after the comma.) This resets the default value for ERROR, and, in effect, resets the default value of "Y" as an answer to the question, "Is the above entry correct?"

That pretty well covers the possibilities for this file. Using these two tricks, you can rewrite as many of the conditional commands as you care to, automating much of the work, and simplifying the actual process of entering the bibliography.

In doing that, though, you pay a price. In order to make it easier to use the program, you have to work a little harder to write it. The program itself, moreover, becomes longer, taking up more disk space and more memory in the computer. In rewriting the first example, four lines became six. In rewriting the second, five lines became nine. Two extra lines here, or four extra lines there may seem like little enough to add, but remember that as the program gets longer, it starts taking longer to run. If you add enough "conveniences" it may eventually take longer to create a bibliography with the program than without it.

This brings up an important point about programming in general. As a programmer you have to make choices and compromises. The choices you make are often a matter of personal taste, but you should always be aware that the choices are there.

THE POSSIBILITIES FOR LONGER, MORE COMPLICATED PROGRAMS

The bibliography example is a full program in one sense, but only a partial program in another. To be really useful, a bibliography program should deal with all reference items, not just with newspapers. The limitation though, has nothing to do with MailMerge. It is strictly a length consideration. An entire bibliography program would take a great deal more space, and add little in the way of new ideas.

A "full" program, in fact, would consist of a series of separate files, each one dealing with a different kind of entry, and each one similar in concept to N.SLA. In each case, the file would contain the appropriate questions and format directions for a particular item—books, articles in magazines, or whatever.

These separate files would be linked through a single menu. After starting with the sign-on file, you would be sent to the menu by way of a file insert command. After finishing each bibliographic entry, you would again be sent back to the menu. Each time you returned to the menu, you would be given the same set of choices for your next bibliographic entry.

In effect, each file would be a subroutine within the program as a whole, while the menu would function as the master control routine for the program.

Here are two versions of the Menu file. The first example does not take advantage of the conditional print commands, while the second one does.

Neither of these menus, incidentally, is complete. There are other choices you would have to add to handle other reference items.

FILE NAME: MENU

*Menu File for Bibliography NOT USING
Conditional Print Commands*

```
.DM The next item to be included in the Bibliography is:
.DM
.DM          (1) Article in a NEWSPAPER (Enter N)
.DM          (2) Article in a MAGAZINE (Enter M)
.DM          (3) Article in a SCHOLARLY JOURNAL (Enter J)
.DM          (4) BOOK (Enter B)
.DM          (5) END Entries (Enter E)
.DM
.AV "Enter Menu Item", ITEM
.FI &ITEM&
#
```

The advantage of setting up a menu this way, without using a conditional print command, is that it's short and simple. The letter or letters you enter for each item are names of the file itself. I'm using single letters here to make it easier to choose; you might prefer using longer file names though—NEWS, MAGS, BOOKS, and so forth.

Notice that for the last option to work—that is, to get out of the program—you can enter anything at all, as long as it doesn't match the name of any files on the disk.

The other version of the same menu follows, this time taking advantage of the conditional print commands.

FILE NAME: MENU

*Menu File for Bibliography USING
Conditional Print Commands*

```
.DM Next Item is:
.DM
.DM
.DM          (1) Article in a NEWSPAPER
.DM          (2) Article in a MAGAZINE
.DM          (3) Article in a SCHOLARLY JOURNAL
.DM          (4) BOOK
.DM          (5) END Entries
.DM
.DM
.AV "Enter Menu Number", ITEM, 1
.EX &ITEM& < "6" GOTO REDO
.IF &ITEM& = "1" GOTO NEWSPAPER
.IF &ITEM& = "2" GOTO MAGAZINE
```

```
.IF &ITEM& = "3" GOTO JOURNAL
.IF &ITEM& = "4" GOTO BOOK
.IF &ITEM& = "5" GOTO END

.EF NEWSPAPER
.FI NEWS

.IF &ITEM& = "1" GOTO MENU
.EF MAGAZINE
.FI MAGS

.IF &ITEM& = "2" GOTO MENU
.EF JOURNAL
.FI JOUR

.IF &ITEM& = "3" GOTO MENU
.EF BOOK
.FI BOOK

.IF &ITEM& = "4" GOTO MENU
.EF REDO
.CS
.DM Sorry, I don't know what that means.
.DM Please pick a number from the menu list (1 - 5)

.EF MENU
.FI MENU

.EF END
```

The first thing you'll notice about this file is how much longer it is. It takes nearly three times as many lines as the first menu. If you run through it carefully, though, you'll see that it adds several conveniences.

The best way to learn what this does—and how it does it—is for you to play computer, and follow the directions for each of the choices. Pick item 3, for instance, and see how the program directs you, as computer, from there to **.EF JOURNAL,** and from **.EF JOURNAL** to the proper subroutine. Also notice how the program sends you back to the beginning of the menu after you finish each entry.

To use the first menu, by the way—the one with file insert commands only—each of your subroutine files should end with a **.FI MENU** command to send you back to the menu each time. To use this second menu, they should not end with the same command. When you finish any of your entries, you will automatically be returned to this main menu, and pick up on the next command line.

With either version of MENU, though, there should be no conditional commands at the end of the subroutine files asking you whether to continue. Each of these subroutine files should end by returning you to MENU, which already gives you the choice of what to do next.

One of the real advantages of this second version of MENU, and one of the things that makes it worth the extra work, is that, unlike the first menu, it won't dump you out of the program just because you entered the wrong menu choice. Take a look at how the first conditional command (.EX &ITEM& < "6" GOTO REDO) is used to test your answer, and how it sends you back to the beginning of the menu if necessary. Also take note of the helpful hint it gives you when that happens.

Another minor advantage of this menu over the other is that it frees you to name your files in any way.

WHY—AND WHEN—TO USE MAILMERGE FOR PROGRAMMING

The point of this exercise is that whether MicroPro intended it or not, MailMerge is a programming language. That much should be clear by now.

On the other hand, it is just as clearly a limited language. It cannot, for example, deal with numbers, or do any calculations. If you're familiar with programming, moreover, it should be painfully obvious that the program can't do loops very well either, which is a sorely missed capability.

The question, then, might be: Why should you bother using it as a language? After all, there are enough "real" languages available—programs that were written as language programs, and that include the capabilities that MailMerge lacks.

The answer is that MailMerge serves the same kind of function as a calc program.

You can write any application in BASIC that you can write with a calc program, but you can write it faster and more easily with the calc program.

Similarly, you can write any application in BASIC that you can write with MailMerge. But you can write it faster and more easily with Mail-Merge. If you're dealing only with text, if the format is complicated, if the output will be going to disk or printer or both, try it with MailMerge.

The only limits that count are in your imagination.

16

Ancillary Programs
SPELLING, PUNCTUATION, INDEXING, AND MORE

Programs Covered
Spelling Checkers
  ProofReader
  SpellStar
  The Word Plus

Punctuation, Typographical, and Style Checkers
  Strunk and White: The Program (Formerly Grammatik)
  Punctuation + Style

Others
  MagicPrint (Proportional Space Printing, Footnotes)
  Math* (Allows Arithmetic from Within WordStar)
  StarIndex (Indexing and Table of Contents Generator)
  Random House Electronic Thesaurus (An Online Thesaurus)

As I've pointed out earlier, this book would not be complete without a look at some programs that go beyond basic word processing. In this chapter, you'll find reviews of an assortment of programs. Some are designed specifically to work with WordStar, others can work with virtually any word processor. Since this book is about WordStar, though, the reviews will only look at the programs in terms of WordStar.

A couple of general comments first. Ancillary programs that work with WordStar fall into two categories. One kind functions, like MailMerge, as an overlay file. These "overlay" programs are used from within WordStar, which gives them many advantages. But they also have the disadvantage that they must match the particular version of WordStar that you're using.

The second, more common, kind of program works independently of WordStar. Most spelling checkers and grammar checkers, for example, work this way. You can call up these programs directly from your operating system, make corrections and mark your files, then go back into the files with WordStar for further editing or formatting.

You can usually call these programs up from within WordStar as well, thanks to WordStar's "Run a Program" command. Simply go to Word-Star's opening menu, enter **R** for Run a Program, then enter the name of the program. When you're finished, you'll automatically return to Word-Star.

Most of the programs we'll look at here fall into this second category, which means you don't have to worry about matching them to your release of WordStar.

One other point: These programs are by no means the only ones that exist. They are, to my mind at least, the most interesting, and the most worthy of notice. In some cases, I've covered two or more similar programs and compared them. Where I've done that, I've offered my opinion on the strengths and weaknesses of each, but I've also tried to differentiate between opinions based on personal biases and opinions based on objective criteria. With a little luck, I've succeeded in making clear which are which.

SPELLING CHECKERS

The most obvious program to buy along with a word processor is a spelling checker. It is such an obvious companion program, in fact, that most word processors have some sort of spelling module available either as part of the basic package or as an option at extra cost.

WordStar is no exception to this, of course. Inevitably, if we talk about using WordStar with a spelling checker, we have to look at SpellStar.

Unfortunately, as much as I like WordStar, I have never liked Spell-Star. Not only is it the weakest module in the WordStar package, it's the only part of WordStar that I think is an objectively weak program.

SpellStar 3.00 had some serious bugs. These seem to have been fixed in version 3.3, but even when SpellStar works perfectly, it is still only marginally useful as a spelling checker.

To begin with, the SpellStar dictionary is too small—20,000 words. To appreciate what this means, consider a list of more than 1300 words generated during roughly a year's use of SpellStar. I spell-checked this list with The Word Plus, which we will look at shortly. The Word Plus, with its 45,000 word dictionary, recognized well over 1000 of the words that Spell-Star hadn't recognized. Many of the remaining words were proper nouns.

At a conservative estimate, each of these 1000 words represents at least one full minute of work: looking up the word, typing it in, and double-checking it before adding it to SpellStar's dictionary. That's 1000 minutes, or more than 16 hours, of unnecessary work over a year's time. That trans-lates to two full workdays.

A second problem with SpellStar is speed—or rather, the lack of it. I timed it on a 7200 word chapter of this book (using a 4 megahertz ma-chine). It took 1 minute 57 seconds to read the file and check it against the dictionary, plus another 2 minutes 30 seconds to flag the errors in the chapter. That's a total elapsed time of 4 minutes 27 seconds between start-ing SpellStar and finally starting to correct the errors.

The Word Plus checked the same file in 1 minute 56 seconds. And don't forget that The Word Plus is checking the file against more than twice as many words in its dictionary.

A third program, ProofReader—which we will also look at shortly—took 3 minutes 15 seconds to check the file. Not bad when you consider that ProofReader was using an 80,000 word dictionary.

Another problem worth pointing out about SpellStar is that it has a severely limited working memory. If you tell SpellStar to add a word to its dictionary, it will, theoretically, not show you that word again while check-ing the file. (The actual addition to the dictionary takes place later.) In practice, though, it doesn't always work out that way. If you give SpellStar more than a few words to remember in any one session, it will forget the earliest words entered, and start showing them to you again if you've used them later in the file. If you are not good at spelling to begin with, you may find yourself having to look up the same words two or three times in the same session.

In all fairness to SpellStar, it does have one advantage over other spelling checking programs. It puts you directly in WordStar when you make corrections. This gives you all of WordStar's editing capabilities, and lets you reformat the text, if necessary, as you go along. With other pro-grams, you have to go back to the file and reformat as a separate step if any words have changed length. This feature will save you a minimal amount of time in reformatting the file, but it will not save you as much time as you are losing elsewhere.

This one advantage to using SpellStar, moreover, also turns out to be a disadvantage. In order to work along with WordStar the way it does, the SpellStar overlay file has to match the WordStar release. In other words, if you update your WordStar, you can't use your old version of SpellStar.

There is, finally, one other important feature missing from SpellStar. Unlike many spelling checking programs, SpellStar will not look words up in its dictionary for you. This means that whenever it finds a word, you ei-ther have to know the correct spelling yourself, or you have to look it up in a printed dictionary. If you're good at spelling, you might not miss this look-up capability, but the lack of it means that SpellStar is really less of a spelling checker than a typo checker. All it does, really, is point out possible typographical errors.

If your word processing is confined to short items—one or two page letters, for example—and if you're good at spelling, then SpellStar is perfectly adequate as a typo checker. I cannot recommend it as a spelling checker.

PROOFREADER AND THE WORD PLUS

ProofReader from Wang Electronic Publishing, Inc. and The Word Plus from Oasis Systems are, for the most part, comparable programs. I can recommend either one wholeheartedly.

Let's start with ProofReader. (Wang Electronic Publishing, by the way, used to be Aspen Software. It is now a subsidiary of Wang Laboratories, Inc., which accounts for the name change. ProofReader has not been changed.)

One of the nice things about ProofReader is that you can get it with any of several sizes of dictionaries, depending on which one fits on your system. The smallest dictionary contains 32,000 words in 72K of disk space. The largest contains 80,000 words in 182K of disk space.

To use ProofReader, you enter "**PRF**" followed by the name of the file to check. ProofReader reads the file, checks the words against its dictionary, tells you how many unknown words it found, then gives you a list of choices for what to do next. The only one we'll bother with is the program's WordStar Mode, in which it will correct the words, plus mark any that change length. (Notice, by the way that this is only important if you are using right justification. If your file is ragged right, it doesn't generally matter if the length of a line changes by one or two characters. ProofReader also gives you the option of not marking words that change length.)

Once in WordStar Mode, ProofReader shows you one unknown word at a time: once in context (meaning with the rest of the sentence it comes from), and a second time separately, where it is clearly labeled "UNKNOWN WORD." This may seem like overkill, but it can't do any harm, and it can help avoid confusion.

With each word, you get seven choices:

1. You can tell the program you want to correct the word, then type in the new spelling.
2. You can look the word up in the program's dictionary.
3. You can put the word in the auxiliary dictionary.
4. You can tell the program to accept the word for the rest of the session, but not to put it in its dictionary.
5. You can tell the program to accept the word just once, but show it to you again if it shows up later in the file.
6. You can abort the session, and put everything back the way it was before you started.
7. You can exit to the operating system, but save all changes to that point.

The interesting choices here are the first two. If you tell ProofReader that you want to correct the word, it asks you to type in the replacement word. Instead of just accepting what you type, though, the program then checks this new word against the dictionary. If it isn't there, the program comes back and tells you. You can then tell ProofReader to accept the spelling you've given, or you can try correcting the word again, or tell it to look the word up in its dictionary. This feature—the automatic checking of the corrections as you enter them—is a real boon if you think you know the correct spelling for a word, but aren't sure. It saves you from having to double check-in a printed dictionary. (It also saves you from sloppy typing.)

The other interesting choice is the second one—asking the program to look a word up in its dictionary. If you pick this one, ProofReader will display 20 "near matches." Most of the time the correct spelling will show up in these 20 words, especially if you are using the 80,000 word dictionary. An even nicer refinement is that when you tell the program to look up a word, it gives you the option of entering a different word to look for. This is especially useful with words that use the prefix "re." These are very often not in the dictionary, but thanks to this feature, their stems—without the "re"—can still be looked up.

The one problem with ProofReader is that the actual process of correcting the errors is slow. After each correction, the program has to search for the next error before it can display it on the screen. It also takes the time to write the corrected version of the file to disk piecemeal as you go through the file. I would rather that the program store the corrections somewhere, then write them into the file later, after my part is finished. That way I can go elsewhere while the program does its housecleaning chores.

The extra waiting with ProofReader is tolerable up to a point, but the longer the file, the less tolerable it gets. This is clearly a matter of personal bias, but I think I'm typical of most computer users in this respect. I'm just too spoiled to feel comfortable about sitting around twiddling my thumbs while waiting for my computer to give me something to do. For Proof-Reader, my tolerance wears thin on files longer than about 3000 words. Let me stress, though, that this opinion is based on using ProofReader with floppy disks. Since the waiting time is dependent on disk-access time, the speed of the program improves considerably if you have a hard disk or a disk emulator.

THE WORD PLUS

A general description of The Word Plus makes it sound very much like ProofReader.

To run The Word Plus, you type "**TW**" followed by the name of the file to be checked. The program comes up showing you what it plans to do: it gives you the name of the file to check, notes whether it will mark words that change length, shows what marking character it will use, and so forth. You can change any of these options, or just tell the program to go ahead and check the file.

When it's finished checking, The Word Plus will do pretty much what

ProofReader does—show you the words one at a time, and give you a chance to correct them. As with ProofReader, The Word Plus gives you several options.

1. You can add the word to the update dictionary.
2. You can add the word to a special dictionary of your choice.
3. You can mark the word so you can find it and check it later in WordStar.
4. You can tell the program to ignore the word for this session.
5. You can correct the word.
6. You can look up the word in the dictionary.
7. You can ask to view the word in context.

In addition, The Word Plus gives you the option of backing up and looking at earlier words. This gives you the chance to change your mind, or correct an error if you accidentally hit the wrong key.

On the surface, this list of choices doesn't look much different from the list of choices in ProofReader, but there are differences.

First, in addition to adding words to a "standard" update dictionary, you can also add words to a special dictionary of your choice. This means that you can keep as many different special dictionaries as you need, and that gives you some interesting capabilities. You can, for example, create a special dictionary of jargon that's appropriate for your business or technical papers, but not appropriate elsewhere. By using this special dictionary only when called for, you can have The Word Plus bypass the jargon on your technical or business files, but stop and point it out in other files. Then you can either replace the jargon on the spot, or tell the program to mark the word, so you can go back later in WordStar and rewrite the sentence when necessary.

Another difference between The Word Plus and ProofReader is that The Word Plus will not show you the word in context unless you ask to see it. This speeds things up considerably, because it means the program can show you a list of words, and ask for your corrections without having to hunt up the context for each word as it goes. And indeed, most of the time—on proper names, for example, or obvious typos—the word itself is all you need to see. On the other hand, if you do need to see the word in context, you have to go through the extra step of telling the program to hunt it up and show it to you.

The other differences between ProofReader and The Word Plus are more subtle. At least they are not immediately obvious from the list of options.

For example, the programs use different schemes for looking up words. ProofReader looks for the spot in the dictionary where the word would be, if it were there. It then takes twenty words from the immediate area, and puts them on the screen. The Word Plus uses a more sophisticated scheme. It looks for similar words throughout the dictionary that almost match the target word, but that have either one letter different, one letter extra, one letter fewer, or two letters transposed.

In practical terms, this means that if you misspell "incidentally" as "incidently," ProofReader will find the correct spelling in its dictionary for you; The Word Plus won't. On the other hand, if you misspell "puerile" as "peurile," The Word Plus will find the correct spelling, but ProofReader won't. This is partly made up for in ProofReader, though, by its ability to let you enter alternate spellings to look for. Also, the ProofReader scheme for looking up in the dictionary is simpler, and, therefore, faster.

Another difference between these programs is that when The Word Plus puts the words on your screen, it puts numbers or symbols next to each one. To correct the spelling, you only have to enter **"C"** for "Correct" followed by the appropriate number. Being lazy, not to mention being a rotten typist, I find this extremely useful.

A more important difference is that ProofReader lets you add words to its main dictionary, while The Word Plus doesn't. Oasis Systems has left this capability out purposely, on the grounds that it's too easy to put misspelled words in the dictionary. The problem, though, is that the program won't look up words unless they are in the main dictionary, which means that you lose the look-up capability for any words you added yourself. My own feeling is, in this case at least, I'd rather not be protected from myself, thank you.

One last comment about The Word Plus: as of this writing, a new version of the program is actively under development. It may be available by the time you read this book. This new version will add some features to the program: it will check your corrections against the dictionary, let you look up alternate spellings in the dictionary, and also look up words in the special dictionary for you. The version reviewed here is release 1.2

PROOFREADER VS. THE WORD PLUS

ProofReader and The Word Plus are both good spelling checking programs. Each has much to recommend it.

With ProofReader, for example, I like having an 80,000 word dictionary. I like the fact that it checks my corrections against its dictionary. I like being able to look up alternate spellings while I'm doing my corrections. And, most of all, I like being able to add words to the dictionary where they can also be looked up.

With The Word Plus, I like the "oops" feature—the ability to back up and change my mind or correct a mistake if I hit the wrong key. I like the fact that it handles capitalization better than ProofReader, generally maintaining the correct capitalization automatically when it corrects a word. But most of all, I like its speed.

Overall, for me at least, when working on a floppy disk machine, The Word Plus beats ProofReader out. The real question for a spelling checker is: How long does it take to correct a given file? The answer: It takes me less time with The Word Plus—even though it means I sometimes have to look up words in a printed dictionary as I go.

In addition to its speed, The Word Plus has a few additional capabilities. It will unscramble anagrams for you, it will hyphenate words, it will give you a quick word count of any file (a useful facility for writers), it will give you a list of the words in any file along with a count of how many times each word was used, and it will do what amounts to a multiple global search and replace—deleting or changing any number of words on a single pass through the file. It will even give you some help with homonyms if you want it. (Homonyms are similar-sounding words that are easily confused in spelling—like "waiver" and "waver." The Word Plus will mark homonyms, if you tell it to, so you can check them out.)

Notice, though, that my major problem with ProofReader is speed. If you run the program on a disk emulator, or even on a hard disk, you will probably find that this isn't a problem after all. Also notice that each program has several features that the other doesn't have.

I stand by the statement I started with. I can wholeheartedly recommend either program. Even at $150, The Word Plus is my first choice. But ProofReader is one dynamite $50 program.

The Word Plus is available from Oasis Systems, 2765 Reynard Way, San Diego, California 92103.

ProofReader is available from Wang Electronic Publishing, Inc., P.O. Box 339, Tijeras, New Mexico 87059.

PUNCTUATION, TYPOGRAPHICAL, AND STYLE CHECKERS

Somewhere "beyond spelling checking" (as the ad says) are programs that can check punctuation, non-spelling typographical errors, and even writing style in some limited sense. Here again, I'll be comparing one program from Wang Electronic Publishing (Strunk and White: The Program), and one from Oasis Systems (Punctuation + Style). Here again, the two programs are comparable in most respects.

Strunk and White, by the way, is the second generation version of Grammatik. The program takes its new name from a well known style guide by William Strunk, Jr., and E. B. White. The official title of the guide is *The Elements of Style,* but nearly everyone who uses it calls it Strunk and White. The book is famous for being brief, informative, witty, and useful. The program uses the book as a basis for choosing which errors to look for, but is no substitute for the book. Each copy of the program, though, comes with a copy of Strunk and White. Whether you get the program or not, the book is highly recommended.

Before we take a look at the particular programs, here are a few general comments to keep in mind.

First, understand that while programs like this may be "grammar checkers" in some vague sense, they are actually doing several different things at once, and there are severe limits on what they can do. A program can draw your attention to a comma or period that follows a blank space. Similarly, it can check that each "open parenthesis" is matched to a "close parenthesis," or each toggle-on character (for boldface for example) is matched to a toggle-off character. It cannot check (at the present state-of-the-art at least) to make sure that the subject of a sentence is in agreement with the verb, or that a pronoun is in agreement with its antecedent.

Second, understand that aside from questions of how well the program works as a piece of software, the usefulness of this kind of program is highly dependent on how closely your writing biases match those that are built into the program. This extends from trivial mechanical questions on up to serious stylistic questions.

On the mechanical side, for example, the accepted standard for manuscripts is to put two spaces after a period. It's perfectly natural, then, to design a punctuation checker to look for those two spaces. If you happen to prefer using a single space, though, and don't want to change, you'll find it annoying to use a program that stops at the end of each sentence to point out the missing space as an error.

Much more serious, though, are stylistic biases—like whether you agree that the word "lastly" is preferable to "finally." (I don't. To me it sounds pompous. But the program Punctuation + Style will stop at "finally" and suggest the substitution.)

As a writer I am certainly concerned with questions of style and the use of words. In fact, two of the three books that stay on my writing desk at all times are the *Harper Dictionary of Contemporary Usage* and Strunk and White's *The Elements of Style*. (The third book is *Roget's International Thesaurus*.) In addition to being concerned with questions of usage, though, I am also aware that in many cases the "correct" usage is simply a matter of opinion. For example, is it "The data is . . ." or "The data are. . ."? The *Harper Dictionary* asked a panel of one hundred thirty-six recognized wordsmiths (writers, editors, and public speakers) and came up with a nearly even split.

My point is that I have some reservations about the concept behind the style-checking portions of these programs. If you are already sensitive to correct usage, then you probably don't need a style checker. If you are not sensitive to correct usage, I'm not sure how much this kind of program will help. At the very least, though, it may improve your writing simply by making you aware that there is such a thing as correct usage to worry about.

A related problem with the style checking portions of this sort of program is that the program will always stop at any word or phrase that is listed as suspect, whether it's being used correctly in that given instance or not.

One example: as shipped, both Strunk and White and Punctuation + Style will stop at "sort of" and suggest "somewhat" or "rather." This is a useful correction if you've written, "It's sort of hot today." It is not useful—or even meaningful—if you've written, "this sort of program."

Here again, if you are already careful about correct usage, the style checking portion of these programs will tend to be more annoying than helpful. Both Wang Electronic Publishing and Oasis Systems recognize this as a possible problem. Strunk and White and Punctuation + Style are each designed to let you customize the list of words and phrases being checked, or even turn off the style checking completely.

In both programs, there's much to be gained from customizing the phrases. Not only can you delete words and phrases that you never misuse, you can add words and phrases that you know enough to look out for even if they sometimes creep in.

This customization capability will, for example, let you build a phrase dictionary to spot jargon or technical terms when you're writing for a general audience. It will also help you spot any errors that you know you make on a regular basis. I have a strong tendency, for example, to type "your" when I mean "you're." This is something I never did on a typewriter, but it's a habit I can't seem to break when writing on a computer. Since I've added this and a few other personal devils to my phrase dictionary, I feel much more comfortable about my finished work.

Despite the overwhelming similarity between Strunk and White and Punctuation + Style, finally, there are also some important differences. Here's a quick look at each, beginning with Strunk and White.

STRUNK AND WHITE: THE PROGRAM

To begin with, Strunk and White is essentially a single program that does all its checking in one pass through the file. An additional module, called PROFILE, will give you an alphabetized list of all the words in a file, along with a count of how often each word was used. This is useful, but tangential to the main function of Strunk and White as an error checker. PROFILE, not so incidentally, is exactly equivalent to the WORDFREQ module that comes with The Word Plus. More on PROFILE and WORD-FREQ later.

To use Strunk and White, you enter "SW" with or without the name of the file to check. The program comes up telling you what it plans to do: which phrase dictionary it is set to read, which kinds of errors it is set to look for, and so forth. Once you're satisfied with the way the options are set, you hit RETURN to start checking the file.

Among the options is the choice between having Strunk and White stop and show you each error, or simply having it mark all possible errors in the file using a number sign (#).

The first choice lets you eliminate obvious non-errors from being marked, and saves you the trouble of having to delete the markers from your file later.

The second choice saves you from having to go through the file twice—once with Strunk and White to mark the errors, and once with WordStar to make the changes.

My experience is that the first approach will save you time overall until you've customized the phrase dictionary so that most of what the program finds are real errors rather than non-errors. The point, though, is that you have the choice. (You have the same choice in Punctuation + Style, incidentally.)

If you've chosen to have the program stop when it finds each error, it will show you the error, identify the kind of error, and show you a suggested correction. You can then tell it to mark the error, ignore the error this time only, ignore the error for the rest of the file, ignore this *kind* of error for the rest of the file, or to quit checking.

When Strunk and White is finished, finally, it shows you some statistics about the file it's just read. This includes the number of sentences in the file, the total number of words, the length of the shortest and longest sentences, and something called the Flesch Grade Level index and a corresponding Reading Ease Score. (More on Flesch shortly.) Strunk and White will also tack these statistics onto the end of your file, if you ask it to, when it writes the corrected file to disk.

Frankly, I'm not convinced that any of these statistics are at all useful in improving writing style. That, of course, is a personal bias that has nothing to do with Strunk and White. (Meaning the program only—the book doesn't deal with such foolishness.) Still, this underlines the point I made earlier. The usefulness of this kind of program is highly dependent on how well your writing biases mesh with the biases built into the program. In this particular case, of course, you can simply ignore the statistics when they show up on your screen, but you still have to pay a price. The program has to spend some minimal amount of time calculating these statistics whether you want to see them or not.

One last note on the Flesch Grade Level index and Reading Ease Score, in case you're not familiar with it.

This is essentially a statistical measure of the readability of any given piece of writing. To determine the Flesch Reading Grade Level:

Multiply the average sentence length in the piece by 1.015

Multiply the number of syllables per 100 words by .846

Add the results together, then subtract that number from 206.835

The result is the Flesch Reading Ease Score. This number will be somewhere between 0 (unreadable) and 100 (very easy to read). This Reading Ease Score can then be matched to a school grade reading level—from grade school to five years of graduate school (Ph.D. level).

Whether you agree that this statistic tells you anything useful about your writing or not, you may still find it handy to have a program that calculates it for you. This is particularly true if you're writing for the school market, where books are routinely graded by this formula to determine their suitability for any given grade level.

If you want to know more about the Flesch Grade Level index or Reading Ease Scores, take a look at *The Art of Readable Writing* by Rudolf Flesch.

PUNCTUATION + STYLE

Punctuation + Style is really two programs. Cleanup checks for punctuation errors, paired symbols and toggle switches, and other miscellaneous typographical errors. Phrase, as the name suggests, is the style-checking module.

Cleanup and Phrase were designed as separate programs precisely because accomplished writers are more likely to be annoyed by a style checking program than helped by it. In the words of the manual, "Phrase is not for everyone." If you don't find Phrase useful for your purposes, this makes it easy to skip it.

On the other hand, if you want to use Phrase, you have to go through the file twice to look for errors instead of doing everything on a single pass.

Whether you consider this two-program approach an advantage or disadvantage, then, depends very much on your own needs.

Using Cleanup or Phrase is similar to using Strunk and White, except that neither module shows you a list of options when you call it up. Instead, you store your options in a file created with WordStar. You can also change some of these by adding commands to the command line when you call up the program.

To use Cleanup you type "Cleanup" followed by the name of the file to check, followed by any option "switches" you want to use. The option switches cover pretty much the same choices as the options in Strunk and White. One additional choice lets you change the error marking character. (The usual character is @.)

If you've told Cleanup to stop after it finds each error, it will do much the same thing that Strunk and White does, namely, show you each error, identify the kind of error, and give you the choice of marking the error, ignoring it, or quitting the program.

Using Phrase is much the same as using Cleanup. You call up the program by typing "Phrase" followed by the name of the file to check, followed by any option switches you want to use. These switches are mostly the same as in Cleanup.

If you've told Phrase to stop after each error, it will show you the error and suggest a replacement. It will then give you four choices. You can mark the error in your file, ignore it, print the sentence on your printer, or suppress the sentence. This last choice is the most interesting; it tells Phrase not just to ignore the supposed error this time through, but to ignore it on all future runs through the file. (The mechanics of this involve creating a file that "tags along" with the text file and tells Phrase which sentences to ignore. The program does this automatically, though; you don't have to worry about it.)

STRUNK AND WHITE VS. PUNCTUATION + STYLE

Strunk and White and Punctuation + Style are both useful programs, though each has its limitations. The drawback to Strunk and White is that it simply doesn't find as many errors as Cleanup, which means that for miscellaneous typographical errors and the like, Cleanup is better than Strunk and White.

The drawback to Phrase is that unlike Strunk and White or even Cleanup, it will not identify the kind of error it thinks it's found. This is an unfortunate oversight. Many of the words and phrases that the program matches are wrong in some contexts, but right in others. This oversight in Phrase is enough to make Strunk and White better than Phrase for style checking.

Overall, Strunk and White and Punctuation + Style are equal. Each has capabilities that the other lacks, but the strengths and weaknesses of the programs pretty well balance each other out. I can recommend either one, with the warning that the one that works best for you will be largely a matter of personal taste.

OTHER ANCILLARY PROGRAMS

StarIndex

StarIndex is MicroPro's new WordStar-compatible indexing program. Because it is a separate program, rather than an overlay file, it will work with any version of WordStar.

Using StarIndex is a two-step procedure. First you go through your text file, entering the information StarIndex needs—marking the words to be indexed, for example. Next, you run StarIndex, and the program generates the index for you. In addition, the program will create a table of contents, a list of figures, a list of tables, and more.

StarIndex can automatically add print commands to the body of your text so your headings will print with boldface, underlining, double-strike, or spaces between letters.

It can also automatically add numbers or letters to your titles and section headings. When numbering, you can tell it to use Arabic numerals or Roman numerals—and if Roman, you can tell it to use uppercase or lowercase.

The StarIndex manual, like all the new WordStar manuals, provides an excellent introduction to the program. In addition, StarIndex comes with a sample file that demonstrates all the important features in the program. Between the manual and the sample file, you should have little or no trouble learning how to use StarIndex.

Basic indexing is simple. For indexing words within the body of the text, you simply mark the beginning and end of the item to be indexed. The usual character is **^PP,** which means a word to be indexed looks like **^Pthis^P** on your screen. The **^PP** will not interfere with WordStar's proportional space feature. When StarIndex creates the index, it also writes a new file to disk. This output file is distinguished from the original file by an ''SI'' ending for StarIndex. The SI file differs from the original file in several particulars. Among other things, it's been stripped of the markers on the indexed words. You go into this second file, add the **^PP^PA,** for proportional space printing, and print as usual.

StarIndex also gives you a ''Master Index Entry'' marker, which works the same way as the ''General'' marker, except that the entry will be numbered in boldface in the index. You can use this to identify a page where the item is defined, or first introduced, or whatever.

In addition to embedded index commands, the program also has dot commands that let you add an index entry that is not contained in the body of the text. This lets you take a section on the Space Shuttle, for example, and index it under ''Space Flight,'' even though the indexed phrase doesn't show up anywhere in your file. Here again, using the command is simplicity itself. You only need to enter the dot command followed by index entry:

.II Space Flight

(Nearly all the StarIndex dot commands, incidentally, begin with **.I,** which makes them easy to remember. The second "I" in this case is for "index entry." For a closer look at the commands in StarIndex, take a look at Appendix C.)

In addition to the indexing commands, the program contains commands for "Outline Design." These again are dot commands. You enter them on the line before the heading, table, or figure that they apply to. You can designate four levels of headings: chapter, section, sub-section, and sub-sub-section.

(One point about the dot commands. The program doesn't care what version of WordStar you're using; it will index the files properly in any case. Earlier versions of WordStar—meaning anything before release 3.3—won't recognize the StarIndex dot commands, and will put a question flag in the right-hand column of your screen. This has no effect on the functioning of StarIndex, though.)

Other commands in the program, finally, deal with format or numbering of one kind or another. If you've told the program to number headings, for example, you can tell it to have the numbers preceded by higher level numbers (as in 1.1.3.5) or not (as in 5). Finally, you can have different formats for the table of contents, the body of the text, the appendices, and the index.

One of the nice things about StarIndex, by the way, is that despite the flexibility of the program, you don't have to learn all the commands. The vast majority of them deal with formatting. Odds are that you can ignore these entirely.

The program comes with a module called STYLE. This is a menu driven question and answer program that you can use to create a format file. In most cases, you should be able to create one or more standard format files and let the indexing program get its formatting information from those. Of course if you'd rather put the format commands in the text files themselves, you can do that instead. The choice is yours.

Overall, StarIndex is an impressively flexible and useful program. If you need the indexing capability, I can recommend it without reservations.

SYNERGY

Synergy is not the name of a program (at least not that I know of). It is, rather, a way of saying that the whole can be greater than the sum of its parts; in this case, it is the result of putting two programs together and finding out that by using them both, you can do more than you might have reasonably expected.

In discussing The Word Plus, and later Strunk and White, I mentioned that each program includes a module that will read a file, and produce a list of words that were used in that file. This list can be a good starting point for choosing the words you might like to index.

The basic trick works this way:

When you're ready to index your file, start by running the WORDFREQ module from The Word Plus, or its equivalent. This will give you a list of the words in the file along with a count of how many times each word appears.

Next, go through the list, choosing the words you want to index, and deleting the rest.

All that remains is to do a global search and replace on your file, replacing each **word** you want indexed with the same ^**Pword**^**P** surrounded by the index markers.

The Word Plus has an additional module that makes this job even easier. The module is MARKFIX, and you can use it to do a multiple global search and replace.

There are at least two ways that this can help. First, you will find that on anything long enough to warrant indexing, WORDFREQ will produce lists with hundreds or even thousands of words on it. The vast majority of these words, though, will never need indexing in any context: The, For, In, At, Majority, and so forth. If you take the time, *once*, to create a list of these words, you can eliminate them from your file automatically with MARKFIX on a single run through the file. This will bring your lists down to a manageable size.

Second, once you've chosen the words you want indexed, you can use MARKFIX to mark all the words with the indexing marker—again on a single run through the file.

Unfortunately, not having been designed for this task, MARKFIX won't let you do this in a single step. The problem is that it will not write the control character into the file when doing the search and replace. If you tell MARKFIX to find **word,** and replace it with ^**Pword**^**P,** it will simply ignore the ^**P**, and replace **word** with **word.**

The way around this limitation is to tell MARKFIX to replace **word** with ***word*,** using either the asterisk or some other printing character that you know you have not used in the file. Then you can go back into the file with WordStar, and do a global search and replace, looking for ***,** and replacing it with ^**P.**

Be forewarned, though, that if you do this, you should also double-check capitalization of the words being replaced, since MARKFIX will treat the asterisk as the first letter of the word.

Also, make sure you treat this trick as a convenient way to *start* your indexing, not as a way to generate the complete list. Don't forget that there will be phrases as well as individual words you'll want to index.

MagicPrint (Proportional Space Printing, Headers, Footnotes) MagicBind (MagicPrint Plus Mailmerging)

Every so often you run across a program that does almost everything you want it to do, but misses by just enough, in just the right ways, to be maddening. For me, MagicPrint 2.00, from Computer EdiType Systems, is that kind of program. MagicBind 1.00, which is essentially MagicPrint 2.00 with mailmerging capabilities added, falls in the same category. In each case, I find myself in a love–hate relationship with the program. I suspect I won't be alone in that reaction.

First the good part.

What the program does, it does well. It will work with any of several printers: the Diablo 1610/20, Diablo 630, Diablo 1640, and any of the NEC 3500 or NEC 7700 series. It will print your files as advertised: with proportional spacing or not, with right-justification or ragged right, using a single-column or multi-column format. It will automatically number footnotes for you, and put them in the proper place on the page. It will also let you use multiple lines in headers or footers.

The proportional spacing with MagicPrint gives more of a typeset look than WordStar's proportional spacing. This comes from subtle differences between the way the two programs distribute blank space within words and between them.

The result, quite simply, is that MagicPrint's proportional spacing produces a more attractive page than WordStar's (unsupported and abandoned) proportional spacing. This holds true even if you ignore the bugs in the WordStar version, and even if you just leave MagicPrint at its default settings. In fact, if you ask anyone at MicroPro about proportional space printing, you will usually be referred to MagicPrint.

If better looking proportional spacing isn't enough for you, Magic-Print contains a fair number of useful print features that you won't find in WordStar at all.

There is, for example, a command to right-justify partial lines, a command to control underlining so you can make it broken or solid, and a command to move the paper backward for multi-column printing.

Instructions in the manual show you how to fine tune the program to match your taste and your printwheel.

For the truly fussy, there is even a local pitch command that lets you change pitch within a line to make minor adjustments within words when necessary. (This is known as *kerning,* and is a standard typesetting trick.)

In addition to a local conditional page command, there is also a kind of global conditional page command. This lets you tell the program that whenever it gets to the last so-many-lines of each paragraph, it should check to make sure they will all fit on the page, and if not, it should start a new page. Default on this feature is set to automatically avoid orphans. (This is a typesetting term. Orphans are single lines left over at the end of a paragraph that won't fit on the end of a page. A related feature of the program also prevents the first line in a paragraph from printing as the last line on a page.)

So much for the reasons I love MagicPrint. Now for the reasons that I hate it.

There is much about this program that smacks of throwing the baby out with the bath water. The program functions not by adding new print features to what already exists in WordStar, but by replacing WordStar's print function entirely.

To use MagicPrint, you either call it up through the Run a Program command from WordStar's opening menu, or you call it up directly from the operating system prompt. You don't even need WordStar on your disk to do this; you only need MagicPrint and the text file you want to print.

What MagicPrint does, for starters, is throw away the "what you see is what you get" aspect of WordStar. This willingness to ignore the on-screen formatting is precisely what lets MagicPrint produce more attractive copy. The trick is accomplished by moving words to other lines, and adjusting the blank spaces as necessary.

My problem with this is that the on-screen formatting feature is precisely the reason I bought WordStar in the first place, and the major reason I continue to use it. I don't think I'm alone in that either. For most people, I suspect, on-screen formatting is one of the most important features of the program—if not the most important.

Anyone who wants to improve on WordStar should give me more on-screen format features, not less. If you can't give me the proportional spacing on-screen while editing, with right justification and so forth, at least show me which words are going to show up on which lines. This would be analogous to what WordStar already does with embedded print commands, adjusting the width of the line on-screen, to show the ^B, or ^S, or whatever.

I'm well aware that what I've just suggested is not a trivial programming problem. At the very least, it would involve writing an overlay file to work with WordStar and modify the on-screen display. As things stand now, no such program exists. MagicPrint 2.00, though, has been improved tremendously by including the option of "printing" to screen, so you can at least see where each page will end without having to print a test run on your printer.

A second important problem with MagicPrint is that you lose all Mail-Merge capabilities (except for print-time line-forming commands. These are replaced by MagicPrint's own commands.) This is largely offset in MagicBind, which adds mailmerging features to MagicPrint's formatting capabilities.

MagicBind, by the way, has some features that MailMerge lacks. It will automatically number sections and paragraphs, for example. Also, if you've printed eighty letters, and then found a mistake in page three of the fifty-third letter, MagicBind will let you print the correction using a simple, straightforward command. You can do the same thing with MailMerge easily enough, but only if the pages are numbered continuously. If they are reset with each record, with a .PN command at the beginning of the file, you have no way to tell MailMerge which page to print. MagicBind, finally, includes a utility that will check to see that you have the right number of fields in each record in a data file. The same utility will also check number fields, such as zip codes, for the right number of digits. These are all useful features, but overall, MagicBind is simply not as flexible as MailMerge. In particular, it lacks the repeat command and the conditional print commands.

Still another problem is that MagicPrint paginates the file differently from WordStar. This means you lose the ability to generate an index or table of contents with programs like StarIndex that are designed to work with WordStar. This problem will also be somewhat offset by a new program, MagicIndex, which is designed to work with MagicPrint. As of this writing, MagicIndex is actively under development, and should be available by the time you read this book. This means buying another program, though. If you've already paid for one indexing program, you may not be all that anxious to buy another. (MagicIndex is expected to sell for about $150.)

There is, finally, one additional problem that is annoying, but would be relatively easy to fix.

MagicPrint includes both dot commands and embedded commands (for boldface, underlining, and so forth). In the standard version of the program, none of these commands bears any relationship to their equivalents in WordStar. In the WordStar version, though, the embedded commands have been changed to match the equivalent WordStar commands. Unfortunately, the dot commands have not been changed. This means that you have to learn an entirely new set of commands to use MagicPrint. Worse, if you want to use MagicPrint on some things, but stay with WordStar or MailMerge on others, you have to keep bouncing back and forth between the two sets of commands. This is simply an unnecessary complication that makes it more difficult to use the program than it should be.

(An aside here: MagicPrint's dot commands aren't dot commands; they're double-dot commands. This was done to avoid the question flags that WordStar puts on the screen when it doesn't recognize a dot command. With the double-dot, WordStar reads the MagicPrint command lines as comment lines, and ignores them. Comment lines, meanwhile, have to be entered with three dots, or else MagicPrint will read them as command lines.)

There you have it—the good and the bad. I love MagicPrint for what it does, I hate it for what it forces me to give up in order to use it, and my recommendation is decidedly ambivalent. Still, keep in mind that if the program weren't so good at what it does, I'd simply ignore it instead of getting upset over what it doesn't do. As of this moment at least, it has no competition. There is nothing available that will print your WordStar files so they look as good as or better than they do with MagicPrint.

One last note: If you decide to buy the program, I strongly suggest getting MagicBind, not MagicPrint. The difference in price is $55 ($195 for MagicPrint, $250 for MagicBind). If you buy MagicPrint first, however, then decide to move up to MagicBind, the additional cost is $200. To me, this seems excessive for what amounts to an upgrade, but you can sidestep the whole issue by simply buying MagicBind in the first place, even if you have no immediate use for the mailmerging features.

MagicPrint and MagicBind are available from several distributers, including: Lifeboat Associates, 1651 Third Avenue, New York, N.Y. 10028.

For further information, contact: Computer EdiType Systems, 509 Cathedral Parkway 10A, New York, N.Y. 10025, (212) 222-8148.

Math*

Math* (read as "Mathstar"), marketed by Force Two, Limited is a useful little program that functions as an overlay file from within Word-Star.

Quite simply, the program gives you what amounts to a four-function calculator without having to leave the file you're editing. Besides letting you add, subtract, multiply, or divide, Math* will automatically format the answer for you. You can tell it how many decimal places to use, to add commas, to add a dollar sign, or to use parentheses instead of minus signs for accounting applications.

Using the program is about as simple as you could hope for. Enter the numbers along with the function signs, then give the calculation command along with any of the formatting commands. (The calculation command is ˉM or @M depending on the machine.) Math* doesn't even care whether you enter a formula vertically or horizontally.

Incidentally, unless you tell the program otherwise, Math* will assume that you want the numbers added. This means that if you're entering a column of numbers in a letter or report, the program will add them up without your having to enter plus signs all the way through.

The only important limitation to Math* is that the entire line or column of numbers must be on-screen during the calculation. If you're adding more numbers than will fit on your screen at once, you can get around this easily enough by chaining the equations together, then going back and re-editing the one or two lines where the seams show.

Math* has two obvious applications. First, if you write letters, reports, bills, or anything else where you have to enter numbers along with totals, Math* will take care of the arithmetic for you.

Second, you can use Math* to replace your calculator in general. In writing this book, for instance, there are several places where I've demonstrated something that "requires a little arithmetic." With Math* you can do that arithmetic without leaving your keyboard. Simply enter the equation, using the screen as a scratch pad. Let Math* give you the answer, then delete the equation. If you have a numeric keypad on your computer, moreover, you'll find this use particularly attractive.

The secret to Math*'s ease of use lies in its installation procedure, which actually modifies the WordStar program. The calculation capability becomes, in effect, an additional feature within WordStar that you can call on whenever you need it—it's instantly available. There isn't even that slight delay from disk access time that exists with, for instance, WordStar's ^Y (delete line) command. (And there is no interference with any of the normal WordStar features.)

In order to modify WordStar the way it does, Math* must be matched to the particular release of WordStar. As of this writing, versions exist for WordStar 2.26, 3.00, and 3.2x. An updated Math* version for WordStar 3.3 in both Z-80 and IBM PC versions should be available by the time this book is published.

The one drawback to Math* has been it's price. Until recently, the list price was $125. Clearly, you have to do an awfully lot of arithmetic while writing before you can justify spending this much just to replace a $10 calculator. The list price, though, has now dropped to $90.

The price may still be a little high, but the program is certainly a more reasonable purchase now—especially if you buy it through discount mail order. That's fortunate, because I happen to think Math* is a good program. It's useful, fast, and seems to be bug-free—at least if there *are* any bugs I haven't run across them. If you do much arithmetic while writing, you should at least consider Math*; the more you use it, the more impressed you'll be by it.

Math* is available from: Force Two, Limited, 9932 Courthouse Woods Court, Vienna, Virginia 22180.

THE RANDOM HOUSE ELECTRONIC THESAURUS

The Random House Electronic Thesaurus, from Wang Electronic Publishing, Inc., works in much the same way as Math*; the installation procedure modifies your WordStar file, adding The Thesaurus as a new feature that you can use while editing a file. (The WordStar interface section of The Thesaurus, incidentally, was written by the same individual who wrote Math*.)

There's really not all that much to say about The Thesaurus. The program is pretty much what it sounds like—an online thesaurus that's based on the print version of the *Random House Pocket Thesaurus*. In fact, it comes with a copy of the print version.

Using The Thesaurus is easy enough, and is exactly equivalent to using a printed thesaurus. When you can't think of just the right word to use, you look up a near miss, and the thesaurus shows you some alternatives. With the online version, the program looks up the word for you, without leaving the file you're editing. You only have to type in the near miss, then hit ESCAPE twice; or, if the word is already on-screen, simply place the cursor on the word or the space immediately after it, then hit the ESCAPE key twice.

The program will either show you a list of alternate words, or if your entry is not listed in The Thesaurus, it will show you a list of the alphabetically closest words that are listed. You can then choose one of these alphabetically close words to look up instead.

If you see a word you like, you move the cursor to it, and tell the program to replace the near miss with the chosen word. If you don't see a word you like, you hit RETURN to tell the program not to change anything. Either way, you are returned to the text you're editing. If you didn't find the right word, you can try again, using another near miss.

The Electronic Thesaurus works. As a computer program it is simple, straightforward, and easy to use. Its only major drawback, from my point of view, is that it's modeled on the wrong kind of thesaurus.

Printed thesauri (or thesauruses, if you prefer) come in two forms. One kind, including *The Random House Pocket Thesaurus*, is set up much like a dictionary. You look up the near miss version of the word, and you are given a list of alternatives. The other kind, *Roget's International Thesaurus* being the prime example, is set up differently.

In case you're not familiar with it, with Roget's you look up the near-miss word in the back of the book, and are given a list of several senses in which that word can be used. Sometimes the word you want will be in this first list. Each item on the list, though, refers you to another section in the front of the book, where words are listed by meaning rather than alphabetically. More often than not, I have to look at one or more of the sections in the front of the book before I find the word I want.

Clearly, my preference for the Roget-style thesaurus is a personal one. But if you share my bias on this, be aware that The Random House Electronic Thesaurus is no substitute for *Roget's.*

The Thesaurus, by the way, cannot be installed on the same copy of WordStar as Math*. Each of these programs modifies WordStar by adding itself to the WordStar COM file. This makes the COM file larger, which means it takes up more space in the computer memory. There simply isn't enough room to run both programs on a 64K machine. The Thesaurus by itself—added on to WordStar—requires a minimum of 57K of available program memory. This generally means that you need a 64K machine (or better).

Finally, The Thesaurus, like Math*, must be matched to the version of WordStar that you're using. If you have WordStar version 2.26 or 3.00, The Thesaurus is available from Wang Electronic Publishing. According to Wang, though, the version for WordStar 3.3 and later versions has been licensed to MicroPro and will be marketed as a WordStar module much like SpellStar or MailMerge. I haven't been able to get MicroPro to confirm this, but the program may well be available by the time you read this book.

A Final Word

One last word on ancillary programs: Nothing in this industry stays still for long. In the few months it has taken me to write this book, I have seen several programs that I've covered here go through two versions, and in some cases three versions. Most of the comments that you'll find here will apply to later releases of these programs as well, but keep in mind that programs do change—usually for the better, but sometimes not.

Also keep in mind that new programs are continually coming on the market. I've made an effort to cover the programs that seem most interesting to me at this moment, but by the time you read this book, there may well be others available. Keep an eye out for them.

Appendixes

APPENDIX A: DOT COMMANDS

If you are familiar with WordStar, then you probably already know what dot commands are. If you're a little shaky on the subject, though, this appendix will serve as a quick review of, and convenient reference for, the basic WordStar commands. For comments on MailMerge dot commands, take a look at Appendix B. StarIndex commands are covered in Appendix C.

A **dot command** is an instruction that tells WordStar to do something. It is called a dot command because it always begins with a dot, or period. **.PA,** for instance, (read "dot P A") tells WordStar to start a new page no matter how much room is left on the current page.

The dot, or period, must be in the first column of a line. This positioning is what tells WordStar that it is dealing with a dot command rather than a period at the end of a sentence. The difference is that WordStar will print a period, while it will interpret a dot command as an instruction to do something. The **.PA,** for example, tells WordStar to go to the top of the next page before it prints the next line.

Normally, dot commands do not print; they affect the way the rest of the file prints. (If you want WordStar to print the dot commands instead of obeying them, tell the program to suppress page formatting when you print the file.)

The following dot commands are recognized and obeyed by Word-Star itself (as opposed to MailMerge or StarIndex). For convenience, they are listed here in the same order that you'll find them on your WordStar quick reference card. This list includes both the range of permissible settings and the default settings for each command, where appropriate. In many cases, the permissible settings go far beyond any reasonable range. A page offset of 255 columns, for example, will put your left margin well past the right edge of your printer.

.BP   **B**idirectional **P**rinting.
     Settings: .BP On   (.BP 1)
              .BP Off   (.BP 0)
     Default: .BP On   (If installed for a bidirectional printer)
This is used to turn bidirectional printing on and off (assuming you have a bidirectional printer. See Chapter One for comments about using this command when printing with proportional spacing.)

The **.BP** command can be used with either the On/Off settings or the 1/0 settings. The two variations are equivalent. Release 3.2 and earlier will put question flags on the screen if you use "On" or "Off" rather than "1" or "0," but they will obey the commands at print time either way.

.UJ   Microjustification.
     Settings: .UJ On   (.UJ 1)
              .UJ Off   (.UJ 0)
     Default: .UJ On   (If installed for a printer capable of microjustification)
As with the Bidirectional Print command, release 3.2 and earlier will put question flags on the screen if you use "On" or "Off" with this command instead of "1" or "0." As with the **.BP** command also, though, WordStar will obey the commands at print time either way.

.PO   Page Offset
     Settings: .PO 1 through .PO 255
     Default: .PO 8 (measured at ten pitch)
The Page Offset command determines the left margin on the printer. More precisely, it determines which column on the printer is printed as screen column one.

.CW   Character Width
     Settings: .CW 1 through .CW 255
     Default: .CW 12 (Ten pitch)
The Character Width command determines the distance between characters when using a printer capable of incremental spacing. The measurements are in $\frac{1}{120}$ of an inch, so that **.CW 12** equals $\frac{12}{120}$ inch, or $\frac{1}{10}$ inch between characters.

.IG   or   ..   Ignore command
The Ignore command allows you to enter comments in the file. Any line starting with either **.IG** or **..** will be ignored during printing.

.CP Conditional Page

    Settings: .CP 1   through .CP 255

The Conditional Page command is used to tell WordStar to start printing on a new page unless there are some minimum number of lines left on the current page. **.CW 9,** for example, tells WordStar that there must be at least nine lines left on the current page.

.FO Footing

The Footing command is used to enter a line once, and have it print on the bottom of each page.

.FM Footing Margin

    Settings: .FM 1   through .FM 255

    Default: .FM 2

The Footing Margin adjusts the distance between the last line of printed text and the footing, if used. Note that this is distinct from the bottom margin command, which adjusts the distance between the last line of printed text and the bottom of the paper.

.HE Heading

The heading command is used to enter a line once, and have it print at the top of each page.

.HM Heading Margin

    Setting: .HM 1   through .HM 255

    Default: .HM 2

The Heading Margin adjusts the distance between the heading, if used, and the first line of printed text. Note that this is distinct from the top margin command, which adjusts the distance between the top of the paper and the first line of printed text.

.LH Line Height

    Setting: .LH 1   through .LH 255

    Default: .LH 8   (six lines per inch)

The Line Height command determines the distance between lines when using a printer capable of adjusting the vertical movement of the paper. The measurements with this command are given in increments of $\frac{1}{48}$ of an inch. **.LH 8,** for example, equals $\frac{8}{48}$ inch, or $\frac{1}{16}$ inch between lines, which translates to six lines per inch.

.MB Margin at Bottom

    Setting: .MB 1   through .MB 255

    Default: .MB 8

The Margin at Bottom (or bottom margin) command adjusts the distance between the last line of printed text and the bottom of the paper.

.MT Margin at Top

    Setting: .MT 1   through .MT 255

    Default: .MT 3

The Margin at Top (or top margin) command adjusts the distance between the top of the paper and the first line of printed text.

.PA   New Page

The new page command forces the beginning of a new page, regardless of how many lines are left on the current page.

.OP   Omit Page Number

As delivered from MicroPro, WordStar will number the pages at the center bottom of each page unless told otherwise. This command turns that numbering off. If you have reinstalled your WordStar so that it will not number the pages unless told to, then the only time you might need this command is if you have previously entered a **.PN** command in the file.

.PN   Page Number

The Page Number command serves two functions. First, you can use it to set the page number if you want to start printing with some number other than 1.

Second, if you have used an **.OP** command earlier in the file to turn off the automatic page numbering, or if your copy of WordStar is installed so that it will not number unless told to, then you can use this command to turn the page numbering back on.

.PC   Page Number Column
    Settings: .PC 1   through   .PC 255
    Default: Center Column

The Page Number Column command sets the column at which the page number will print, assuming the automatic page number function is active.

.SR   Subscript/Superscript Roll
    Settings: .SR 1   through   .SR 255
    Default: .SR 3

The setting on the Subscript/Superscript Roll determines how far the printer will roll the paper up and down when given the commands for subscript or superscript (assuming your printer is capable of supporting this feature). See Chapter Two for comments about how to use this command for two column printing.

.PL   Paper Length
    Settings: .PL 1   through   .PL 255
    Default: .PL 66

The setting on this command determines how many lines WordStar will count on each page before starting a new page. See Chapter Two for comments on how to use this command with two column printing.

A Last Word on Dot Commands

In all the examples in this book, I have been careful to put dot commands in upper case. I've done this only for consistency, and to make the files easier to read. It doesn't matter whether you use upper- or lower-case or mix the two. It doesn't even matter whether you put space between the dot command and whatever follows it. (**.cW 8** is exactly equivalent to **.CW8,** for example.) At least it doesn't matter as far as WordStar and Mail-

Merge are concerned. It does matter, though, for people—including yourself, if you ever go back to the file to adjust it. Whatever you do, make sure your file is readable.

APPENDIX B: MAILMERGE COMMANDS

This appendix covers MailMerge commands only, including dot commands. For WordStar dot commands, see Appendix A. For StarIndex Commands see Appendix C.

The commands are grouped here by function.

SETTING VALUES FOR VARIABLES

Variable Names

Variable names are used to indicate the places in a file where MailMerge should insert variables. Permissible variable names follow three rules:

> A variable name can be anywhere from one to forty characters long.
>
> Variable names can consist of letters, numbers, and dashes (–). Spaces and other characters are not allowed.
>
> The first character in a variable name must be a letter.

(For further information see Chapter Four.)

/O Omit
    Form: &VARIABLE-NAME/O&

The Omit command is used in a MailMerge format file along with the variable name. It tells MailMerge that if a variable has a null value, it should ignore the variable name altogether. If the variable is the only item on that line, the line itself will be skipped. Without the Omit command, MailMerge would "print" a blank line on the page. (For further information, see Chapter Four.)

.AV Ask for Variable
    Form: .AV VARIABLE-NAME
                  or
      .AV "PROMPT", VARIABLE-NAME

Either of these can be followed with a comma and number to define a maximum length for the variable.

The Ask for Variable command puts a prompt on the screen at print time, asking for the value to use in printing the particular variable. In the absence of a specific prompt, enclosed in quotes, MailMerge will use the variable name as the prompt. (For further information, see Chapter Four.)

.SV Set Variable
    Form: .SV &VARIABLE-NAME&, Value

The Set Variable command is used within the body of the file to set the value of a variable. When using this command be careful to avoid extra spaces at the end of the line, since the variable on the left side of the comma will be set to **exactly** the value on the right side of the comma, including the extra spaces. The space between the comma and the value is optional. (For further information, see Chapter Six.)

.DF   Data File
.RV   Read Variable
    Form: .DF FILENAME
          .RV &VARIABLE1 &, &VARIABLE2, &VAR +
                    OR
          .DF FILENAME
          .RV &VARIABLE1&, VARIABLE2&
          .RV &VARIABLE3&, &VARIABLE4&

The Data File and Read Variable commands are used together to tell Mail-Merge to read the value of the variables from some given file. The Data File command gives the name of the file to read. The Read Variable command lists the variables that will be assigned values. (For further information, see Chapter Eight. Also see the CHANGE command below.)

Other "Basic" Mailmerge Commands

.FI   File Insert
    Form: .FI FILENAME

The File Insert command is used to insert a file into the MailMerge format file at print time. If used in the middle of a file, the files are said to be *nested*. If used at the end of the file, the files are said to be *chained*.

    Nested files can be up to seven levels deep.

    Chained files can link any number of files together.

Note: *The File Insert command line should never be the last entry in a file.* When chaining files, be sure to follow the .FI command with a blank line so that your screen looks like this.

    .FI FILENAME   M (MailMerge flag)
               <

If you leave out this last carriage return, the **.FI** command will often fail to work properly.

    (For further information, see Chapter Six. Also see the CHANGE command below.)

Change
    Form: .DF FILENAME CHANGE
               or
       .FI FILENAME CHANGE

The Change command can be used along with the Data File command or the File Insert command. In either case, when MailMerge sees this command it will stop, and prompt you to put the proper disk in the machine.

    (For further information, see Chapter Six.)

.DM Display Message
Form: .DM Message

The Display Message command will display any message you want to see at print time. This can be used along with the Ask for Variable command to put more information on the screen than can fit on one line in the file. (For further information, see Chapter Four.)

.CS Clear Screen

The Clear Screen command is used to clear the screen of any earlier messages displayed by the .AV command or the .DM command. (For further information see Chapter Four.)

.RP Repeat
Form: .RP n
(where n is the number of times you want the file to repeat.)

The Repeat command is used to tell MailMerge to repeat a file. As with the .FI command, the Repeat command line should never be the last entry in file, or else it may not work properly. (For further information see Chapter Four.)

Print-Time Line-Forming Commands

The Print-Time Line-Forming commands control the printed format of the file, making adjustments for inserted variables, and for changes in format when desired. (For more information on these commands, see Chapter Five.)

.PF Print-Time Line-Forming
Settings: .PF On
.PF Off
.PF Dis (Discretionary)
Default: .PF Dis

This is the basic Print-Time Line-Forming command. When left at the default setting, it functions as a kind of automatic pilot that will almost always adjust the printed format correctly.

If set at **.PF Off,** MailMerge will not reformat the lines at print time. *This must be set at **.PF On** in order to use the other Print-Time Line-Forming commands properly.*

.OJ Output Justification
Settings: .OJ On
.OJ Off
.OJ Dis (Discretionary)
Default: .OJ Dis

The setting of the Output Justification command determines whether the printed output is right justified or not. If left at the default setting, the justification of the printed output will match the justification of the file as edited—either right justified or ragged right.

.IJ Input Justification
  Settings: .IJ On
       .IJ Off
       .IJ Dis (Discretionary)
  Default: .IJ Dis

The Input Justification command has much the same effect as the Output Justification command. If **.PF** is set to "On" or "Dis," and if **.OJ** is set to "Dis," then turning Input Justification on or off will determine whether the printed output is right justified or ragged right.

.LS Line spacing
  Settings: .LS 1   through   .LS 9
            or
         .LS (Dis)
  Default: .LS (Dis)

At the default setting, Line Spacing on the printed output will follow the spacing of the file being printed. Otherwise lines will be spaced as indicated by the command.

  NOTE: This command is obeyed by release 3.3, but it is not recognized while editing. WordStar will put a question flag on the screen.

.RM Right Margin
.LM Left Margin
  Settings: .RM n or .RM (Dis)
            .LM n or .LM (Dis)
            (Where n equals the column number for the left or right margin respectively.)
  NOTE: These two commands are not recognized or obeyed by release 3.3.

Conditional Print Commands

  (Only on Wordstar 3.3, and only on CP/M-80 and MP/M-80 versions.) (For further information on the following, see Chapter Seven.)

.IF ... GOTO (If . . .)
.EX ... GOTO (Except when . . .)
  Form: .IF &VARIABLE-NAME& = "Value" GOTO
            or
        .EX &VARIABLE-NAME& = "Value" GOTO

The If and Except When commands are the basic choices for the conditional print commands.

  The **.IF** command is used for conditional statements that take the form "If this is true . . ."

  The **.EX** command is used for conditional statements that take the form "Except when this is true . . ."

  In either case, the conditional statement includes a variable name, a value, and a comparison character for specifying the relationship between the two.

The six possible relationships, or comparison characters are:

=	equals
< >	not equal
>	greater than
<	less than
> =	greater than or equal to
< =	less than or equal to

GOTO is the part of the conditional command that tells MailMerge what to do if the conditions are met. This can be written as "GOTO," "goto," "G," or "g." It can be followed by a label or not.

.EF
The **.EF** command serves as a marker to tell MailMerge where to skip to if the conditions in a conditional command are met. If the conditional command includes a label (. . . GOTO LABEL), MailMerge will skip to the first **.EF** command that also includes that label (.EF LABEL). If the conditional command does not include a label, MailMerge will skip to the first **.EF** command that it finds.

.AND.
.OR.
    Form: .IF . . . .AND. . . . GOTO
          .IF . . . .OR. . . . GOTO
.AND. and **.OR.** are used to create complex conditional commands. *Both of these commands must be in upper-case, and both must include a period before and after in order to function.*

You can use the **.AND.** and **.OR.** in any combination, to link as many commands together as you like. The only restriction is a one hundred character maximum for the command line.

APPENDIX C: STARINDEX COMMANDS

This appendix covers the StarIndex commands, grouping them by function. It is meant primarily as a reference guide. In addition to explaining each command, it also contains some helpful cross references to related commands. You should find it useful when you need more information than you can find on the StarIndex reference card.

You can also use this appendix as a quick introduction to StarIndex. Be aware, though, that it assumes you are at least vaguely familiar with the program—either from having used it or from having read the StarIndex section of Chapter Sixteen.

The commands are divided into two sections: Basic StarIndex Commands and Style Override Commands (print and style directives).

The basic section covers only those commands that must be entered in the file if they are to be used at all.

The style override section covers the StarIndex functions that can be controlled either by entering commands in the file or through a separate FMT file.

Two points to help you remember the commands: With one exception (see the page break command), all StarIndex dot commands begin with a **.I.** The second letter is usually a mnemonic.

Many of the commands are toggles. They are toggled "on" with "1" and "off" with "0." Other commands use the 1/0 choice to toggle between upper-case and lower-case.

Basic StarIndex Commands

Indexing Commands

Index Entries by Topic

.II   General Index Entry
.IM   Master Index Entry.
    Form: .II Entry
          or
        .IM Entry

These two commands are used for adding index entries by topic when the wording you want in the index is not already contained in the text. *Entries marked with the* **.IM,** *or Master command, will be numbered in boldface in the index. Entries marked with the* **.II** *command will not be.* The two commands are otherwise identical. You can use boldface numbering to indicate anything you like; it can, for example, be the page where the item is defined, or the page where the item is accompanied by a figure explaining it.

With either version of the index command, the command line should be entered immediately before the line that is being indexed.

You can use a comma in the command line to indicate subentries in the index. You might, for example, have these two lines at different places in your file:

.II Entry, undesired
.II Entry, desired

They will show in your index as:

Entry
   desired, 7
   undesired, 3

Notice that StarIndex alphabetizes the sub-entries within the major heading.

You will occasionally need a comma when it is not meant as a sub-entry—in a name, for example. In that case you enter a backslash before the comma:

Widgets\, Inc.

This will show in the index as:

Widgets, Inc.

INDEXING WORDS IN THE BODY OF THE TEXT

^PP　General Index Entry (Shows on screen as ^P)
^PK　Master Index Entry (Shows on screen as ^K)
　　　Form:　^Pentry^P
　　　　　　or
　　　　　　^Kentry^K

These two commands are used to index words within the body of the text. Enter the **^PP** or **^PK** before and after the word or words to be indexed. As with the **.II** and **.IM** commands, the "master" index entry, **^PK**, will print the page number in boldface in the index. The "general" entry, **^PP**, will not. Once again, though, the two commands are otherwise identical.

Notice that once you've chosen a word to index, you can use the global find and replace function to let WordStar find and mark that word throughout the file.

.IO　Indexing Off, or On
　　　Form:　.IO0 (Turn Indexing Off)
　　　　　　.IO1 (Turn Indexing On)
　　　Default: .IO1

You can use this command to turn indexing off, then on again, if you want to skip a section.

Headings (Outline Design)

StarIndex allows for four levels of section headings. These are:

.IA　Major heading
.IB　Section heading
.IC　Sub-Section heading
.ID　Sub-Sub-Section heading

　　　Form: .IA or .IB or .IC or .ID
　　　　　Followed by section title on next line

With each of these section commands, the command line goes on the line just before the section title. StarIndex uses these markers in several ways.

You can, for example, tell StarIndex to add one or more level of heading to the index. You can also tell it to include only certain levels of headings in the table of contents.

You can tell it to add print commands: to boldface and underline one level of heading, double strike another, and so forth.

You can also have StarIndex number the headings for you, in which case it will number them as 1, or 1.1, or 1.1.1, or 1.1.1.1, depending on the level you designated for the heading. (You can also use letters instead of numbers, or even mix the two.)

If you're making use of any of these functions—either through an FMT file created by STYLE.COM or through Style Override commands—it's obviously important to mark the headings appropriately.

Two points to keep in mind. First, StarIndex will not change case for you. If you want a heading in upper-case, or you want the first letter in each word to be upper-case, you have to do that manually.

Second, if you've told StarIndex to add any of the toggle commands (for boldface or underlining for example) do not add them yourself as well, otherwise you'll wind up with a double toggle (^B^B) before and after the heading, and lose the print enhancement.

.IE   Heading for Figures
    Form: .IE
        Followed by Figure Title on next line
This command tags figures, if any, so StarIndex can number them and can generate a list to go with the table of contents.

.IT   Heading for Tables
    Form: .IT
        Followed by Table Title on next line
This command tags tables, if any, so StarIndex can number them and can generate a list to go with the table of contents.

Setting Values Within the File

A1   Indicates the beginning of the appendices, if any.
    Form: .IAA1
        Appendix Title (First Appendix)
This tells StarIndex where the chapters end and the appendices begin. All major headings after this (meaning all headings preceded by **.IA**) will be listed in the table of contents under the heading "Appendices" (or whatever you've changed it to).

In addition, if you are printing the chapter number and page number on each page (1-1 for example), this command will tell StarIndex to substitute the Appendix letter (or number) instead. If you are using letters to "number" the appendices, then, the page numbering will take the form A-1.

The **A1** command can only be used with the **.IA** command.

A0 Indicates the beginning of the index.

> Form: .IAA0
> Index

This command is included as the last entry in your file. Note the word "Index" on the second line; it tells StarIndex to enter the word "Index" in your table of contents.

In addition, if you are printing the chapter number and page number on each page (1-1 for example), this will substitute the word "Index" for chapter number in the index itself, so it will take the form Index-1.

The **A0** command can only be used with the **.IA** command.

.IN Set the chapter number

> Form: .INn

This command is roughly equivalent to the page number command in WordStar, except that instead of setting the page number to n, this sets the chapter number to n. If you are printing with chapter number and page number (1-1 for example), this will force the chapter number to print with the desired value.

The **.IN** command line must come before the **.IA** command for the chapter.

New Page Command
.PA

> Form: .PAO
> .PAE

The new page command in StarIndex is an extension of WordStar's page command (.PA).

.PAO forces a new page, and tells StarIndex to begin printing on the next ODD numbered page.

.PAE also forces a new page, but tells StarIndex to begin printing on the next EVEN numbered page.

In either case, StarIndex will insert a blank page if necessary.

StarIndex will also recognize the **.PA** command by itself, and will carry it over to the SI output file.

Using Headers or Footers with StarIndex

StarIndex recognizes all the usual heading and footing commands including the special print character "#" which will be carried over to the SI output file, and will print as the current page number, whatever that happens to be.

In addition, StarIndex recognizes an additional special print character: @.

The "@" does for chapter numbers what "#" does for page numbers. If you enter a header or footer as "Chapter @ page #," for example, StarIndex will insert the current chapter number where it sees the @. It will then write a separate header or footer command for each chapter when it creates the output SI file. (**.HE** Chapter 1 page #, **.HE** Chapter 2 page #, and so forth.)

Chaining Files with StarIndex

.FI   File Insert

StarIndex recognizes the MailMerge file insert command, and uses it to chain individual files together. This means, for example, that if you have each chapter of a book in its own file, you can use the **.FI** command to chain them so that StarIndex can create a single index for the entire book.

You can also create files with nothing in them but **.FI** command lines, and have StarIndex work from the command file. A note of warning here though: StarIndex is more particular than MailMerge about how you set up the file. If each file is a chapter in a book, for example, and if you want each chapter to start on a new page, you will probably want to end each file with a **.PA** command line. With MailMerge, you can end each file either with:

    .PA <RETURN>

or with:

    .PA

In the first case, you would enter your command lines one after the other in the command file. In the second case, you would enter a blank line (with a hard carriage return) between each **.FI** line. Either approach will work.

With StarIndex, you must take the first approach, and end each file with a hard carriage return. If you try the second approach, you will find that StarIndex will not paginate the table of contents properly.

STYLE OVERRIDES (PRINT AND STYLE DIRECTIVES)

Unless told otherwise, StarIndex will generate its various files—the index, the SI text file, and the table of contents—according to the format and print instructions contained in the file FORMAT.FMT.

You can change the instructions in FORMAT.FMT, or create alternate format files at any time, using the StarIndex command file STYLE.COM. If you always make your format changes through an FMT file you can ignore the rest of this appendix. If you are using a special format for a specific file, though, and you never expect to use that format again, you might prefer to enter the format and print commands in the file itself. This has the advantage of saving the commands with the file, so you don't have to remember which FMT file goes with which text file. The disadvantage, of course, is that if you ever use the same format again, you have to re-enter the commands in the new text file.

StarIndex gives you enough override commands, or directives, to alter just about anything you can think of in the various formats. You are free to use as many or as few of these overrides as you need for the particular file. Except where StarIndex sees a specific override command, it will continue to obey the instructions in the format file.

Once again, the commands are grouped by function. The "defaults" for each function will vary depending on the settings in your FMT file.

Print Directives

StarIndex includes six print directives that can be added to the file to modify the instructions in the FMT file. The print directives are:

B   for Boldface

D   for Double Strike

E   for Elongated Letters
   (works with dot matrix printers only.)

S   for putting extra Spaces between letters
   (L I K E   T H I S)

U   for Underlining

X   for normal print (no print enhancements)

Any combination of these (or any non-contradictory combination) can be used in any of the following command lines:

.IA   (Major heading)

.IB   (Section heading)

.IC   (Sub-section heading)

.ID   (Sub-sub-section heading)

.IE   (Figure heading)

.IT   (Table heading)

.IR   (Except for .IRI—see below)
   (.IR is Rename title)

Entering a print directive in any of the heading commands will affect all the headings on that level—meaning all section headings, for example, or all sub-section headings.

INDEX HEADINGS: Indexing Overrides

I0   Headings at this level do NOT go in index

I1   Headings at this level DO go in index

M1   Headings at this level go in index as MASTER entries (Page number is boldfaced)

Form: .IAI0 (or .IBI0 etc.)
   or
   .IAI1
   or
   .IAM1

Any of these commands can be used with any of the heading command lines—**.IA**, **.IB**, **.IC**, or **.ID**.

INDEX: Format Overrides

L0 Alphabetizes entries in index, but does not print individual letters as "headers"

L1 Alphabetizes entries in index, and adds "headers" of individual letters

The L0 or L1 command is used with the **.IR** command.

Form: .IRL0
   or
.IRL1

This command can be used with or without a print directive. **.IRL1B** will print the individual letters in the index in **boldface**. **.IRL1BU** will print the individual letters in **boldface** and <u>underline</u> them.

TABLE OF CONTENTS: Format Overrides

.IL   Set line lengths (or line widths) for lines in Table of Contents
   Form: ILn   where n is the number of characters in the line (usually 65)

Controlling Page Numbering in Table of Contents

N0 Omit page numbers in Table of Contents
N1 Number pages consecutively in Table of Contents
R0 Use lower-case Roman numerals to number pages in Table of Contents
R1 Use upper-case Roman numerals to number pages in Table of Contents

Form: .ILN0
   or
.ILN1
   or
.ILR0
   or
.ILR1

If using any of these commands, the **.IL** command line must come before the **first .IA** command line in your file.

Controlling Section Numbers in Table of Contents

T0 Section numbers in table of contents are NOT preceded by higher level numbers.

T1 Section number in table of contents ARE preceded by higher level numbers.

Form: .IAT0   (or .IBT0 etc.)
        or
     .IAT1

Either of these commands can be used with any of the heading command lines—**.IA, .IB, .IC,** or **.ID.**

(See also H0/H1 for adjusting section numbers in the body of the text. All other numbering options in the table of contents—numbering or lettering, Arabic numbers or Roman, upper-case or lower-case—will match the options chosen for numbering the headings.)

Headings: Format and Numbering Overrides

Controlling Section Numbering

R0   Chapters numbered with lower-case Roman numerals.

R1   Chapters numbered with upper-case Roman numerals.

Form: .IAR0
        or
     .IAR1

The R0 or R1 command can only be used with a .IA line. It will control how chapters are numbered in both the body of the text and the table of contents.

Do not confuse this R0/R1 command with the other R0/R1 command that is used in the **.IL** command line. This command affects how the CHAPTERS are numbered. The other use of R0/R1 affects how the pages of the table of contents are numbered.

N0   Sections at this level and lower are NOT numbered

N1   Sections at this level are numbered consecutively

L0   Sections at this level are "numbered" with LOWER-CASE letters

L1   Sections at this level are "numbered" with UPPER-CASE letters

Form: .IAN0   (or .IBL0 etc.)
        or
     .IAN1
        or
     .IAL0
        or
     .IAL1

The above overrides can be used with any section heading command. They will control how headings at that level are numbered in both the body of the text and in the table of contents.

Do not confuse this N0/N1 command with the other N0/N1 command which is used in the **.IL** command line. This command affects how SECTIONS are numbered. The other command affects how pages in the table of contents are numbered.

H0   Section numbers *in the body of the text* are NOT preceded by higher level numbers. (Sub-sub-section is numbered "1.")

H1   Section numbers *in the body of the text* ARE preceded by higher level numbers. (Sub-sub-section is numbered "1.1.1.1.")

Form: .IAH0

        or

        .IAH1

The H0/H1 commands can only be used on a **.IA** command line. (See also T0/T1—for adjusting section numbers in the table of contents.)

NOTE: Where section numbers are preceded by a higher level number, the punctuation between them can be controlled.

The desired punctuation (or lack of it) is placed between two back-slashes (\ \).

Examples:

.IA\ \   Eliminates punctuation between major headers and section headers.

.IB\:\   Puts a colon between section numbers and sub-section numbers.

Controlling Page Numbers

#0   Pages will be numbered consecutively throughout

#1   Page number will be reset to "1" at each **.IA** command line.

Form: .IA#0

        or

        .IA#1

This must be placed in the first **.IA** command or it will be ignored.

TITLES and CAPTIONS: Changing Text

Changing Titles

.IR   Rename with supplied text

used with any of the following identifiers:

A   for Appendix title in table of contents

C   for table of Contents

F   for list of Figures

I   for Index prefix

N   for Notes (blank pages)

T   for list of Tables

Form: .IRA\New name\

The **.IR** command changes the text that StarIndex uses to label the item identified in the command line. The FORMAT.FMT file on your distribution disk, for example uses "Figures" as the title for the list of figures. You can change this to "Illustrations" with the **.IRA** command.

The new title can be up to twenty-five characters long. It is typed between two backslash characters as shown above.

The **.IR** command line can also include print directives, in which case the print enhancements will be applied to the title. (Except for the Index Prefix. Print directives will have no effect on a **.IRI** command line.)

Changing Captions
To change the captions for figures and tables, use the same backslash characters as above, but with the **.IE** command for figures on the **.IT** command for tables.

Form: .IE\New text\
or
.IT\New text\

APPENDIX D: REINSTALLING YOUR WORDSTAR

There are several places where I've mentioned that you might want to reinstall your WordStar to change one or more of the default settings. The instructions for doing this vary from one release of WordStar to the next. So does the ease with which you can do it. These instructions are already in your WordStar reference manuals, but depending on the release, you may have to wade through a lot of other material to find them.

The instructions here assume that your WordStar is already installed, and that you only need to change the defaults. For first time installation, see your manual.

Also note that you need the correct version of the installation program for the particular release of WordStar that you're reinstalling.

RELEASES 2.26 AND 3.0

To reinstall release 2.26 or 3.0, you need a previously installed copy of WordStar and a copy of the installation program, INSTALL.COM. (WordStar 2.26 uses INSTALL 3.8. WordStar 3.00 uses INSTALL 4.2. Although these two INSTALL programs are slightly different from Word-Star's point of view, they look the same to the user. The instructions here apply to both programs, but make sure you're using the right one.)

This example assumes that both the WS.COM file and the INSTALL. COM file are on the same disk.

When you call up INSTALL, it will begin by asking whether this is a normal first time installation of WordStar. Answer no, and you'll see this menu:

A   INSTALLation of a distributed WordStar, INSTALLING WSU.COM,
    producing WS.COM, and then running the INSTALLed WordStar.
B   INSTALLation or re-INSTALLation of a WordStar COM, file
    of your choice, placing the newly INSTALLed WordStar in a file
    of your choice, and then exiting to the operating system.
C   Same as B except run the INSTALLed WordStar.

D   Modification of the INSTALLation of a WordStar COM file of
    your choice. The modified WordStar replaces the original
    file. The modified WordStar is then run.
PLEASE ENTER SELECTION (A, B, C, or D):

Choose B, C, or D, depending on whether you want to replace the original file and whether you want to go into WordStar when you're finished.

You will then be asked for the name of the file to be installed. Enter WS.COM, or whatever you're using as a name for your WordStar command file.

If you've chosen B or C, you will then be asked for the filename to use in saving the reinstalled file. Enter whatever name you want to use. (If you enter WS.COM, you will lose your original file. If you leave off the COM ending, INSTALL will supply it for you.)

INSTALL will then show you a series of installation menus for your printer and terminal. You don't want to change any of these. Just keep hitting RETURN until you see this prompt:

ARE THE MODIFICATIONS TO WORDSTAR NOW COMPLETE?

IF THEY ARE ANSWER YES TO THE NEXT QUESTION.
IF YOU WISH TO MAKE ADDITIONAL PATCHES TO WORDSTAR'S
USER AREAS, ANSWER NO TO THE NEXT QUESTION.

OK (Y/N):

Answer "N."

INSTALL will repond with two paragraphs of instructions, ending with this prompt:

LOCATION TO BE CHANGED (0=END):

From this point on, you can enter any of the following changes or not. Each entry must be followed by a RETURN. After each entry, WordStar will return to the "location to be changed" prompt.

Notice that some of the entries require colons. If you leave the colon off, you will get an error message and be returned to the "location to be changed" prompt.

To change the default for right justification, Enter:

INITWF+1

WordStar will respond with a message like this:

ADDRESS : 0386H   OLD VALUE: FFH   NEW VALUE:

For default of Right Justification ON, Enter: FF
For default of Right Justification OFF, enter: Ø
To change the default for printing page numbers at the bottom center of each page, Enter:

ITPOPN:

WordStar will respond with a message like this:

ADDRESS: 03D3H OLD VALUE: FFH NEW VALUE:

For default of page numbers omitted, Enter any number greater than 0. For default of automatically printing page numbers, enter 0.

Changing the marker for variable names (the variable name delimiters) requires two changes, since the beginning marker and end marker are entered separately.

To change the beginning marker, Enter:

VARCH1:

When WordStar asks for the new value, enter the ASCII code for the new beginning character, using the Hex value. (See below.)

To change the end marker, Enter

VARCH2:

Once again, when WordStar asks for the new value, enter the ASCII code for the new beginning character, using the Hex value.

To change the marker for field delimiter, Enter:

RVELIM:

When WordStar asks for the new value, enter the ASCII code for the character you want, using the Hex value.

The hexadecimal values for the ASCII symbols are as follows. (If you don't know what hexadecimal means, don't worry about it. Just enter the numbers and letters that match the symbols you want to use.)

Hex Value	Symbol	Hex Value	Symbol
21	!	3B	;
22	"	3C	<
23	#	3D	=
24	$	3E	>
25	%	3F	?
26	&	5B	[
27	'	5C	\
28	(	5D	]
29	)	5E	^
2A	*	5F	_ (underline)
2B	+	60	`
2C	,	7B	{
2D	— (Minus)	7C	|
2E	.	7D	}
2F	/	7E	~
3A	:		

When you are done with your changes, Enter "0."

WordStar will ask you to confirm your terminal and printer selections. You didn't change any, so just hit RETURN. WordStar will then write the reinstalled version to disk, ready to be used.

There are other changes you can make. You will find some of them in the 3.0 reference manual on pages 8-1 and 8-2. You will also find some printer patches on pages 7-1 through 7-4. These will let you do things like change the number of strikes used for "double strike" to get still darker printing.

RELEASE 3.2

Release 3.2 does not give you any easy way to change the defaults, although you can change them through DEBUG. This is a programming tool, which you ideally should never have to use—unless of course you are interested in programming.

There is a program available that will change the defaults for you though. It was written by John Schnell, for the first issue of *PC: The Disk Magazine*, which is put out by the same people who publish *PC Magazine*. *The Disk Magazine* is available by subscription, or in most retail computer stores.

RELEASE 3.3

The install program for release 3.3 has been rewritten to make the installation, or reinstallation, of the program as painless as possible. You can change most of the important defaults through simple menu choices. There is also a "hidden" label patcher that lets you make changes that aren't on the menu.

The installation program for 3.3 is called WINSTALL.COM.

When you call it up, it tells you what it does, and asks if you want to continue.

Answer "Y" for yes.

It then asks you which program you're working with. (WINSTALL is also used to install other MicroPro programs.)

Enter WS for WordStar, as shown on the menu.

You will then see a help screen, with some pointers on how to use the program. Hit any key to continue, and the program will guide you through the procedure step-by-step. The instructions are well written and carefully designed, complete with error checking messages to protect you from mistakes.

When you get to the installation menu, enter E, for "Menu of WordStar features."

The Features Menu will give you a choice of items that you can change the defaults for. These include the justification toggle, the data field delimiter, the variable name symbol, and fifteen additional possibilities. (The MS-DOS version includes a sixteenth choice: to change function keys.) To change any of these, you pick the appropriate letter from the menu. WINSTALL will show you the current value, either as a number or as a symbol, as appropriate. It will ask what to change it to, and, finally, return you to the Features Menu for your next choice.

When you're done, enter X to exit from the Features Menu, enter X again to exit from the installation menu, and follow the instructions for leaving the program.

If you're familiar with INSTALL for WordStar version 2.26 or 3.00, finally, you may notice that there are patches available for WordStar—particularly printer patches—that aren't on the WINSTALL menu. You can still make these additional changes, though, with the hidden label patcher I've already mentioned. Simply go to the main menu in the install program and enter +. (This is not a menu choice, but it works.) This will send you to the label patcher, which works the same way as the label patcher for 3.00. (See the discussion of 3.00 for details.) I am told by MicroPro that the patcher uses the same labels as the 2.26 and 3.00 patcher.

Index